STATE OF THE ARTS

STATE OF THE Arts

CALIFORNIA ARTISTS TALK ABOUT THEIR WORK

Barbara Isenberg

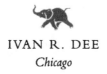

IVAN R. DEE
Chicago

www.ivanrdee.com

Library of Congress Cataloging-in-Publication Data:
Isenberg, Barbara.
  State of the arts : California artists talk about their work / Barbara Isenberg.
    p. cm.
  Originally published: New York : William Morrow, 2000.
  ISBN 978-1-56663-631-5
  1. Arts—California. 2. Artists—California—Interviews. 3. Entertainers—California—Interviews.
I. Title.
NX510.C2184 2005
700' .92'2794—dc22   2004065667

Contents

Introduction

The photographer Edmund Teske once told me what first lured him to California in the forties: thoughts of walking at the ocean's edge, invisibly, near Greta Garbo. The California of John Muir and Walt Disney, Billy Wilder and the Beach Boys, easily accommodates such romantic notions.

Much has been written about California as the locus of exotic cults, colorful eccentrics, Hollywood debauchery, gang warfare, jammed freeways, fires, floods, earthquakes, riots, and other natural and unnatural disasters. But what has long intrigued me is why so many accomplished painters, writers, composers, and other artists have spent their creative maturity working here despite all that.

Given both my own love of California and my sense that something here truly stimulates creativity, I was immediately intrigued by word that the Los Angeles County Museum of Art was putting together the exhibition *Made in California: Art, Image, and Identity, 1900–2000*. At its helm was Stephanie Barron, an innovative curator whose work I began to follow during my years as an arts reporter for the *Los Angeles Times*. Her ambitious plan was to both chronicle and comment on the state's cultural history in what was to become the largest show the museum has ever mounted.

I first simply "observed" the exhibition. I was invited to listen, then summarize two days of exploratory talks the museum hosted in late 1997 for its curators and assorted artists, writers, philosophers, and others. Hooked immediately by what I heard, I arranged to meet with curator Barron to talk further.

Over coffee at a West Hollywood diner, we explored the idea of my interviewing painters, sculptors, photographers, and other visual artists for both a complementary book and, through audiotape excerpts, the exhibition itself. We came up with a list of about twenty people, including David Hockney, Robert Irwin, Edward Ruscha, Alexis Smith, and other internationally known artists who had long been associated with California.

Given that my curiosity about California culture doesn't end with the visual arts, I next added the poet Lawrence Ferlinghetti, the architect Frank Gehry, the choreographer Bella Lewitzky, and a few other arts pioneers who also had to be in any book on California creativity. Dave Brubeck took West Coast jazz around the world, while playwright David Henry Hwang vividly dramatized not just the Asian American but the larger California immigrant experience. And could one actually write a book about California without a visit to Joan Didion?

As my list edged past thirty, I continued looking for people who reflected the state's cultural heritage through either their own experiences or the experiences of those who influenced them. Toward that end, I consulted a wide range of scholars, curators, historians, and other experts, keeping in mind my original selections, as I tried to fill in gaps of age, experience, geography, and discipline.

Though I intentionally shied away from film, television, and pop music because artists in those fields are included in so many other books, I somehow couldn't exclude the creators of such significant California anthems as "I Love LA" (Randy Newman) and "Hotel California" (Don Henley). Robert Towne, who wrote the quintessential California film, *Chinatown,* clearly belongs here. So, I feel, does Clint Eastwood, the man who both inhabited San Francisco detective Harry Callahan—"Dirty Harry"—and served as mayor of Carmel, as does Carol Burnett, who so profoundly realized the Hollywood dream.

After months of research and conversations, and a potential list of nearly one hundred names, I began to send out letters. While a few people didn't respond to persistent wooing, nearly everyone I asked was eventually receptive.

In each case I asked people how they became artists and how being an artist here is different than being an artist somewhere else. I asked them about childhood influences and mentors, about what they longed to be and what they became, about who or what prodded them in this or that direction. I asked them why they came here and why they stayed. How did their work change here?

They spoke of their parents and grandparents, those who came before them and those who followed. Again and again they referred to Raymond Chandler and Frank Zappa; Delano grape fields and Central Avenue jazz clubs; the Watts Towers and the Hollywood sign; gold rush towns, Point Lobos, and the blue Pacific.

Conversations were punctuated with talk of not just museum exhibitions and MacArthur "genius" awards, but of the Mexican Revolution, the Great Depression, wartime internment of Japanese Americans, and Chinese immigration. Personal memories led into communal memories of Italian Americans in fifties San Francisco, rock musicians in seventies Los Angeles, artist and playwright communities in eighties Southern and Northern California.

The topic was creativity, but the context was the California of family, friends, teachers, and memory. What can we learn from these artists about art, California, and the creative process? What is the impact of environment on creativity? And why does California have such extraordinary impact far beyond its borders?

While such people as the clown Bill Irwin, the novelist Carolyn See, and the playwright Luis Valdez were born here, fewer than half of the artists in these pages are native Californians. Yet in both groups nearly everyone describes California as a frontier, a place to both be a maverick and enjoy the freedom to fail.

Gone are the European émigrés who settled here in the thirties and forties, but still flourishing is the legacy of training or inspiration they gave people like Brubeck and conductor Michael Tilson Thomas. In the Santa Monica house where Austrian director Berthold Viertel and his wife, screenwriter Salka Viertel, entertained such guests as Arnold Schoenberg and Thomas Mann in the forties, theater producer and director Gordon Davidson and his wife, publicist Judi Davidson, host Arthur Miller and Edward James Olmos.

American-born émigrés, too, came to California for the weather, the light, the space, and the opportunity. Seeking something better or something new, many compare their odysseys west in the United States to the odysseys their ancestors made from Europe, Mexico, and elsewhere. Here they could find, explore, invent, or reinvent themselves. They could start over and change not only the present and future but the past as well.

Sometimes they changed careers, other times their very identities. Robert Towne's father took his new family name from the ladies' clothing shop he purchased in San Pedro, while artist Judy Cohen assumed the surname of Chicago, the city that resonates so strongly in her speech patterns.

As in any book about California, Hollywood is, of course, a crucial supporting player. Luis Valdez's father was a mule driver in the film *Cimarron,* Michael Tilson Thomas's father headed out to the desert to write Westerns, and Matt Groening's first job in California was as a movie extra.

Everybody talks about the movies. David Hockney says he grew up in Bradford, England, and Hollywood, and nearly all the artists I spoke with were influenced by what they saw on the screen wherever they were. The difference is that once in California, they could meet the people they saw in the movies. They could shop with them and, often, dine and dance with them as well.

There is also persistent nostalgia. Artists speak of the Los Angeles or

San Francisco that was, of places and people that no longer exist. They conjure a Santa Clara Valley replete with orchards rather than high-tech office buildings and factories, and a San Fernando Valley where the air was sweet with the smells of oranges and lemons, not exhaust fumes.

Lastly, these are not written essays, but rather my edited transcripts of conversations I had with each person. I've reordered and cut them for length and repetition but I have not rewritten them. I tried very hard to stay in the voice of the person speaking.

Most of these conversations occurred in the speaker's home or studio, whether in California or elsewhere. Artists also met with me at my home, friends' homes, and in hotel rooms and restaurants. Several Northern California artists talked with me in a recording studio in San Francisco's Mission District, while Lawrence Ferlinghetti and I chatted in an otherwise deserted Los Angeles hotel ballroom.

All the interviews I conducted are included in these pages; nobody was excluded once I interviewed them. My selection of artists reflects my interests and judgment and sprang from a hunch that within these fifty-seven people dwelled fifty-seven wonderful stories.

STATE OF THE ARTS

Part I

Native Sons and Daughters

bella **LEWITZKY**

The choreographer Bella Lewitzky was born in 1916 in a Mojave Desert colony not far from Los Angeles. Raised on her father's chicken ranch in San Bernardino, she studied dance as a child and was performing at the Hollywood Bowl with choreographers Agnes de Mille and Lester Horton by the thirties. Horton's principal dancer from 1934 to 1950, she worked briefly on Broadway and in films but primarily as a modern dancer. The first dean of the California Institute of the Arts Dance School, Lewitzky formed the Bella Lewitzky Dance Company in 1966, leading it on tour throughout the United States and abroad to great acclaim before disbanding it in May 1997. She has been married to the architect Newell Reynolds since 1940 and lives in Albuquerque, New Mexico.

I think I must feel about the light in California the way the painters did about the wonderful light in Provence. Ever since I was a child it has been an important part of my awareness of my environment.

I lived in a valley surrounded by high mountains, and that suited me just fine because it meant you didn't know what was on the other side. This made it wonderful and exciting and mysterious. Having a place to go over formed part of my philosophy of life. You could throw your arms out as wide as you wanted wherever you were in the valley and never touch the mountains. They were all still very far away.

I spent my first two years at Llano del Rio, a socialist colony in the Los Angeles environs. My father was the political cartoonist, and he was also the baker. Everybody did as many jobs as they felt they could undertake.

My father, who came to the United States from the Ukraine, moved here from Philadelphia because it was suspected that he was consumptive. He had nothing actually wrong with him at all. Poverty was the only thing that ever really troubled him.

My father bought a chicken ranch in San Bernardino, but he had studied art and continued to paint. Always. That was the first real lesson I learned about life and probably the most important: You work at anything to earn a living, but only if you have already found a way to make your life worth living. He never taught it. It was by example, which is probably the most passionate, strong, and long-lasting way that one can learn anything. I learned that my father remained a full man. I learned by my own cognizance, looking at him, watching him, knowing what he chose. Never by lecturing.

The only thing my father did that was close to lecturing was when I would trail him through museums. He would say, "Look at that mountain and see in it how many colors there are." He just pointed out what moved him. He was a wonderful liver of life, which made him an absolutely splendid teacher. So I learned life lessons when he talked about the art he loved. His paints, his easel, his charcoal—that's what enriched him. That's what described his life.

None of this did he ever tell me. All this I learned by watching and by listening. When I was quite young, he treated me as an adult. All children are really adults—they're just less experienced adults. One reason I became such a good teacher is that my father was such a good teacher. He taught children as human beings—they had fewer experiences but they were not less intelligent or less capable of seeing the world.

My sister and I used to guard his paintings. It was the act of making the painting that was complete for him. He had no need to keep it or have somebody else look at it. Since my sister and I were not complete in the act of making them, our completion was to have them to look at. We were the appreciators. Canvas was very expensive, and he would paint over his paintings to save canvas. We learned to grab the ones we loved and hide them somewhere so we'd have the paintings, and he'd have the act of painting.

We were of humble origins. Richer than anyone could possibly be but poor in terms of actual monetary worth. He would set up a still life on our dining room table, and people would come in and would reach to take some food on the table to eat. My sister and I then had the job of yanking the food away from them because we knew it was a still life, not something to eat. My father would never say, "Don't eat that." He was hospitable, kind. I never met anyone who didn't love my father— he was that kind of person. Even to his own destruction, he would let them eat his still life.

My father was an admirer of certain painters who lingered from his life into mine. Cézanne was one of his heroes and remained one for me also. In my mind Cézanne was the forerunner of modernism and the art we knew later. I've always had a love for those people who ran ahead of their time by a little bit, and Cézanne was for me that kind of painter. I think that was why I fell in love with Satie's music. I never used any of Satie's dance pieces—I thought they were very contrived—but I adored his other material.

As early as I can remember, I was a mover, in ways you don't consider dance. They're movement experiences. I would try to fly, and if I ever met anyone who'd never tried to fly, I'd say, "Go back. Your life is missing something."

I learned about motion when I was quite young, maybe seven, and many a bruised bone did I have jumping off our chicken ranch roof. I was sure what was wrong was merely timing. I had not put my arms and legs in the right places at the right time to sustain myself in the air. Otherwise, of course, I could fly. Other times I was positive that if there was a good strong wind and you knew how, you could sit in it and the wind would support you and carry you forward. Many a bruised bottom came from this assumption. But those were important movement experiences. I knew I could fly if I got it right. I knew I could sit down in the wind, and the wind would support me if I got it right.

The thing I learned, probably from my father, was: Dream it, then bring it into practice. I still use that, I realize, except now I know better how. I don't fall down, and I don't break my neck trying to jump off the roof.

I also did other less interesting things like make up movement plays. That's when I learned that when you are the maker of the piece, you can also cast yourself in the best role. I learned that very young. So a lot of just-plain-reality experiences guided me. You have to have a vision. You have to have a place to go. You have to have a stairway to heaven to be able to move to another place, always of course to a better place.

I remembered my father's lessons when I danced in films. If you were a dancer in films, unless you were favored or somebody liked you for the wrong reasons, you were a fill-in, an environment. You didn't do much. My friend Dorothy and I were short, and you had to be leggy, tall, and buxom to be selected for films. We were very good dancers, and nobody had any need for dancers. I found working in films as humiliating as anything could possibly be. I wasn't cut out for it. I did it for the money, so I could afford to concertize. Therefore I could tolerate it.

In the late sixties, when Herbert Blau was assembling his faculty to launch California Institute of the Arts, he was having a hard time finding a dance person. I'm sure he contacted a lot of people before he contacted me because I had no large name at all. It was very likely that the strong dancers would have been turned off by theater being so dominant, because where there's a theater person, believe me, as a dancer you are not on a par at all; you are the handmaiden of theater. But at that point in my life what I wanted more than anything else was a group of people that I could bring together and train for a longer period of time. I had done that on my own for about six months, and it was so exciting and so successful that I knew it was something that I needed to continue doing.

I had dancers with whom I worked, but not a dance company at that point. He said, "Well, my program is to make art," and I said, "Fine, that's my program." So we bonded. My object was to train dancers for every need they might have. They had to be creative, know how to light a show, know how to tear a show down; they had to do the publicity, the works. I realize now that I was looking for the same thing I was always looking for—independence. You couldn't turn to a light designer and say, "Make it green." God knows how many shades of green there are. When I auditioned dancers, I didn't care much that they be pretty in the vogue of the day. I cared that they had intelligence and need. Those are two very driving forces to gain independence.

People asked me, "Why are you here? How can you stay here?" And I said, "I love it, it feeds me." The light feeds me, the space feeds me, and I think that would be true still. I would curl up and die in New York. When I went to New York with Lester Horton as a dancer for the Folies-Bergère, it was horrible. I used to find a vacant lot, bend down, and just pick up the earth. It was like a repeat of *Gone With the Wind*.

I stayed in California when everybody else found it essential to fly off to New York to earn money, make a living, be where the influence was. I understood it completely, but I could not do that because my fuel was the sun and the light in California.

dave **BRUBECK**

Raised in the dual worlds of his cattleman father and pianist mother, the musician Dave Brubeck worked on the ranch, wrote music, and played in dance bands by the age of fourteen. Born in 1920 in the San Francisco Bay Area town of Concord, he went to the nearby College of the Pacific in Stockton to study veterinary medicine. He soon switched to music and, after the war, studied with avant-garde French composer Darius Milhaud at Mills College in Oakland. By the early fifties Brubeck had come up with a West Coast jazz of polyrhythms, unusual time signatures, classical influences, and improvisation that landed him on the cover of *Time* magazine in 1954. For more than four decades the pianist, composer, and bandleader has taken jazz to college campuses, the White House, and overseas, and his landmark 1959 recording, *Time Out,* featuring saxophonist Paul Desmond's "Take Five," still sells well today. Although he is a longtime resident of Connecticut, he says his close friends and family are still in California, and "We never really left."

I was born in Concord, California, where my mother was born. There wasn't even a high school in Concord then, so she and other people went around to different farmers and got them to sign that they would support a high school; she was in the first graduating class of Mount Diablo Union High School.

My mother went to a conservatory in San Jose, and after her three sons were born, to Europe to study piano with Tobias Matthay and Dame Myra Hess. She took my oldest brother, Henry, with her, and my brother Howard and I lived with neighbors. My dad lived on a cattle ranch in Clayton and would pick us up on weekends and take us up to the ranch.

It was just a natural thing in our house to play the piano, and she started teaching me piano when I was four. There were five pianos in the house—two grand pianos in the studio part of the house, another piano in the dining room, and another in the library. I can't remember where the fifth one was.

We moved to Ione, about ninety miles above Stockton, when I was in the eighth grade. Concord had 2,600 people when I was born. Ione had 250. My dad managed a 45,000-acre ranch. I had chores before I caught the school bus, and I'd start early in the morning to keep the woodblocks full, milk the cow, and, in summer, haul water from the spring in the meadow. I remember the hot sun, the sticklers going down my back.

My dad was a champion roper. He won the Salinas calf-roping and the double-team steer-roping competitions. I thought of him as a figure bigger than life, which in some ways he was.

In the summer I would ride with my dad. You can't imagine how many miles long the ranch was. He might send me to start the pump so the cattle had water. I had to ride there and start it, and the pump had great rhythm. I'd lie down and the pump on the two-by-fours would make vibrations. And when the horse would walk or trot or gallop, it would put rhythms in my head, polyrhythms in my head. Same way with the pump.

My first job was when I was fourteen, at Mokelumne River near Clements. The guy who collected laundry at the ranch heard me practicing, thought it sounded good, and asked me to play in his band. It was an outdoor dance hall with very warped wooden boards on the floor and bare lightbulbs strung above.

I played at the Jumping Frog Jubilee Dance in Angels Camp. We played Sutter Creek, Jackson, Mokelumne Hill—all those foothill towns in Amador County, where the gold rush was. In those days you often had a dance hall on top of a store or a blacksmith shop, and that's what it was in Sheep Ranch—on top of the store.

I wanted to be a cattleman like my dad and play in those bands. That would have satisfied me fine. I didn't want to go to college. My folks said I had to, like my brothers, Henry and Howard. I was pushed into going, and the idea was that I'd do premed at the College (now University) of the Pacific in Stockton, then go to U.C. Davis, which had a strong veterinary department. I didn't like chemistry and zoology and everything I took, but it came in handy when I switched to music; I'd done it my freshman year.

I met Art Tatum when I was still a student. Cleo Brown was working in Stockton, and I played intermission for her. Art Tatum was working at a place called Streets of Paris in Hollywood, and I said I wanted to hear him. She gave me a note to take to him, and I went to Los Angeles and to the club. It was early evening, and there was not one soul there except the bartender, Art Tatum, and me. That shows you how little attention was paid to him at times. All the musicians were aware, though, and to this day he's probably still considered the greatest jazz pianist who ever played.

When he got off, I showed him the note. We talked awhile. He could barely see out of one eye. He asked how Cleo was playing, and when I said she had the fastest left hand I've ever heard, Art immediately took me back to the bar. He showed me a high bar stool he wanted me to sit on, which would be as close as you could get to his left hand. Then he went around the oval bar and opened a hinged part, walked in, and went up two or three steps to where the piano was. He looked down to see if I was seated where he placed me, stuck his right hand straight up in the air, and proceeded to play, amazingly, with just his left hand. And then I knew who had the fastest left hand.

I studied with Darius Milhaud at Mills. My brother Howard was teaching there as his assistant, and I hitchhiked from Stockton to Oakland to see him. Milhaud said I could study with him after the service, and when I got out in '46, Mills even took male undergraduates on the GI Bill. He said if you wish to express America, you should use jazz in your compositions.

Before that, when I was stationed at Fort Irwin, forty miles into the desert from Barstow, I had hitchhiked into Los Angeles to see the composer Arnold Schoenberg. He told me to write something and bring it back. I did, and he said, "Why do you write these notes?" I said, "Because they sound good." And he said, "That's no reason; there has to be a reason." He also said, "I can say what the next note should be because I know more about music than any man alive." No doubt he was right, but that was my last lesson with him.

I didn't get to San Francisco until after the war. I had a good job, finally, at the Geary Cellar. It attracted people like Stan Kenton and Benny Goodman and Duke Ellington and became the place for traveling musicians to hang out. Word started spreading from our work there, and we were getting known away from the local scene. Ellington told people in New York about me, that they should hire me, and you can't beat that when you're unknown. The same with Benny Goodman—the first night we opened in New York at Birdland, Benny was at the first table, with his brother-in-law, John Hammond, the jazz critic.

Also, my friends started studying with Darius Milhaud. We had a group called the Jazz Workshop Ensemble, that became the Dave Brubeck Octet. It was such an advanced group. It predated the *Birth of the Cool* [recordings] and Miles Davis and Gerry Mulligan, that wonderful group that came out of New York. Neither group influenced the other, but we started way before them.

People wonder if there's a San Francisco sound. In jazz there's always been a sound that comes from St. Louis or Chicago or Kansas City or Memphis. When you're in the middle of it, you don't think about it. You just do it. But you are creating with the people in your area and environment, just as jazz has always done.

One time I played a concert at Northwestern, probably in the late fifties, and hadn't noticed who would be on the show. But it turned out to be all San Francisco people—Johnny Mathis, the Kingston Trio, Mort Sahl, and our quartet. So that shows you that what was popular all over the country was coming out of San Francisco. It was like a new wave, and we were all different. Johnny was going pretty strong, Sahl came out of the nightclubs, and there were Lenny Bruce and Lawrence Ferlinghetti—San Francisco was very alive then. We weren't just local people—we were starting to get a name all around the country.

So many people were associated with California, like Chet Baker, Gerry Mulligan, Shorty Rogers, Stan Kenton, and the list goes on and on of great musicians who came to Los Angeles to work in the studios. You had people the stature of André Previn in the studios.

I was playing a concert a few years ago at University of the Pacific on the same stage I was on when I was a student, and before the concert, in the afternoon, students could come and ask me questions. One student asked me, "Where did you meet your wife?" and I pointed to a door at the left of the stage and said, "Coming through that door."

The next time we played there, the dean came out at intermission and said they had a surprise for me. A light from the balcony focused on that door, then moved to the left of it where there was a black cloth hanging. A student pulled some cords to unveil a plaque that said something like, "Dave Brubeck and Iola Whitlock started their musical life coming through this door."

There were many different universities and establishments that wanted our archives, but that's what really sold me and my wife. There could never be anything equal to that wonderful feeling we got from seeing that plaque on the door where we first saw each other. And it has deeper meaning than just the plaque. It says a lot more about where we grew up.

robert **TOWNE**

Screenwriter and director Robert Towne was born in 1934 and raised in the Southern California port town of San Pedro. After college he studied acting with Jeff Corey in the fifties, roomed with classmate Jack Nicholson, and kept many of those ties as he moved into screenwriting. He has written films like *Chinatown, The Last Detail,* and *Without Limits,* for which he was credited, and worked on many more, including *The Godfather,* for which he received no screen credit (although Francis Ford Coppola did thank him publicly on receiving an Oscar). Once called by Larry Gelbart the best scriptwriter writing, Towne drew extensively on San Pedro places of his childhood in crafting *Chinatown.* The 1974 script, which won him an Oscar, ranks among the most honored and studied in recent memory, and launched him into the small circle of screenwriters who seem always to be working. The grandson of a Gypsy fortune-teller, Towne readily acknowledges his debts to both Carey McWilliams and Raymond Chandler, two California writers he feels "walked down the same streets."

M y dad's father was a tanner in Minneapolis. My dad was the seventh son and by far the most interesting of the lot. He was a remarkable man. He had to quit school in the ninth grade because his father died and there was nobody to take care of his mother.

One day he woke up in Minnesota and looked in the basin, in which there was water frozen, in the house, and he figured that was it. He got a job as a straw-hat salesman and went on the road. When he got to California, he said, "This is for me," and moved out here. Later he opened, with great success, a ladies' apparel shop on Sixth Street in San Pedro. It was called the Towne Smart Shop. He adopted that name after a lot of people started calling him Mr. Towne.

Across the street from the shop there was, and still is, a magnificent movie theater, the Warner's Theater. My parents loved the movies. Since the theater was right across the street, I could go alone, but usually I went with my mother unless it was a Saturday matinee. They had serials, a cartoon, double feature, news, announcements about the war—it was a whole way of life. It had to be four hours in the theater. And, as I recall, from the age of five or six, I did go to the movies by myself during the day.

I remember growing up with fishermen, merchant marines, sailors, defense plant workers, and people who ran shops like my dad. Every year there was a blessing of the boats, and it took over the whole town. My earliest memories of fishermen were how much they loved kids and how safe you always felt with them. I remember being lifted onto the boats, and looking down at the pier, and if you dropped, you dropped a thousand miles, but I never worried about that. It was a tremendous feeling of security.

It was indicative of how different things were in San Pedro. There was a market about two or three blocks away—the Ideal Market. My mother would give me a dime and say, "Go buy me a loaf of bread," and I'd do that. I'd leave the house on Saturday, play all day, and come back at night and nobody would ever worry; you were forever playing in the street—baseball or football or kick the can, or some kind of war game. We were a bunch of kids chewing fresh tar, lying in the street, or getting slivers of ice from the iceman.

Milkman, iceman, baker. It was a time when no matter how poor you were, these guys would come by your house. I think back on the extraordinary number of conveniences for poor people. We had no money. We weren't broke, but this was not a wealthy neighborhood. There was a bakery called DiCarlo's, and when they were baking, all of San Pedro smelled of fresh bread. One of the ways you could go to the movies for free was you'd save up DiCarlo bread wrappers.

We moved to Los Angeles when I was fifteen, but to me Southern California *was* San Pedro, and in a way it always has been. Los Angeles just seemed like a mess, and by that time—1950—it had changed anyway. I just didn't like it. But I wanted to stay in California, and I went to Pomona College. It was very much the old California, off Route 66, and Claremont was a classic kind of town, surrounded by orange groves in the foreground and a snow-capped mountain in the background.

I was thinking of going into journalism or some kind of writing like that. Then I started reading James Agee. There were two volumes of his. One was a collection of his reviews for *Time* magazine and for *The Nation,* and the other was several of his screenplays. It was the first time I saw a screenplay in print.

I remember reading something like, "I've often been bored by a bad play, but I've never been bored by a bad movie." Well, that's sure changed. But at that time the B movies, no matter how bad they were, were lively and fun, and I thought, That's how I feel. I don't care if movies are disreputable; I want to write movies. It was not considered a very reputable thing to do in the late fifties, early sixties. Good writers came out here to take the money and run, go back, and write a play or a novel. It was just not considered respectable.

I came late to Raymond Chandler. The *Los Angeles Times*'s old *West Magazine* had an article about Raymond Chandler's Los Angeles, and there were a half dozen photos taken as of that time. One was of a Packard convertible parked underneath the porte cochère of a beautiful house in Pasadena, others of a Plymouth convertible in front of Robinson's department store, the Bradbury Building downtown, Union Station. I remember thinking, This is the Los Angeles that I remember, and that it would be possible to re-create it as it was. I knew dozens of places that, selectively photographed, put you right back in that time and place. I had nothing in mind at that time, but I started reading Raymond Chandler mainly for the descriptions of Los Angeles. His descriptions made me realize the things that mattered to me.

He used to speak of the tomcat smell of eucalyptus and the red wind of the Santa Anas. See that pepper tree in the backyard? That was a birthday present from my wife, Luisa. Pepper trees were one of the things I remember most vividly as a kid, walking along the sidewalks and crunching the BBs that fell from the trees. Just that sense of time and place.

I remember the first day it hit me. I was walking with an old friend along the Palisades. There are a couple of trails down by the ocean, off Sunset, and you can hike up onto the bluffs overlooking the ocean. I was walking along with this guy, and suddenly I felt like I was about ten years old. And it was because I could smell the grass having turned to straw on the vacant lots up there and the eucalyptus trees and the ocean all at once. I realized *that* was why I felt like a kid, because all the scents I remember being in the air when I was a kid were there. It reminded me how almost invariably they weren't there. I would drive up Western Avenue with my dad, and in the evening, you could smell the orange blossoms in the air. You could smell the tar in the road. Good luck today—it's not going to happen.

It was so quiet, not like now where you've got every kind of motorized insult to your ear—car alarms, house alarms, leaf blowers, cars backing up with the little dings on them, dump trucks and garbage trucks that are motorized. Your head is ringing like a tuning fork.

They weren't in evidence then. It was so quiet. When somebody was washing his car, half a block away you could hear the chamois on the car, squeaking the way a chamois squeaks. And there's a moment in *Chinatown* when Gittes hears the squeaking of the chamois. He literally looks, and it's a guy cleaning a car. You were so much more attuned to little things like that. The loudest thing you'd ever hear was a Good Humor truck. Or the Helms Bakery man.

Carey McWilliams speaks about the mining mentality of California. It's the place where people come to mine gold, oil, and real estate, to come out and make a killing in the movies, to come out and make a killing in setting up some religious cult. This was not a place in which to build communities. It was a place to cut the land up and sell it any which way you could. You were selling pieces of the dream in Southern California.

Southern California is, I suspect, particularly congenial for *film noir* because everybody here is a stranger. Everybody's an outsider because everybody here came from somewhere else. There are no communities in the sense they were in the East. There are no little blocks and neighborhoods that have been there. Everybody is in pursuit of a dream of one kind or another. Parking-lot attendants are going to be movie stars—or, even worse, screenwriters now. Everybody is on the road to being something else. People feel that just because they're here, they're going to be rich and famous.

In any case it's a place where, in the genesis of *film noir,* all these things were going on. There were people coming out for their health, people escaping from unpleasant situations in the East, the Dust Bowl, prejudice in some cases, to the land of fresh starts, and along with that a certain hustler, a criminal element escaping from the law. People were looking for people: People get lost in the mail somewhere between here and Poughkeepsie. You see that a lot in Chandler.

So it was ripe for *film noir*. What you require is a land of outsiders, so nobody is quite what they appear to be. There's no set community against which you can really feel a sense of time and place. Everything is kind of slippery, like the hustlers, and it's all in an atmosphere of lazy sunshine and a place that is, physically at least, very congenial. It's got an idleness that has a kind of malevolence to it because there's no industry, no people hustling and bustling, no sense of direction. Cults. Kids without families coming here and getting surrogate families. I think it's very congenial to that.

In the East and Midwest, just as in medieval towns, there was a place for everything and everything was in its place. That's the reason why people tried to break away. They were weary of being landlocked or tied to a specific place and a specific profession, not unlike my father. The flip side of the coin is that the village idiot had a place in that town: "Hey, there's the village idiot. Hello, village idiot." Everybody knew him; he wasn't a stranger. Is anybody watching out for the village idiot today? So many of these crimes are committed by people saying, "Notice me," because they get out here and there's this desert, psychologically as well as physically, and they're worse off than they were before. Their dreams did not automatically come true. Nobody knows them, and nobody cares.

amalia MESA-BAINS

The daughter of migrant and domestic workers, Amalia Mesa-Bains put herself through college canning fruit and tomatoes, bottling maraschino cherries and cocktail onions. She was born in Santa Clara, California, in 1943, received a B.A. in painting in 1966, a Ph.D. in clinical psychology in 1983, and a MacArthur Foundation "genius" fellowship in 1994. Often using traditional Chicano altars, the artist and activist creates room installations and other artworks that explore memory and history—her own and her ancestors'. A prominent lecturer, writer, and teacher, she is a former San Francisco arts commissioner. She is director of the Institute for Visual and Public Art at California State University, Monterey Bay, and lives with her husband, musician and teacher Richard Bains, in Monterey.

M y grandfather Rafael was on the wrong side of the Mexican Revolution. He was a merchant who provided supplies for the army, and eventually he was executed by the revolutionaries. Two of my uncles were taken by Pancho Villa. So around 1917 my grandmother collected her three remaining brothers, my father, and my uncle, and came to the United States.

They went to work in Pueblo, Colorado, and eventually found their way into California by the early twenties. They lived as a migrant family, and my whole childhood was filled with these wonderful stories of their migrant years, trapped in Blythe during the heat waves or in the snow in Colorado, and all the different places they lived and worked.

My mother, who was also born in Mexico, came in through El Paso with her mother to clean houses on the American side, and eventually they just stayed. She wound up in Los Angeles, where she met my dad through a community of domestic workers. He was a gardener and sometime handyman, and she was a maid and governess. All these young people would get weekends off and go to dances in Santa Monica near the pier.

After my parents were married, they went north, following work. When I was born, in Santa Clara, it was still an orchard area. It wasn't the Silicon Valley that we know now. We still would contract orchards where the whole family would go out and pick together—apricots, almonds, things like that.

By the time I was school age, we had a permanent home in Sunnyvale. My father worked on a ranch, and very early I felt part of the tradition of families who made things grow. One of my very first jobs, when I was thirteen or fourteen, was working in a hothouse pinching the buds on carnations so all the nutrients would go into the main flower. I cut apricots, and when I turned eighteen, I went to work in the canneries to save enough money to go to school.

I feel as though my life, like the lives of many Mexicans, is inherently tied to this human food chain. We are the community that plants, harvests, and trucks it. We prepare, cook, and serve it, and we clean it up. We've been doing it probably for a couple of centuries now. I always think if former California governor Pete Wilson had actually been successful in deporting Mexicans, he would have starved to death his very own self, because there would be no food in California and, for that matter, the rest of the country.

On my drive to and from California State University at Monterey Bay, where I teach, I often travel through what's known as "the Salad Bowl of America." The road is called Blanco Road, which means "the

White Road," and which I always think is so ironic because 99 percent
of the people I pass working in the fields are either Mexicans or Central
Americans.

I have these flashbacks when I'm driving down the White Road.
About my childhood and why I'm doing what I'm doing now. Where I
am, and why these things have not changed. In fact, students of mine
who interviewed field workers found that income has actually *decreased*
for farmworkers in the last thirty years.

While I'm far away from the fields now in terms of my education
and the class that I've moved into, I'm really back there again because I
drive these roads. I'm teaching the first generation of farmworker kids
just like I was the first generation that went to college.

My mother worked cleaning houses when I was a child, and I used
to go with her to keep her company. That was when I really learned all
of these enormous class differentiations. Because you go in side doors or
back doors and you get their hand-off and cast-off goods, you get to see
a part of their lives that other people don't get to see.

My father and uncle raised English bulldogs, and they were dog han-
dlers for wealthy people. So I was always going with my dad to these
wealthy people's homes and seeing dogs that had their own little play-
rooms with trains. The dogs would sit and watch the trains go around.

Within my extended family, creativity and problem solving were
very routine. My father's family produced artists, inventors, and musicians, and there were always groups of people playing guitars and making up songs and singing. Cars were painted with flames and cobras.

So when I showed an aptitude for drawing, people facilitated it. At an
early age I had this habit of sitting on the bus quietly tracing around people with my finger. In order that people would not think that I was a
peculiar little girl—because I also used to spin and dance and jump
around—-my mother had a little pad and pencil that she would whip out.

For as long as I can remember, I was encouraged to make things. My
mother always had a little basket with a pair of scissors and scraps of

paper, and I would spend hours cutting things out. My father used to collect ends of paper rolls from meat markets, and he would stack them with rocks to get the curl out. Those became my drawing paper.

When I was seven or eight, I got an easel, which they kept out on the back porch. The washing machine, the dog's bed, and my studio were all on the same little porch, and I would be able to go splash around and paint.

They bought me a complete oil-painting set—which I'm sure was not within the family budget—when I was in high school. It was very expensive, with the sable brushes and all, and I had my own little painting box that I took off to school. I didn't do well in class because I couldn't follow directions, but I don't think creative people are very good at following directions—nor should they have to.

I went to San Jose State during the sixties, when concepts of new media and material were happening. I constructed some paintings there with metal-flake surfaces, because as a child I had become enamored of the Chicano tradition of car art. I used to go with my cousins to rod-and-custom shows, where we'd see cars with fiberglass-constructed tailfins and fifty layers of lacquer. In 1966 my first prize-winning piece was constructed and spray-painted with metal flake the way car surfaces are.

At San Jose, Luis Valdez was in my class, "The Romantic Literature of England," and I was both mesmerized and terrified by him. I had spent a large part of my life trying to act like a white person, and here was this person with slicked-back hair, army fatigues, and wraparound black Ray-Bans. He was starting then the Teatro Campesino, and some of his actors lived next door to me and would rehearse out in the backyard. I went to the world premiere of *The Shrunken Head of Pancho Villa,* and that had a lot of influence on me. It was my first consciousness that there was another way to be Mexican.

I also met my husband, Richard, at San Jose. He came from a large black family of ministers and preachers and grew up playing first gospel, then folk and rock music. We went to San Francisco in the mid-sixties to join the music movement, and by '69, I had connected with Chicanos in the Mission District who were forming galleries.

The stories I'm telling you are the basis of what I make in art. They're the narratives that hold the whole process of being an installation artist together for me. I take these little odd fragments and bits and pieces, and they all come together in the installations.

When I try to tell people what I do, they say, "Are you a sculptor? Are you a painter?" I say, "Well, I'm sort of a sculptor who makes pictures." I had already been making art for almost fifteen years before people applied the term "installation art" to what I did.

In truth my work came out of community celebration. It came out of reclaiming traditions in which you made offerings—*ofrendas*. It came out of my earliest childhood experiences with my grandmother keeping her prized objects on top of the dresser, which I now realize was an altar. It came from my godmother's yard shrine, that I spent hours sitting in front of. It came from my upbringing as a Catholic girl sitting out in the grotto behind this tiny old church and praying. All of those things are the connective tissue for what it is I do that other people now call installations.

My mother grows roses and dries the petals for potpourri I can use. The interviews and research, having my women friends over to sew, all the process of family and community that goes into my work, is as important as the actual installation. I've never made an installation on my own. All of them are filled with other people's efforts.

The way in which I made work for close to twenty years, in an impermanent fashion, really came out of the Mexican tradition of ephemeral art, where, for example, a whole village spent days before a great festival lining the streets with designs made out of flower petals. Or they'd make paper cutout flags that would fly on strings in the street, then be washed or blown away when wind or rain came.

It is the fugitive power of the ephemeral that makes it so important. Because it can only last for a few days, it is more valuable to you. For those few days, you have this very intense quality of the momentary.

That idea attracted me to doing ephemeral work, and I used to recycle. I might turn my kitchen drawer into a box for my Dolores del Rio installation, then paint it and turn it into something else for my Frida Kahlo altar. I didn't really start making anything even remotely permanent until the early nineties.

I've struggled for a lot of years trying to explain not just my own work but also what it was as Chicanos we were doing. Now I call it "cultural reclamation."

I discovered that memory is the most powerful tool we have. It is the bridge between the past and the present, between the living and the dead. My work has had so much to do with the dead, and at first I wondered why it attracted me. Then I realized that honoring the dead is mainly a practice of recalling. It's the way in which memory really serves you.

The dead are never completely gone from us, as long as we have one single memory of them. And so making the *ofrendas* and the altars was really the pursuit of memory. Walter Benjamin, the cultural critic and theorist, talks about how anecdote is the antidote to history, and as Chicanos we have suffered not from an absence of memory but really a memory of absence. All the things that we've lost are so clear to us.

What is the *corrido,* the tradition of the running song? Nothing more than pieces of memories sung and strung together over time. Every so often you add another verse on to it. Or the family fables that my parents told me, and my friends' parents told them. They're only memories being recalled for us so that we will never forget where we come from.

But I think there's something else to it. Part of the reason that our families have told us these stories and encouraged us to remember is because they know that in the remembering we are made stronger, that in the remembering is the kernel of resiliency.

I think it's hard for people to understand that all the time California has been California, it's always been Mexico. There is a Mexico within the memory, the practices, the politics, the economy, the spirituality of California. It's invisible to everyone but Mexicans. We've known it, we see it, we live in it, but Californians don't know it. They think it's Hollywood. They think it's Silicon Valley. They love their oranges and their lettuce, but they don't understand all it is built upon.

Within Chicano political theory there is the concept of internal colonization—that we were engulfed by a manifest destiny and a westward movement that swallowed us up and turned our class system upside down—that took our land from us; that through the Treaty of Guadalupe Hidalgo promised us linguistic rights, cultural rights, and the rights to the land, and we have none of those now. We're living through the most xenophobic, anti-Mexican, antibilingual period since the early days of the Mexican/Southwest annexation. And yet we are still Californians.

I've been working on a piece called *Private Landscapes and Public Territories,* and it's about that first orchard that I remember as a child. Whether I go out in those fields anymore is not the point. I am one of the people who will always advocate for those people who *do* go out in the fields.

My most important art began the day I made art in the service of my community, and I've never really changed that viewpoint. Whether I'm showing in the Smithsonian or LACMA, or any other major museum, my intention in some way is to shine a light on the conditions of our past and our present as California Mexicans. And I feel that's a job that will never be totally done.

Yet even when I'm trying my best to make people pay attention to some political fact or event in history, I also want them to lose themselves in my work. I want them to forget who they are and to remember someone else's life. Or to find a connection between their life and my life, or their life and our life.

We always felt there were two Californias, the one that is understood by the larger society, and the Mexican California that we're a part of. The two don't seem to have a connection to each other, and that's because part of being in California is this impossible dream. You're at the edge of the ocean. There's this future that's totally open to you. There are no obstacles. You can reinvent yourself anytime you want. There are plastic surgeons. There is virtual reality. And here was this group of people who constantly focused on what others saw as a past that simply didn't need to be addressed anymore.

The Chicano way of moving forward and making art is both of the Californias. It's this constant reclaiming of memory, but it's also this vigorous reinvention of oneself. I'm a Chicana even if I don't speak fluent Spanish. My sister will be a Chicana even if she wasn't part of the movement. You can have a past that recalls the real history and a heritage that allows that future. They're inseparable.

jon robin **BAITZ**

Few playwrights have so successful a New York debut as Jon Robin Baitz did with his 1987 play *The Film Society*. Writing of the playwright, then twenty-five, *New York* magazine critic John Simon said, "Though it's riskier to gamble on writers' futures than on pork bellies, I would invest in Jon Robin Baitz." Born in Los Angeles in 1961, Baitz has drawn on the city again and again in his plays. *The Film Society* may have been set in South Africa, where he spent much of his childhood, but it also reflected the film culture of Hollywood. *Mizlansky/Zilinsky*, his first produced play, came out of his experience as a gofer for two larger-than-life Hollywood producers. A voracious reader, Baitz did not go to college and first began writing plays at Los Angeles's Padua Hills Playwrights' Festival, which he attended for several summers. Also a screenwriter and, occasionally, an actor in friends' films, he lives in New York.

M y first memories of Los Angeles are of bracing cold days like today, with clear skies and picnics at the beach with my family. My father in Ray-Ban sunglasses. Driving out to Santa Monica in our white Ford Fairlane.

My father's work with what was then Carnation Milk took him all over the world, and I left Los Angeles for the first time when I was seven and went to Brazil. We came back, for a minute practically, when I was ten, then left again for South Africa for six years.

I came back when I was around seventeen, which was when I thought the Los Angeles of my childhood was starting to change. Beverly Hills had gone from a relatively sleepy little village with a five-and-dime and clunky little stores to a place with marble surfaces everywhere. You could smell money in some way that was overt. Maybe it was the difference between mid-Wilshire where we'd lived before and Beverly Hills where we lived then. I was also a little older. Anyway, it had changed.

I didn't go to college. I was a relatively lazy academic student and somewhat congenitally disinterested in being any kind of super hyper-achiever. I had a weird contempt for the whole notion of doing well at something—SATs and college all seemed to be unattainable or inaccessible to me. I also didn't really catch up with American life that quickly.

Right after I graduated from Beverly Hills High School, my parents moved to Holland, and I went there to visit them. Took advantage of the fact that they lived in Europe. I wandered around Israel for several months and spent a lot of time in England.

I was maybe twenty when I moved back to LA and my adult life began. I somehow fell in—like Pinocchio falls in—with theater people. I fell in almost by accident with the Padua Hills Playwrights' Festival folk.

I was wandering like a vagabond through a Beverly Hills bookstore, when Beverly Hills still had bookstores, and I met this guy Tony Peyser. He was a writer and journalist who had an office in the Writers and Artists Building ten feet away from Billy Wilder's office, and that was like flypaper to me.

While I was vaguely interested in the theater as a kind of slacker's heaven, Tony actually *read* plays, and he would toss me plays to read. His friends were actors, and I had never really met actors before. I thought that they were a great, great diversion. And this was around 1984 and the Olympic Arts Festival, when there was so much happening all of a sudden. There was this adrenaline-infused theater.

I started to sit down and write a play. My high school friends were all going to Berkeley and Stanford or working at Wolfgang Puck restaurants as waiters, and I decided I couldn't keep floating around anymore. And at exactly that moment, Tony pushed me into contacting the Padua Hills Playwrights' Festival about going as an apprentice playwright.

The Padua Hills Festival had been started by Sam Shepard, Murray Mednick, and a few other folks. At that time, it would gather every summer on the grounds of Pomona College in Claremont, up in the hills, and it was sort of all red earth and olive trees. They would write site-specific plays, some of which remain to this day completely inscrutable. People would come up every summer to see those plays and tromp from spot to spot.

What I shared with the best of the Padua sensibility was bewilderment with this notion of writing as a living. It was a little band of actors and writers drinking tequila all night and sitting in dorms, very impoverished, and utterly on the fringes of what seemed to be consuming the rest of the world: show business and money.

John Steppling, who's the first playwright I really became close to, used to talk about the necessity of embracing failure. That was a very attractive and liberating kind of idea, especially for someone who wasn't going to college and wasn't really hip to achievement.

Meanwhile I had no money and somehow got a job as an assistant to a couple of film producers whose position had been slowly deflating, a little bit like a Mylar balloon. But I didn't realize this at the time. I thought, These men are interesting: They give me scripts to read and I drive them around, pick up the laundry, and go to Nate 'n Al's deli.

It was an entirely new world for me of casual lassitude. Lassitude I knew, but not casual. I knew desperate lassitude, and these guys were absolutely casual skeptics, and brilliant satirists of the Hollywood infrastructure.

I found them and their language exhilarating, specifically the way they talked about one another's position, what was to be ordered for lunch, what girls looked good on the street, the great uses of the speakerphone, who was a hypocrite that day in *Variety*. I liked how they had turned the Californian dream of ease, comfort, and a showbiz sort of glitz into a somewhat murky sideshow in which they were the stars instead of just the supporting players.

When I was at Padua, I was still vaguely working for my Hollywood guys, and I said to Steppling—lying, completely lying—"I'm writing a play called *Mizlansky/Zilinsky*." He laughed at the title, which he loved, and I took his laughter as encouragement. Laughter was the only thing I needed to get me to put on a skit. So I wrote it very quickly.

They were entirely conscious that I was writing about them, and they would correct my notes. In fact, on my first day as an assistant, I was paid the ultimate compliment, which was, "You are going to run a studio one day."

As I wrote my play, all of the grotesquely funny class consciousness and the hierarchy of success in Hollywood poured out. The despair and longing that swirled in their hearts came together to make this sort of ambivalent witch's brew of avarice, greed, and community spirit.

Mizlansky/Zilinsky was first produced by LA Theatre Works in 1985. My old bosses came to see it, and I was grudgingly told that I had romanticized them and that they were in fact much worse than that. I did love them very much, and they were very good to me. They were thrilled that I'd become a writer, even though they thought it was an entirely schmucky profession.

My play struck a chord, and in the nonnarrative twenty-some years of my life, I suddenly had an identity. I was a playwright at a time when opportunities in the theater here were very, very rich for a young writer.

I was still trying to sort out the years in South Africa, and I had started to think about what an unapproachable subject it was. South Africa was something I had blocked out in an effort to deal with the present, the here and now, Los Angeles 1986. And South Africa was exploding. There was a kind of ongoing bloodshed. I would see the news in mute stupefaction, impotent helplessness, and sadness. I felt so distant from it, and it had been such a large part of my life. Once again I was in exile from something I knew very, very well.

Meanwhile I used to have dinner at Musso and Frank's almost every night at the counter, with the film producer Jerry Bick. After dinner one night we wandered over to Book City and into the film section. It was interesting to me, working for those guys, and the culture here is a movie culture. It's wrapped up in a mythology of stardom, escapism, and success, and those models are great and awful both.

I felt very distant wandering in the enormous movie section of Book City. Then I saw this slim English paperback, *How to Start Your Own Film Society,* and I picked it up. It seemed so filled with yearning for community, and it just spoke of an infinitely lonely, desperate life, and infinitely unfulfilled experience in the dark, the dark being the only respite from reality.

My play *The Film Society* built itself up in my head pretty quickly from that moment on, and I wrote it over a couple of months. I wasn't thinking just about South Africa—I was thinking about power and those who haven't got it and how alluring escapism can be. Really what I was doing, in retrospect, was taking the first steps to growing up as a writer.

There's something about being in Los Angeles that helped me write that play. It certainly provided a tremendous counterpoint. It is the world capital of not being realistic, of not facing truth, of not looking in the mirror. It is the universal capital, in fact, of artifice, and it vividly and daily demonstrates haves and have-nots.

The Film Society is very much about retreating from reality and the present. It is about escapism, and for a lot of people LA is a place to lose themselves. For painters it's the light. For writers it's to be tortured.

Anyway, the opportunities were really rich for being a young playwright in Los Angeles. I gave *The Film Society* to Gordon Davidson at the Mark Taper Forum and Bill Bushnell at the Los Angeles Theatre Center (LATC), and the next morning Bill Bushnell committed to it.

LATC had just opened. It was the essence of idealism about reclaiming a part of the city that had long been abandoned. I remember walking out of Bill Bushnell's office and thinking, I'm part of the theater in Los Angeles—the new theater here. It comes out of Padua. It comes out of the avant-garde. It is not part of show business at all. It's art. My brothers and sisters were painters and artists. They weren't screenwriters writing for money.

I knew I was at a literal crossroads. There's this Robbie Baitz that is lazy and easily seduced. It's the Robbie that loved the theater because it was a place for slackers—people who have powerful imaginations and dream lives that take up a lot of time. I'm proud of being from LA, but I absolutely knew I had to leave to not be a full-time screenwriter. Not be a writer for money. And not go into a kind of Dantesque topography of studio development where I once was a playwright. I thought there would be time for that later, and I still do.

That was what LA meant to me then. It meant go talk to someone at Twentieth Century Fox about making a movie about secret societies at Yale. Well, I don't know anything about that, but because I was young and could pretend to be articulate and lucid, central casting in the LA tradition might have sent me over there.

So having become a playwright and stumbled into something I believed in, I had to move to New York. Now, when I come back, the first thing I always do is go to the Farmers' Market and walk around and marvel at the little bit of old LA that's left. Sometimes I take my childhood walk, the walk my mother took with me to the Hancock Park elementary school, stopping at the Sav-On Drugstore for pistachio ice cream, five cents a scoop.

I come into town and see what's gone. Which strip mall has wiped out which relatively inconspicuous but sweet architectural curiosity. I

look at a place like San Francisco, which manages to retain its character. San Franciscans are nothing if not professional romantics. They
specialize in nostalgia and romance. And Los Angeles doesn't. Los
Angeles is voraciously about the future. It is voraciously about the abol-
ishment of traditions and cannibalizing the past to make some glittery
new bauble.

Is there one word I can think of that describes Los Angeles? I think
the word is "heartbreaking." It always breaks my heart. I realize I can't
live there anymore. It might be actually a notion of childhood that
doesn't exist anymore. Maybe Los Angeles has always been about a culture of celebrity, money, and yawning hunger. But now it's that way and
actually feels somewhat charmless, too. There is nothing sadder to me
than that.

carolyn SEE

Born in Los Angeles in 1934, Carolyn See spent most of her childhood in the working-class suburb of Eagle Rock and most of her adult life in the bohemian Topanga Canyon. A writer who has described raw silk as the flannel of the desert, she has written evocatively of her family in the memoir *Dreaming* and of her home state, California, in nearly all her books. Her first novel won second prize in the Samuel Goldwyn Creative Writing Contest at UCLA, where today she is an adjunct professor of English. She has been a Guggenheim Fellow and Getty Scholar and watched daughter Lisa See emerge to achieve her own writing distinction. She lives with her companion, the writer John Espey, in Pacific Palisades.

When I talk to my students about writing, I talk about character and plot, space and time, but, most important, geography. Place has always been where you start. The more specific you can get about a particular place, the better chance you have of making it be universal and of really grounding it.

Geography dictates what you write. I see it with translations of my new novel, *The Handyman.* Imagine *The Handyman* in French or German. You conjure up a whole different guy because he's plodding around with a Germanic mind and German coming out of his mouth. Any novel depends primarily on setting, more even than on the characters.

It seems to me that's why California literature is pretty much an entity unto itself. The potential here is still untapped and hasn't been written, so it doesn't have to be the same old tiresome tragedy. There is a whole quality of hope here that the future is still open ended. In the way that people used to come to America—this is a platitude, but what the hell—to shed their past and fulfill their dreams, now they come from the East to California.

Clara, my younger daughter, works with the homeless in Santa Monica. I was talking to a lady on one of the boards there, and she said, "Our homeless are a cut above because they have the sense to take the bus from downtown where it's so awful to the beach where the climate is better." That whole westward movement is, of course, inherent in all of American literature, but also I think in every one of my books there's been a movement from the center of the city to the beach. When you get to the beach, that's the end and you feel better.

My novel *Golden Days,* which ends on the beach, is set in Topanga Canyon, where people survive nuclear war because of those sheltering walls of earth. And also because they're so damn crabby and ornery.

Topanga shows up in most of my books. When you first turn into Topanga, especially if it's high summer, it's like driving into Africa. It's a parallel universe. It's primitive. Even now, with more houses and some rich people up there, it's never really going to change because it's too steep, too narrow, too dangerous, too hot. It's too wacky.

All of us, I think, want maximum freedom, but then there's that little place where, if you go just a little bit beyond maximum, you're scared to death. You're in chaos and free fall emotionally, domestically, spiritually, whatever. In Topanga you would see that. In fact, that's really partly why we moved out after thirty-two years. You paid for extraordinary physical beauty with catastrophe just all the time.

You pay for everything here. A house in the flats has the illusion of stability, but of course there are going to be earthquakes. You also pay for a house in the flats with boredom to the max. There's a house next to you, and a house next to that. In *The Handyman* somebody says, "I just hated this woman because she'd sold out: she lives in Hancock Park for two stories and a lawn."

Topanga traditionally was full of outlaws fleeing their past. There's a wonderful novel, *Fast One,* by Paul Cain. It's set in the thirties, where the intrepid private eye flees to Topanga and bleeds out his life on the dry earth. Charles Manson lived there for quite a while. There are elements of freedom and of danger. With freedom comes danger. And with security comes safety, but also boredom.

I guess the overriding theme in my books is that we're living in paradise, we don't even know it, and if we wake up, we'll see it. But the counterpoint of that is we could be living in hell. Topanga is a perfect place; it changes back and forth. I have a passage in *Rhine Maidens* where the heroine says she's done enough gardening to know that you can change your world just by changing your glance. You could be looking into an extraordinary rosebush and just look over to see the sun beating down on the weeds. It only takes a glance.

Here in the Palisades we're half a mile from the Self-Realization Fellowship, which has a little tiny lake surrounded by a mad garden. There's every kind of plant, and things go in and out of bloom with demented liveliness. I think the point of the lake shrine is that it's extraordinarily beautiful, and if man can invent or organize that kind of beauty in one little postage stamp of earth, what's to keep him from organizing beauty everywhere else?

A few days ago I was driven through Irwindale, the gravel-pit capital of California, and it's astonishingly ugly. People had to work hard to make it that ugly. So it's like we have the capacity in us to create heaven or hell, and Topanga mirrors that tremendously. It completely depends on the season up there.

When you wake up in Topanga—assuming it's one of those beautiful days—the birds are going crazy, the coyotes have been yapping all night, the trees are just breathing, and the aromas are intense. The acacia is bright, bright yellow. So then you hang out, the same as you would any other place, except you're hanging out in the most beautiful place in the world.

But when the fires are coming, or when it's just high summer, it is *agony*. You wake up in a pool of sweat. You take four showers a day. There are tarantulas in the garage, and rats and snakes, and everybody's in a bad mood because it's so hot, including the rats and snakes and tarantulas. We had air-conditioning but it didn't work; it was hotter than the air-conditioning could handle.

There was a bitch of a fire in 1995. We'd been through a lot of fires, one after another, in our thirty-two years in Topanga. But this thing was traveling so fast, and it started so close to us. It was one of those horrible hot days, and I heard a helicopter, which of course is the worst news you can have. I ran outside, and it looked fine from the living room side, but out back the wind made dust devils of fire on the patio. The helicopter pilot was saying, with a bullhorn, "Get out, get out! Get out!"

Since there'd been fires all over town, we already had the car packed up. We'd certainly gotten out of the house many times. I'd say fifteen times in thirty years. That's what you do when you live up there. You have everything packed up, and then you stay until the last minute.

It's sort of standard procedure if you live in Topanga to always have a list of stuff to take either by your front door or on the refrigerator. My list was always on the refrigerator door: the family Bible, the family photographs, passports, insurance, the portraits by Don Bachardy, and Sleepy and Squarey, the two toys Clara slept with when she was little. Even after she'd moved out of the house, she'd say, "If there's a fire, be sure and pack Sleepy and Squarey." When Lisa was home, we had other stuff.

You're terrified, but you also love it because there's no other time like it. The air is so dry that you're almost dehydrating. You can't catch your breath. You're gasping. Your mouth and eyes are dry. Your breath rattles in your throat. Your adrenaline is so high you're trembling. There are times when the fire goes through and you watch it, and it makes a sound like a train bearing down on you. It sucks the oxygen out of the air.

This last time, our house disappeared in smoke and flames, which led me to believe it had burned down. It hadn't, but we got to see how we behaved in an emergency, which was extremely well. John was saying, "Well, dear, this is just an opportunity for a fresh start." Santa Monica was full of refugees from the fire, motels were giving cheap rates, and the exhilaration was so weird. People were laughing, still out of breath, jittery.

When the floods come, people get very depressed. A flood is a whole different thing. It takes a long time to work itself up into being a flood, and it's cold and damp and nasty. You're wet, and it takes forever to get finished. But the fires go by so fast. They crackle. They're so spectacularly beautiful, so awe-inspiringly dangerous, that you go through a fire on an adrenaline rush. All this stuff is very biblical, you know, which again leads you to write a little bit beyond the constraints of ordinary life.

My mother, who appears in all my books under one guise or another, lived in Victorville in a tiny trailer park. Victorville used to be a little Depression town on the railroad tracks, and now it's kind of a booming semimetropolis, but it's still in the desert.

California to my mind is full of these places. Even in Los Angeles you're just three or four days away from dying of thirst and exposure if anything happens to the water supply, because we're in the desert. This is one of the few cosmopolitan cities that goes so against nature. That's

why people in the East are always foretelling our doom, and they may
be right, although it hasn't happened yet.

There's that giddiness that also may have to do with Hollywood
and the hope that you might strike it rich. It's a sense that although
there are sociological classes, they're still amorphous enough that you
can crash through one class to another. You can still be upwardly
mobile here.

Most of our futures are probably grim, and probably, for most of us,
this is still a vale of tears. But in California there is the gold rush, okay?
Simon Rodia had a vision that had to do with air and trash and he
turned that into the Watts Towers. There are lame-brain starlets who
make it in the movies. There are businessmen who look out on nothing,
see tract houses, and turn from dumb contractors into multimillion-
aires. And there are baggy old crones who go to good plastic surgeons
and turn back into thirty-year-olds.

These are things that you can't get away with in other parts of the
country, I don't believe. People would say, "You're sixty-five, for God's
sake, Mother! How could you humiliate us by changing your
appearance?"

Midwestern books are mostly about endurance and hard times, and
novels set in New York, Connecticut, and those places are about class
and pressure on the individual. Frankly I'm glad that I live out here,
because I love writing about futures that aren't set in stone, and pasts
that you can invent and reinvent.

In my books people pretty much end up on a voyage or on the beach,
going somewhere in a state of hope or in a state of happiness. And that's
true even in *Golden Days,* where I used some of the worst images of
nuclear war that I could find. The sand on the beach melts into glass,
and I thought, Well, okay, what do you do with it then? You windsurf
on it. So when the characters come down out of the canyon, the beach
is glass, it's the colors of a jukebox, and a few hardy souls are
windsurfing.

At a cocktail party in New York some years ago, a gentleman said to me, "Ah, yes, you're from California. I always feel that New York is the brains of America, and California is the genitalia." He gave me this big dumb smile, and I thought, Given that choice, which he presented so clearly, where would you rather be?

Part II

Frontier

frank **GEHRY**

With the Guggenheim Museum Bilbao, the architect Frank
Gehry capped a career distinguished by experimentation and in-
novation. Called the "world's most celebrated new building" by
the *New York Times,* the 1997 museum joined a group of buildings around the world that have dramatically altered the way we
look at architecture. Born Frank Owen Goldberg in Toronto in
1929, Gehry came with his family to Los Angeles in 1947 and became a U.S. citizen in 1950. His own home in Santa Monica, initially disparaged for its chain-link fencing, plywood, and
corrugated metal, has since become an architectural landmark.
Winner of the 1989 Pritzker Prize, the National Medal of the
Arts, and Austria's Friedrich Kiesler Prize, he received the 1999
American Institute of Architects Gold Medal, the institute's high-
est honor. In his hometown of Los Angeles, he continues work
on the Walt Disney Concert Hall and recently completed reno-
vation of the Norton Simon Museum in nearby Pasadena. In addition to designing furniture and museum exhibitions, Gehry
also plays ice hockey and owns part of an ice hockey team. He
and his family live eight blocks from his Santa Monica office.

M y father was one of nine children and hung out in Hell's Kitchen,
New York. He became a boxer in tournaments, came to Toronto
for something, and met my mother there. My mother was born in

Lodz, Poland, in 1904 and when she was nine years old, her family went to Canada. Many who stayed perished in the Holocaust—we counted thirty-three or thirty-four people who were killed at various camps.

My grandfather, her father, had a hardware store, Caplan's Hardware, on Queen Street in Toronto, and I used to go to work there. I loved the stuff, and I used to make pipe fittings with him and cut glass. I would go there every Saturday morning, because my grandfather would go to synagogue, and he would get me to hold the store open for him and watch the place. I used to stay over with my grandparents on weekends a lot, and I would read Talmud with my grandfather.

My grandmother was a healer. She did a kind of mystical thing where she'd go to people's houses when they were sick and write on their hands with a quill. I went with her a few times. I never believed in it, but I loved her, and I was fascinated with it. I was too young to really know whether it was right or wrong, but people believed in it.

She had a woodstove. She used to get wood shavings at the cabinet shops around the neighborhood, and they would be funny shapes, as if cut out on jigsaws. When I was around eight, I spent time with her sitting on the floor of her kitchen making cities out of these wood things—we'd build bridges, car ramps, things like that.

Making these cities was very memorable and pleasant and something I looked forward to. Later, when I was struggling about what to be when I grew up, I remember asking myself what I really liked in my life and I had this image of sitting on the floor with Grandma, making stuff.

We moved to Los Angeles in 1947. My father was sick. He was having a hard time, and the family was living in a tiny apartment the size of this room we're in, with a wall down the middle and pull-down beds. It was in a building in downtown LA that's still there.

I was eighteen or nineteen, and I had to go to work. I drove a truck, and I would sometimes go to movie stars' houses to deliver things. Once I delivered this breakfast nook to Roy Rogers and Dale Evans. Because it didn't fit, I had to fix it. I did a lot of extra work, and they were very appreciative that I got it all done for them for Christmas, so they invited me for Christmas. They just put me in the family. I was a kid from Canada, and I was in awe of the whole thing.

My family used to take me to movie premieres when people would just stand around and gawk at movie stars. They didn't have any money, so they would do that kind of stuff. I remember once I went with them, and Roy Rogers and Dale were in a car with Bob Hope. They recognized me and stopped the car.

I was working full-time as a truck driver because the family was very poor, but I took art and drafting classes at LA City College. My cousin was going to USC, and I would go hang out with him and his friends there. He had a fancy car, and socially, that was very exciting.

I signed up for night and Saturday classes at USC. I got into a ceramics class with Glen Lukens. Glen was building a house by Raphael Soriano, who at the time was hot stuff in LA architecture, and took me to his home one day when Raphael was there. I saw this guy come in with a black beret and a black outfit, and he looked like a prizefighter whose nose has been broken and never fixed. He was very verbose, and he was jumping around and talking about the fireplace and this and that and enjoying his building being built.

I don't know what happened, but it ignited something in me that Glen could see. He called me in and suggested I take an architecture design class. I did, and I really got excited. During that year I also met a very nice man, Arnold Schrier, who was doing graduate work at USC and is now practicing architecture in Montreal. Arnold and I would spend weekends looking at work of other architects. Every weekend we'd have a list of houses to go look at—built work by Schindler, Neutra, Frank Lloyd Wright. I really loved doing that.

I see now that I was building up my own visual vocabulary and trying to understand why things happened the way they did. You slowly started to understand the work of each architect and their language and how they addressed clients, site, and budgets. So it was just a learning process. But it was exciting too. Now I see kids come to look at my Santa Monica house, and I think back to when I did that. And I still go look at people's work, when I can.

My mother had taken me to galleries and concerts when I was a kid, and I loved music, art, and art history. I couldn't get enough of that. And when I got into the architecture school, it bothered me that the artists and architects were in the same building, and they weren't talking to each other. So all the way through school, I kept trying to put them together and create projects where we would work together. I went to all their shows.

But the architects were closed to the artists. I don't know if the artists were closed to the architects. I don't think so. I think it was mostly the other way around: The architects felt the artists' thing was a different world. And I knew it was the same. Right from the beginning I knew it was the same. They've never convinced me that there was any difference, even to this day.

When I graduated from USC, two of my city-planning teachers knew that I didn't want to do rich guys' houses, that I was a left-leaning, city-planning do-gooder. They kept urging me to apply to Harvard Graduate School of Design, which I did, and when I got out of the army, I went to Harvard. I went into city planning and not architecture, but I found that city planning was about statistics, government, economics, and a lot of stuff that I was interested in, but I wasn't ready to do that kind of thing. I didn't have that maturity or something. I tried to turn all the planning classes into urban design, and my teachers hated it, and I had a hard time. They made fun of me. It didn't fit what they were doing.

I was coming from LA, and architecture here was all about Asia. There was a lot of emphasis on Japanese classicism and art while I was in architecture school, and my early works look like they come from Japan. Harvard was Western. My Harvard experience opened the door to the Greeks and Western classicism, and to the French and Le Corbusier. Le Corbusier had a show of his paintings in Robinson Hall where I was studying, and I got very excited about it because you could see him working out his language in paint. I saw his paintings as sketches for his architecture, and I found him interesting. All the people around him who came to Harvard were interesting.

I dropped out of city planning, and they allowed me to attend all the classes I wanted, for no credit, for the rest of the year. It happened accidentally, but that turned out to be an incredible opportunity. It was a better education than the prescribed one.

My family and my first wife's family were in LA, so we moved back in 1957. I worked at different places until 1962, when I started my own practice in Santa Monica. The clients I had didn't have a lot of money, and the workmanship you got was pretty horrible. It was wham-bam, thank-you-ma'am, *slam,* when I'd been trained for perfect details and things that you couldn't achieve.

This was the time when Rauschenberg and Johns were making art with junk. Donald Judd was making art with galvanized steel, and Carl Andre was putting bricks along the floor. Intellectually I connected with them, and not only because the minimalism fit my liberal tendencies. Despite its matter-of-factness, accessibility, and unpretentiousness, it was high art. It was obviously beautiful, and people were responding to it.

I didn't know many artists. Then, in '64, my Danziger house was being built, and when I would go to the site I would find Ed Moses there. And Kenny Price and Larry Bell. Since I knew who they were, I got really excited that they were interested in what I was doing. I was just hot out of the box, and the architects of the period were not so interested in what I was doing. In fact they were critical. So I sort of found a family.

Ed was very important, because he liked what I was doing, and I got to know Billy Al Bengston and Kenny Price and John Altoon and Bob Irwin and Craig Kauffman. I guess I was nice to have around because I was smart and I talked the talk and I loved everything they were doing. I was in awe of them, and it probably was not an unpleasant thing for them to have a few characters like me around. I went to all their shows, and I was very supportive.

I was learning as well, and I think it took them by surprise in the end. But it wasn't like I was there on a secret mission. It was very genuine. I loved them all. I still do. What I learned from the artists was what wasn't happening in the architecture realm. It was a freedom more closely related to what was going on in the world. The artists were more willing to be commentators.

I think a lot of the inspiration for my early work came from the Los Angeles artists' studios. For instance, Billy Al would change his studio every month. He would knock a wall out, make a loft, change the doorway. Every time I went there to dinner it looked different. Billy Al has incredible taste and style. It was hands-on. It was macho. It was very seductive. I was like a sponge, taking it all in.

I was recently at the University of Toronto getting a fancy degree, and I was asked about whether or not my work would have turned out the way it is had I stayed in Toronto. My answer to them was that it wouldn't have because, first of all, I would never have been accepted at the University of Toronto architecture school, because I was too much right brain, and I didn't have the aptitude for all the funny tests they gave. I didn't have the grades, so their system would have put me in trade tech. I might have become a mechanic or something.

I don't think the culture in Toronto would have been nurturing for the kind of work style that existed in the California art scene—the thinking, the stuff people were talking about and doing, that led to my own language. That kind of discussion wasn't happening in Toronto.

California was about freedom because it wasn't burdened with history. The economy was booming because of the aircraft industry and movie business, and things were going up quickly. Everybody could make whatever they wanted, and, while I didn't realize it then, I realize now that's what democracy is about. Democracy didn't say everybody has to have taste.

My own house couldn't be built anywhere but California. I was experimenting with wood and glass and materials that are used here. It's not an expensive construction technique, and I was using it to learn.

The experience of playing on the floor with my grandmother was, in hindsight, like an adult giving you permission to play. Creativity is about play and a kind of willingness to go with your intuition. It's crucial to an artist. If you know where you are going and what you are going to do, why do it? I think I learned that from the artists, from my grandmother, from all the creative people I've spent time with over the years.

It manifests itself in a funny way in my life with the fish image. My grandmother used to go on Thursday and buy a carp and bring it home and put it in the bathtub, and on Friday the fish would be gefilte fish. I used to sit and watch the fish in the bathtub. When the postmodern movement started, and my colleagues started to reject modernism and to regurgitate Greek temples, I in my anger said, "Well, why not go back three hundred million years before man, to fish?"

You know, I didn't really think it through then, but the more I thought about it later, the more I realized that there was something to it. I looked back at Japanese woodcuts and the drawings of Hiroshige.

I looked at fish and their subtle movements. It was just following the end of your nose, not thinking about it. Then it started to evolve, and I made fish drawings and lamps and everything. That freedom to try things from free association, to trust your intuition and move forward, is, I think, the essence of creativity.

michael tilson **THOMAS**

Internationally acclaimed conductor and composer Michael Tilson Thomas was born in Los Angeles in 1944 and was music director of the city's Young Musicians Foundation Debut Orchestra at nineteen. Grandson of Boris and Bessie Thomashefsky, founders and stars of New York's Yiddish Theatre, and son of the screenwriter Theodor Thomas, he won the Koussevitzky Prize at Tanglewood in 1968 and became assistant conductor of the Boston Symphony Orchestra in 1969. A celebrated interpreter of such twentieth-century masters as Igor Stravinsky and George Gershwin, he recalls nearly driving off the road the first time he heard James Brown on his car radio, and has concertized with the Grateful Dead. Formerly principal guest conductor of the Los Angeles Philharmonic and principal conductor of the London Symphony Orchestra, he is founder and artistic director of the Miami Beach–based New World Symphony. Reminiscent of Leonard Bernstein, he has been widely acclaimed for programming as well as conducting at the San Francisco Symphony, where he has been music director since September 1995. He lives in San Francisco.

I grew up in the San Fernando Valley, where we had a small ranch-style house on more than half an acre of property. It had an enormous windbreak of eucalyptus trees, citrus trees, and a real country feeling.

There was a huge cactus garden, which my father nurtured and which began in large part with little souvenir cacti the size of your thumb that he had bought getting off the train at Union Station.

The light was wonderful, and my father had surrounded all of these citrus trees and cacti with fabulous mounds of volcanic rock that he had picked up on his forays to the desert. I used to love going outside just after it had rained, because the color of the earth and all the plants was so vivid, especially in the late afternoon. There was a huge richness to the colors and to the scent of the lemon and orange trees. It was quite idyllic.

After dinner our standard recreation would be to play the piano. Then we'd go for a walk down these other dirt streets, past the stables and the turkey farm, the persimmon and walnut orchards. There was an Armenian family that made their own ice cream sometimes, and we'd stop there and come around back home.

In the middle of this environment were my parents and all their Yiddishist radical friends, talking about Freud and Marx and Dostoyevsky and listening to Beethoven and Schoenberg on 78 recordings, and arguing about who had been the truest spirit on the Yiddish stage or whatever. All these very intellectual, artistic issues were being talked out within the extremely relaxed and beautiful natural environment.

My parents went to Los Angeles in the 1930s, partly to go out west and try something new. Paul Muni, who was my father's cousin's husband, was at the height of his film career. My father, who had worked with Orson Welles at the Federal Theater Project in New York, began doing a lot with the studios, and my mother became the head of research at Columbia Pictures.

They very quickly fell into this crowd of radical Yiddishist young people, many of whom also had done things in the theater or education in New York. I remember always there were parties, barbecues, or big family-style meals. People would bring some things themselves and just sit around and talk ideas. My grandmother might be encouraged to sing one of her old songs or do one of her recitations, and my father would play some on the piano.

Tempers would flare. My father especially could really get into screaming matches with all these people about the merits or purity of a particular artistic idea. For instance, when *The Old Man and the Sea* came out, my father would say, "Ach, God, all these four-letter words, and just these declarative sentences. Somebody teach the man how to use a semicolon, for Christ's sake."

My father was such an amazing poet, musician, designer, painter, such a self-taught kind of master of everything. But he didn't have much small talk of the kind necessary to schmooze your way through studios or Hollywood situations.

He preferred to be sent out on location, making Westerns. He loved being out in the desert, with the colorful characters who used to be on those movies, and he'd sometimes bring home these cowboy extras. There was a musician who was named something like "Bear-Fat Charlie" because he supposedly rubbed his fingers in bear fat before he played the violin.

I went to a cooperative nursery school where I think nearly all of us were the children of radical, Jewish, Hollywood filmmakers of some sort. It was there, for the first time, I perceived that I was going to be a musician and a conductor.

We had a game where the teacher would play piano pieces in different rhythms—marches, waltzes, whatever—and she'd change from one to another. We had little sticks, and we were supposed to bang those sticks together in the rhythm of the music while dancing around to the rhythms. When she changed rhythm, I was instantly changing with her, and I remember noticing that the other kids were still doing the old rhythm. I would run around and try to correct them.

From the time I was the tiniest child, I couldn't walk by the piano without playing something. My father would improvise little pieces with me, and we played duets on tonettes and recorders. We played musical games together, my parents and I, including ones where we would guess tunes by clapping out the rhythms or by leaving out notes and trying to fill them in.

When I was around seven, I was taught to read music, but it wasn't until I was about ten that I moved on to a teacher who was more demanding. My parents really had a fear of my being pushed too far, too fast.

I didn't get that serious about it all until I was around thirteen. My parents hoped that I would go into the sciences because they had observed so many people who had frustrated lives in theater and music. They were hopeful that I would not go down that route, where I could experience some of those same frustrations.

While they had seen my grandparents' colossal success and Muni's big success, they had already seen so many others who were struggling. But as much as they encouraged me to go into science, ultimately my genetic background won out.

My grandmother encouraged me by example. She would tell me stories about the theater and her experiences, and we'd learn songs together. As far back as I can remember, she spoke to me as if I were her peer. She'd say, "You're like me," or "Your parents are very, very nice people but they're really terribly conventional."

She enjoyed that sort of role. And always, when she came to the house, we'd put on a show where I'd play a piece and she'd sing something. Or I would do a dance or whatever. If my cousin was there, we'd involve her in it. I think people were sometimes astounded to come to the house and realize that they were going to suddenly have this whole show presented.

I studied at the University of Southern California's preparatory school with Dorothy Bishop, a very creative music educator who taught me through Bach and Mozart but also contemporary music and improvisation. Through her, I became introduced gradually to the faculty of USC—Alice Ehlers, John Crown, Ingolf Dahl—which really influenced my choice to attend USC.

John Crown and Ingolf Dahl both performed regularly at Monday Evening Concerts, and once, when I was eighteen or nineteen, there was a concert coming up where they were going to play Ives's *Over the Pavements* for piano and chamber ensemble. Ingolf was conducting it, and when I came for my lesson, John showed me a few pages of this outrageous cadenza. He said, "Oh, God, I just have no time to learn this. If I could only find somebody who'd learn it and play it in my place."

I said I'd play it, and I really learned it. I played the hell out of it, and it went very well. I began to be asked to do more things at Monday Evening Concerts, playing the piano and little by little doing some conducting.

I had been seeing Stravinsky conduct since I was ten, and it was always such a treat to watch him work and hear his concerts. At Monday Evening Concerts, I would see him sometimes in the audience, and then the day finally came when I was playing something under his direction. I was there at a rehearsal, hearing him speak, and even speak directly to me, and having him sit over my shoulder watching me play continuo for the Monteverdi *Vespers* in one rehearsal that was held up at his house.

Stravinsky's house was on Wetherly Drive off Sunset. There were lots of dictionaries and atlases, and he was insatiably curious. If he was hearing music, he always looked to see if there was anyone there who had the score that he could look over. I showed him photostats of original manuscripts of pieces. By this time he was an old man and somewhat frail, but there was enormous strength of purpose in his attitude.

Were the pieces that Stravinsky wrote in Paris more important than the pieces he wrote in Los Angeles? Well, probably yes. I mean there were certainly more of them. It was a bigger burst, a more creative period in his life, a younger period in his life. But some of those pieces from the late years in Los Angeles are really very powerful and just now beginning to be really appreciated.

While I never met Schoenberg, I certainly had lots of contact with people who had worked with him very closely. There were also all the film people—[composers] Bronislaw Kaper, Johnny Green, Elmer Bernstein—who, although hugely successful in the quote popular unquote world of music, were enormously involved with classical music and extraordinarily generous in giving money and attention to the development of young artists. And they were all very kind to me.

In the late sixties and seventies there were very heated debates often, about the merits of these different schools of music. It was exciting. People really cared very passionately about these things and were not abashed to duke it out if necessary. We would go eat before the concert, go to the concerts, then go have Irish coffee and talk, talk, talk.

We just took it for granted, but now it seems very much like what you read about going on in Vienna, with people hearing a premiere, then going off to a coffeehouse. That same kind of lively, artistic interchange was a unique feature of the Monday Evening Concerts and of those transplanted émigrés who did so much originally to shape it. Even though, of course, Peter Yates, who was as American as it's possible to be, had first created that concert series with Frances Mullen Yates, his wife.

I had heard my grandmother sing some of those Stravinsky folk songs, and it was just wonderful to then hear them being played by an enormous orchestra. I played those 78 records sometimes right through the record, I had listened to them so many times.

My growing up in a house with that mixture of intellectuals, show business people, and people in the sciences was great because it gave me this sense that there are so many different ways of expressing creativity and so many different ways of pursuing your life, all of which are valid. You can do creative things with nearly any endeavor that you choose.

I think there was less pressure on all of them because they were living in California. I think it was less pressure on me. I think that in a New York environment, I'm the kind of personality that might have been driven too far and too quickly and burned out quite early. That didn't happen.

We had relatives who lived in San Francisco, so it was part of my family's yearly schedule to visit them a couple of times a year. It was a magical place to be. I loved coming up here, and over the years I always made it a point to come here as a guest conductor. When finally I was asked to be music director, I accepted with enormous pleasure.

The main thing I think is great about San Francisco now is that San Francisco is a place in which life is possible, because the city is the right size. Its relationship to the environment is very good.

I love that I can be so quickly in a park or some other kind of natural surrounding, and that on the hiking trails I meet people who say, "Maestro, we just loved Mahler's Sixth last week. Are we going to get the Seventh next week?" People are physically active and conscious of their health and conscious of the environment and also love this great music.

I think my greatest joy still is to be in the desert, and I know that's something that I got from my father. I walk, mostly. Listen to the silence. My father's appreciation of the desert was summed up by his saying it was a place where he could turn his hearing aid all the way up and not hear anything.

lawrence FERLINGHETTI

San Francisco's first poet laureate, Lawrence Ferlinghetti was born in Yonkers in 1919, raised in France and New York, and spoke French before he spoke English. After college and the navy, he studied literature and painting in Paris on the GI Bill and first settled in San Francisco in 1950. Ferlinghetti cofounded the paperback bookstore City Lights with Peter Martin in 1953, and in 1956 first published and then successfully fought against censorship of Allen Ginsberg's *Howl and Other Poems*. City Lights has also published Jack Kerouac and Frank O'Hara as well as what *Booklist* once called "a who's who of post–World War II American modernism."

The author of more than twenty books of poetry, plays, prose, and translation, Ferlinghetti is best known for his 1958 landmark book of poetry, *A Coney Island of the Mind*. Never out of print, *Coney Island* has sold about a million copies around the world; in 1997 New Directions published its sequel, *A Far Rockaway of the Heart*. Demonstrating his traditional antiestablishment views, as well as his sense of humor, he begins the discussion by asserting that "an interview is another form of fiction. It's not necessarily true, anything I say, although I may think it's true when I say it. The dead decades you want to resurrect are lost in the mists of time."

I arrived in California in 1950, overland by train from New York. I took a ferry from Oakland to San Francisco, landed at the Ferry Building, and walked up Market Street with a seabag over my shoulder, not knowing where I was going.

I was of the last bohemian generation, not the beat generation. We were the expatriate generation of the Second World War, displaced and uprooted by going in the army or navy. A lot of the people who were uprooted like that never went back home, or they went back home just long enough to change their clothes and take off, usually for the West. I was in Paris, painting, for almost four years, and after I got my doctorate at the Sorbonne, I left. I stopped in Baltimore to see my brothers and mother, but I was in San Francisco within days of having left Paris.

There was a westward tilt of the continent. You could say there was this massive population shift to the West, like a table had been tilted. It took until the 1950s for everything to coalesce into a new culture, because everything was just streaming westward in the late forties and everything was in an amorphous, fertile, germinating state.

San Francisco seemed like the last frontier in those days, which is why I went there, and it seemed to be separate from the United States and from California. It's an island off the coast, surrounded by water on three sides, and when I arrived in 1950, the people used to have an island mentality. There are parts of South San Francisco that are only a few feet above sea level, and when Arctic icebergs melt enough, it could be an island again.

It seemed to be its own world. It seemed to be the most European of cities. When I arrived North Beach was very Mediterranean, and the street I lived on, which has now changed, was totally Italian.

In Paris my friend George Whitman was just starting Shakespeare and Company. (That's not the original Shakespeare & Company. He had started out as "Librairie Mistral" and taken on the name.) George sold used books, and when I left Paris, my idea was maybe I could start a used-book store.

When I came to San Francisco, I submitted some poem translations of Jacques Prévert, and Pete Martin accepted them for *City Lights* magazine, which was maybe the first pop culture magazine. *City Lights* was just sold locally. I don't think he printed more than five hundred copies, and it only lasted about six issues. He had this brilliant idea of starting a paperback bookstore, of which there were none, to pay the rent for the magazine office. You couldn't get paperbacks except in drugstores and places like that, and the people who sold them didn't know anything about them and didn't know the authors, and they were generally merchandised like toothpaste. So this was really a brilliant idea of Peter Martin's.

One day I was coming up from my painting studio on the waterfront and I saw this guy putting up a sign that said "City Lights Pocket Book Shop." So I stopped and went over and introduced myself, and he said, "Oh, you're the guy who sent me the Prévert." I said, "Yeah," and he said he needed some help getting the store started. He said he had five hundred dollars, and I said, "Well, I have five hundred dollars." So we started the store on five hundred dollars each. I could have driven around to get to my house by another block, and I never would have stopped there. My whole life would have been different.

Earlier in the century, in 1915, Cavalli's Librería Italiana was where City Lights is now, and in the marble on our doorstep it still says Cavalli. In 1935 there was an enormous amount of Italian men who'd come over from Italy and would bring their families over later, and they were living in boardinghouses around Columbus and Broadway. And so in the evening, as is the Italian habit, they would come out and stroll about. Men in dark suits, a lot of them wearing derbies, would fill the street in front of Librería Cavalli, listening to Mussolini on the loudspeakers. There were many, many Mussolini followers in North Beach, and there were also many Italian anarchists, who were naturally opposed to fascism.

Pete Martin was the son of Carlo Tresca, an Italian anarchist assassinated on the streets of New York, and right at the beginning we got Italian anarchist newspapers from Italy. The garbage truck had two Italians working on it. One of them actually wore a derby while he was working on the garbage truck, and he would jump off the back and rush in to buy his Italian anarchist newspaper from us, then jump back on the garbage truck.

The Italian anarchists were really a fascinating group, which Kenneth Rexroth was in touch with. Kenneth Rexroth was the leading anarchist poet, actually the leading senior statesman poet for the whole literary community in San Francisco, including the beats as they arrived from New York. He was the reigning deity in the literary and poetic world and would always call himself a philosophical anarchist.

I got my complete political education from Kenneth Rexroth, listening to him on KPFA and then going to Friday-night soirées at his house in the Fillmore district. KPFA in the early fifties was the most important intellectual influence in the Bay Area next to the University of California. Later other stations were created and it became the Pacifica Network—KPFK in Los Angeles, WBAI in New York, and two or three other stations.

But in those days there was no alternative radio. KPFA was a unique voice, the only alternative radio there was. The intellectual content was really extraordinary. They had people like Alan Watts on there regularly. Kenneth Rexroth had a program. He didn't just review poetry; he reviewed books in every field: astronomy, geology, philosophy, foreign literature translations.

In North Beach fishermen mended their nets in what are now garages for the Mercedeses of upper-class Silicon Valley electronics yuppies who have started to dominate the city. It's changing so fast and losing its distinctive qualities. It's no longer a place where artists and poets can afford to live. The warehouses where painters used to have their studios are now all torn down or turned into condominiums.

My studio is in Hunter's Point Navy Shipyard, which is on the south edge of the city, and we have about two hundred artists out there. When Dianne Feinstein was the mayor of San Francisco, she circulated a questionnaire to all the artists at Hunter's Point asking them what it would take to satisfy their needs in another location. I wrote back, "You're going to have to carry us out like the squatters in Amsterdam," because we didn't want any other location. It's the last holdout of real studio space that an artist can afford.

It's the yuppification of San Francisco. The whole world is converging, and everything is rushing together into a black hole, into the tube of a television or a computer. Everything becomes alike, and every place becomes alike. Travel becomes narrowing, and even a standout place like San Francisco with its island mentality becomes just another part of the amalgam with no distinctive qualities of its own.

Corporate monoculture is sweeping the world, so you can go to cities in the South Pacific and they look like cities in the United States, with skyscrapers and automobiles and traffic lights and the whole schmear. In the days of Gauguin, you could escape civilization by going somewhere like Tahiti. If you go to Tahiti today, there's the Hilton. If you say there must be an island farther out where you can still get away, you go to Mooréa, and there's a Club Med. So where do you go from there?

judy **CHICAGO**

The pioneering feminist artist Judy Chicago was born Judy Cohen in Chicago in 1939. In 1970, she created the Feminist Art Program at Fresno State University, the first such program in the country, and two years later was instrumental in launching both Womanhouse at the California Institute of the Arts and Los Angeles's Woman's Building. Her themes are large ones and often involve hundreds of collaborators in such monumental works as *The Dinner Party, Birth Project,* and *Holocaust Project.* Trained as a painter and sculptor at UCLA, she is perhaps best known for *The Dinner Party,* a multimedia artwork that included place settings for thirty-nine historical women. Complete with individually crafted, painted plates and embroidered runners, and names of nearly one thousand more in floor panels, *The Dinner Party* traveled to fifteen venues in six countries. Author of eight books, including two autobiographies, she lives in Belen, New Mexico, with her husband, the photographer Donald Woodman.

When I was growing up, our house was a center for intellectual and aesthetic discourse, record parties for the Spanish civil war, and discussions, endless political discussions. My father was a labor organizer and trained me very consciously in logic and values. My parents were Jewish liberals, and there were lots of discussions about race relations and equal rights for women.

They raised me to believe that I could do what I wanted and be what I wanted, and making a contribution as an artist was a very major goal of mine for as long as I can remember. It never crossed my mind that my aspiration was at all odd.

I started drawing when I was very young, and when I was four my prekindergarten teacher told my mother that I was talented. My mother worked as a medical secretary but had been a dancer as a young woman and was always interested in the arts. Even though we had limited resources, she made arrangements for me to start going to classes at the Chicago Art Institute.

I came to California in 1957 to attend UCLA, which I knew had a good art school, and it wasn't really until I started my upper-division classes that I began to encounter discrimination as a woman artist. At first, I was very naive and unaware of the social messages. I didn't consciously notice that the teacher used to call only on guys. I'd just wave my hand around so vociferously that finally he'd be embarrassed into calling on me. Now I understand, but I don't think I did then.

When I was in graduate school, Billy Al Bengston came to teach. I used to follow him around, much to his amusement, and I really learned from him about what it means to be a serious artist. I went to his studio, his big white studio, and I saw the seriousness with which he approached his work and the integrity: Nothing else is important except art. Making money didn't figure in at all. Being taken seriously as an artist was what it was about. The whole group at Ferus Gallery lived the high-risk artist's life that one had to live at that time to embark on an art career. I think that that's a type of life that's difficult for women, actually.

They taught me the "something is going to happen" philosophy. How do you live when you don't have a steady job? Well, something's going to happen. And if something didn't happen, you were really up shit's creek. You had to pay your rent.

When I was in graduate school my imagery was sort of biomorphic, female and expressive, and what I saw in galleries had a whole different, highly polished, crafted look. I realized quickly that was a desirable look if one wanted to be taken seriously, which was my big goal at that time. But I didn't know the first thing about how to do that; I had not learned about tools and construction when I was growing up.

John Chamberlain, the sculptor, used to say, "What I should do is go to auto-body school. Those are the guys who really know how to paint." So as soon as I got out of graduate school, I announced I was going to auto-body school. There were 250 guys and me. They made me wear this Mother Hubbard long white smock, just in case I leaned over and one of the guys saw a breast.

I learned not only how to spray-paint, but about respect for the object—that I was actually creating a physical object. There was this show-car painter who taught me then that there's no such thing as perfection. There's only the illusion of perfection and how you create that is what it is all about. He also showed me what you do to make mistakes not be evident to the viewer. Those were all very important lessons. For my graduation I had to spray-paint a Chevy truck.

As everybody knows about LA art and the art scene in the sixties, if described as macho it would be considered an understatement. I concluded that the only possible reason I was having so much trouble in the art world was because I was female. Because of the swagger and bravado of these guys, it never crossed my mind that I was starting to experience the oppressive ways in which artists are treated.

It took me many years to realize that artists are treated very badly in the art world. It's a buyer's market. If one artist makes trouble, there's another compliant artist down the line. It's worse now. There are more artists than there were then, proportionally, after all these years of graduate schools pumping out hundreds of thousands of graduates into what is virtually a nonexistent system.

At least the art scene was open in the sixties, and they were actually looking for young artists. I was very, very fortunate. Despite my gender my work was being written about and shown and caught up in this emerging scene.

But I was still trying to be one of the guys, and the ultimate manifestation of this period came quite by accident when I was having an exhibition at the Jack Glenn Gallery. Jack came to me with this idea that we would go down to the gym where Cassius Clay, now Muhammad Ali, trained, and take a picture of me in the boxing ring. We all trooped down, me with my short haircut and wearing shorts, big boots, boxing gloves, and this sweatshirt emblazoned with "Judy Chicago."

When we walked in, well, you can imagine how these guys reacted. I thought they were going to collectively drop dead. I liked the idea, not because I was really butch and tough, but because it was a parody of all these ads with the guys from Ferus Gallery: the studs, the war babies, with their big muscles and their cigars.

Well, it just happened that the boxing-ring photo coincided with the beginnings of the women artist movement around the country. And it sort of symbolized that women were about to come out fighting. I had begun to travel around the country, and I discovered that everybody had the boxing-ring photo up in their studios. Male artists would say to me, when they'd meet me, "Oh, you want to box?"

I was born Judy Cohen, but I had this ferocious Chicago accent, and Rolf Nelson, when I started showing with him, used to call me Judy Chicago. At that time artists in LA had this habit of listing their phone numbers in the phone book under underground names. It was a little in-joke, and I started listing my phone number under Judy Chicago.

At the end of the sixties, when I was fed up with the antics of the art scene and had enough of fighting the sexism, I decided to formalize my protest by changing my name.

I always say that at the beginning of the women's movement we didn't have forums of our own so we borrowed freely, notably from the

Black Panthers. I feel like I chose my name and created my own identity, and it is who I am. I particularly like going to Chicago, because people always say, "Judy Chicago? You've gotta be kidding. What a great name!"

I wanted to infuse more personal content and subject matter into my art. At the same time I thought, Maybe if I go back and work with young women, I can encourage them to make art without having to assume male drag. I was genuinely concerned, even then, by the fact that there were more women starting out with me when I first came out of school, and as I moved up a little bit on the ladder, there seemed to be less and less women.

I started looking around for a place to teach. I actually can't remember how I happened to light on Fresno, maybe an opening came up, but I started recruiting female students. I commuted to Fresno for one semester, then moved into a supermarket in a small town twenty miles south of Fresno called Kingsburg, which had three thousand people.

Already formulating in my mind was the idea of creating new forms of art, art education, and art history, which I called "feminist art," "feminist art education," and "feminist art history." I invented those terms, and I feel proud of them. When young women don't use the term "feminist," it's because they probably don't remember when it didn't exist.

It was my coming up as a young artist in Southern California that gave me the freedom to dream that I could create a new approach to art history. I don't think there's a chance in hell that I could have done it in New York. Absolutely not. There was an openness here to new ideas that was very, very essential.

I think it's no accident that the feminist art movement was born on the West Coast, precisely because the West Coast at that time was much less in the shadow of the whole looming tradition of art. It was new, and there was no real international art scene here yet. There was a burgeoning local art scene, and there was beginning to be an interchange with New York in terms of visitors and things like that. But LA was looked at as sort of la-la land by the New York art scene. So there was a combination of openness and bravado, and I think that had a big influence on me.

That year in Fresno was a really important year for me. Not only did I start the women's program, but I was embarked on what I now call a vision quest, looking for my history as a woman. Like a lot of young women, I grew up without knowing anything about the women before me. It was as if there had been no women before me.

Some of these ideas were certainly stimulated by the early women's liberation literature that was starting to happen on the East Coast, and I knew that there were other women who were beginning to also think about these things. So buried away in Fresno, my students and I were reading women's literature, collecting slides, and assembling a very primitive art history. It was a pretty exciting time. After all, there had been no concept of female-centered art at that time—none whatsoever. And even though it was in a very early form, that was what was being born in Fresno.

I met the artist Miriam Shapiro, and she and her husband, Paul Brach, offered me the possibility of bringing my program and some of my students to California Institute of the Arts. I was ecstatic. We would have our own space, with a real art historian to work on these art history files that we were assembling in ragtag fashion. We had this big caravan—all these young women and their boyfriends, pets, and trucks—and we all went down the freeway two hundred miles to LA.

The Cal Arts building in Valencia wasn't ready, and we found this old house. We invited some women artists to work with us, taught women building skills, and renovated the house. We did consciousness-raising sessions, like I had started to do in Fresno. Womanhouse opened in January of 1972 in LA, and in a month nine thousand people came to see it. It was one thing to create female-centered art in Fresno, but it was another thing to do it in LA. I think it was in *Time* magazine. It really hit the big time in terms of media and interest.

Around that time I wrote a piece called "My Struggle as a Woman Artist" for a local feminist newspaper. Anaïs Nin told me she had read and admired it, and she invited me to visit her. We became friends, and she was a tremendous mentor for me. I would tell her everything, about how confused I felt and about how I was trying to create female art. I could hardly get the words out fast enough. What a women's movement does, I think, is create a context for women in which their behavior does not seem odd.

By the time we moved into the Woman's Building, I was chomping at the bit to get into the studio. I was in my early thirties, at the prime of my art-making energies, and I really didn't want to teach anymore. I didn't want to do anything but work.

By the spring of 1974 I was starting to make plans for *The Dinner Party,* although it wasn't called that then. I wanted to tell women's history through art, and I'd been studying china-painting, which is traditionally done on domestic objects like plates. I went to visit a woman who had painted complete place settings for sixteen people and set them up on her dining-room table, and I thought to myself, "For men it's *The Last Supper*. Women have dinner parties." I think that was when it crystallized for me that I was going to do a female analogue to *The Last Supper*.

The Dinner Party was such a popular success, the art-critical assault on it was confusing to me. I had to get away, and I went to Benicia, a small, wonderful town near San Francisco, which provided me solace during that period and where I did *The Birth Project*. Again I found big, inexpensive space—this time at an old army installation. Again it was out there where nobody noticed anything, and I could continue my activities, which were always against the grain of the art world.

By the mid-eighties, I was coming to the end of my interest in the subject of what does it mean to be a woman. I started going to New Mexico to paint, and for the first two years I never saw anybody. I worked entirely by myself. I never planned to stay there, but in 1985 I met my husband, Donald Woodman, the photographer.

After I finished my series, *Powerplay,* we embarked on *The Holocaust Project* together. That ended up taking eight years, and when we finished in 1993, I wanted to move back to California. But Donald had been in New Mexico since '72, felt very rooted there, and did not want to come to California, even though I tried desperately to entice him into the glories of California living. I still miss California.

helgi **TOMASSON**

Born in Reykjavík, Iceland, in 1942, Helgi Tomasson has been involved with dance since he first saw a visiting Royal Danish Bal-
let troupe when he was five. At fifteen he was working with the
Pantomime Theater in Copenhagen's Tivoli Gardens, and at sev-
enteen he so impressed Jerome Robbins that Robbins arranged
for him to study with the School of American Ballet in New York
City. After dancing with both the Joffrey and Harkness Ballets,
Tomasson won the Silver Medal at the First International Ballet
Competition in Moscow in 1969—Mikhail Baryshnikov won the
Gold—and a year later joined the New York City Ballet. In 1985
Tomasson moved to San Francisco to become artistic director
of the San Francisco Ballet, the nation's oldest professional bal-
let company, where he has choreographed twenty-nine ballets as
well as commissioned works by Mark Morris and others. *New
York Times* dance critic Anna Kisselgoff called his work with the
company "one of the spectacular success stories of the arts in
America." Tomasson lives with his family in San Francisco.

I have wonderful memories from Reykjavík. I thought it was a quaint,
beautiful little city. I remember summers being wonderful because
there were twenty-four hours of daylight. Winter, of course, was the
opposite with only four or four and one-half hours of daylight. It was
tough going to school, to get up in the dark, then wait at the bus stop in

the snow with the wind howling. By the time you got out of school, it was dark again.

I think something about the weather there also shapes you. That's how it is. You just accept it, and you learn to live with it. Maybe that's something that stayed with me. People say about me that I don't give up. If I set my goal, I'm very determined. That's it. Don't be in my way.

There were always dramas and classical music on the radio, and school buses took us to the theater and concerts. The arts were accessible. For a city of one hundred thousand at that time, there were at least two professional drama theaters going full time, a ballet school that gave performances, a symphony orchestra. It has been said about Iceland that there are more books sold there per capita than anywhere else in the world. I remember as a child of twelve or thirteen, I would get eight or nine books for Christmas, and that was not unusual for a child that age. It was in the culture.

I was about five when I first saw the Royal Danish Ballet. My mother had gone with her twin sister, and they thought I might enjoy it. We lived very close to the theater, so during the intermission they went home and brought me back for the second half. I don't remember any particular ballet or dancers, but I do remember beautiful lights and colors and people moving around and jumping.

We were living then in the Westman Islands, basically a well-to-do fishing village of maybe fifteen or twenty thousand people. It was a very small troupe of soloists from the Royal Danish Ballet, and I don't think they came through before or ever again. Why they ended up there, I don't know.

My mother told me later that whenever there was music on the radio, I seemed to be trying to imitate what I had seen on the stage, turning and jumping, so it must have had some major effect. She put me in ballet school to get it out of my system. It didn't quite work.

We moved back to Reykjavík, and I was enrolled in a local ballet school once or twice a week. The following year the National Theater had been built and established a ballet school. My local Icelandic teacher advised my mother to take me there to study.

So my mother enrolled me with Erik and Lisa Bidsted. The school only operated from early October to early April, when the Bidsteds would have to leave and go back to Copenhagen. He was ballet master at the Pantomime Theater at the Tivoli Gardens there, and she was the leading dancer. I began to go to Denmark with them, and then, at fifteen, I started working with the Pantomime Theater.

People would go to Denmark or abroad to educate themselves. When I went away, it was the norm. I couldn't make a career in Iceland, so I had to go somewhere else. I decided to stay in Copenhagen during the winter months and study and do shows to pay for my room and board and education.

I went home to visit in 1959, and I arrived there about the same time that Jerome Robbins's Ballet USA was there. I was encouraged to audition, although it was not a permanent company. I received a letter from Mr. Robbins a very short time later that he had arranged for me to come to New York on scholarship to the School of the American Ballet to do some further study. That was how it all started.

I was with the Joffrey Ballet two years, and then with the Harkness Ballet. I joined the New York City Ballet in 1970. By the 1983–84 season, I decided to stop dancing, and I gave myself a year to wind down. I had just started to choreograph, and both Balanchine and Robbins were very encouraging. I was teaching as well as dancing, and it became too much. I knew something had to give. I had had a long wonderful career, so I knew it would have to be the dancing that would go.

Within a short time I got an offer from the Royal Danish Ballet to become ballet master, which almost happened. I went over there two or three times, and there were negotiations. As I was waiting in New York for that to happen, I received a call from Lew Cristensen, the director

of the San Francisco Ballet. He said, "Don't sign anything. Let me talk
to you first."

Lew passed away soon after that, and when a search committee was
formed, I felt I owed it to Lew to at least go to San Francisco and take
a look, which I did. I saw a community that was very supportive of the
arts. There was a wonderful building that indicated the board and community were very serious about supporting the ballet. There were some
talented dancers here.

When I went back to New York and contacted Copenhagen, nothing
was happening there and I said, "Fine, okay, I'm not interested." I was
voted in here, and I had this job one week after my last performance in
New York.

I had been here on tour, and I had seen the San Francisco Ballet in
Brooklyn a few years before, but this was a situation that presented
itself unexpectedly out of nowhere. I have to admit that I was very
much a New Yorker. Having come from Europe to New York more
than twenty years before, I had my whole career there.

It was a big move. But I took over the company, set an agenda, and
went to work. Bob Joffrey was one of the first ballet company directors
to invite choreographers from the modern side of dance, and that had a
great deal of influence on me as a young dancer. I was trained as a classical dancer, and I was being cast in ballets that technically were foreign
to me. But it was challenging. Also, at the New York City Ballet, where
Balanchine and Robbins were the two primary choreographers, there
was always something new. When I started to direct, all that made me
who I am and why I have chosen this kind of repertory.

I received many applications from Europe and elsewhere, from
dancers who knew of me and what I stood for, and I hired them not
because they were foreign but because I needed dancers. Maybe, in
some instances, part of it is because I was born in Iceland. I could never
have had a career there, and I was given chances, first in Denmark, then
in this country.

The diversity of the San Francisco Ballet very much represents the community of San Francisco. That was the norm here and was fine with me. There are a lot of good dancers out there. I want a little bit more than that. There should be something special. We're all looking for individuality. I look for personalities, for people not all looking the same. The city of San Francisco has an enormous ethnic community, be it Chinese, Filipino, Vietnamese, Japanese, black, or Hispanic. It's all a melting pot here. I always felt the company reflected what the community is like in San Francisco.

I think the people of San Francisco take their arts very seriously. For the size of the city, the support it gives to the arts is astounding. People stop me in supermarkets or restaurants to tell me about that program, this ballet, that dancer. It's not a very big city when you think of it. Maybe that's part of it. But we have wonderful audiences here, and people seem to be quite passionate about dance.

I always felt, when I came out here, that this was a place that would allow me to choreograph *my* way. It allowed me a certain freedom to explore what I wanted to do and say and how I wanted my dances to look. I felt if I had stayed with the New York City Ballet in some capacity, I would have choreographed very differently.

Speaking generally, we think of California as not being burdened by tradition. You are not locked into doing things a certain way because that is how it has been done and should be done. It has a reputation as a place that starts new trends, and by living here, you can't help but be influenced. California's very casual, particularly compared to some of the European countries, and maybe that fosters, Let's try that or do that, I know it hasn't been done before, but maybe we should try it.

Definitely, being here has influenced me and how I work. Yes, I take my experiences with me. But mixing that with what I have been allowed to do—the freedom to totally choose and do what I thought would be right for the company—could only have happened here. I would not have been able to accomplish this much, I don't think, anywhere else.

julius **SHULMAN**

Photographer Julius Shulman has documented California's distinctive architecture since the thirties. Born in 1910 in Brooklyn, he moved with his family from a farm in Central Village, Connecticut, to Los Angeles in 1920. He knew nothing at all about architecture and little more about photography when, in 1936, by chance he took some photographs of Richard Neutra's Kun House that so impressed the architect he essentially hired Shulman on the spot. Neutra introduced him to Raphael Soriano, and in a short time Shulman was working for architects from Rudolph Schindler and Frank Lloyd Wright to the lesser-known Bruce Goff and John Lautner. Largely self-taught, he guesses he's taken "thousands upon thousands" of photographs over the years, most of them published in books and magazines. Architectural historian Joseph Rosa has compared Shulman's views of Los Angeles to Atget's of Paris, and an international reputation soon followed his documenting of early California modernist architecture. The subject of recent exhibitions in New York, Milan, and Berlin, as well as at USC's Fisher Gallery, Shulman lives in the steel-and-glass Hollywood Hills house Raphael Soriano designed for him in 1949.

⌐⌐

was raised on a farm in Connecticut. Central Village, Connecticut, had 293 people, and we walked a mile and a half to school every morning.

My father and mother both came here from Russia, and how they ever became farmers is a mystery. The water came from a well, and there was no electricity. The heat came from a coal and wood stove in the kitchen, where my mother did the cooking. She bathed us in a laundry tub on the kitchen floor.

When I was ten, my father announced one day that we were going to California, where he'd been told the streets were paved with gold. We got on the train, and five days later we landed at the Southern Pacific Station in downtown Los Angeles.

It was a warm, beautiful September day. I remember we took off our warm, heavy Eastern coats and bathed in that wonderful sunshine.

Boyle Heights was a favored location because it had better weather conditions. My parents' New York Dry Goods Store was tremendously successful, and I was the only one of the five children who didn't work in the store.

In 1927, when I was in the eleventh grade, I was given the opportunity to take one of the nation's first classes in photography. In those days every family had an Eastman Kodak box camera—a Brownie—and I was imbued with some natural desire to take pictures.

One of our assignments was to go down to the Los Angeles Coliseum to photograph a track meet. I walked around the coliseum, found this spot where the track meet was being set up, and snapped my picture the moment the hurdlers came over the first hurdle. The timing was perfect.

My photograph showed the coliseum, the audience, and the hurdler; it told the story of a track meet. It was the same thing I later did in my architecture photography. I would photograph not the house alone, exterior-wise, but its location and how people lived in the house.

A few years later I got a Kodak vestpocket camera as a birthday present. I began taking snapshots all over the city, around the railroad tracks, around the bridges over the LA River. I took that camera with me to UCLA, where I first went to become an engineer, and when I went to UC Berkeley. I took snapshots at Berkeley, especially of buildings. I made some eight-by-tens, framed them with a simple frame, and sold them in the campus bookstore for $2.50 apiece. It paid our rent.

Why I photographed those buildings, I don't know. It's almost mystical. I had no training in architecture, photography, or art.

In 1936, after being seven years away auditing classes at UCLA and Berkeley, I thought I'd been gone long enough. So I drove back home. And everything changed within a two-week period of the time I came home from Berkeley.

My older sister and her husband had a pharmacy near Silver Lake, where the Richard Neutras lived, and Neutra's new apprentice had rented their spare room. A week or so later, she said to me, "Julius, you should meet this young man who works for Richard Neutra." I did, and drove with him one day to a house that Neutra was building.

I didn't know who Richard Neutra was. I had never met an architect. I wandered around and took six pictures with my little Kodak camera, then made prints and gave this young man a set of eight-by-ten prints. I just thought maybe he'd like to see them.

At the end of that week he called me and said he had shown my photographs to Mr. Neutra. Mr. Neutra wanted to meet me and buy more copies of my photographs.

So Saturday, March 5, 1936, I drove over to Silver Lake and met Mr. Neutra. He had my pictures on his desk in front of him, and he asked me if I was an architectural student or studied photography. I said no and briefly told him how I had been going to the university for seven years.

It was as if I was ordained to wait the seven years until I met Mr. Neutra. Here was this very distinguished-looking man who, I was told, was a famous architect. I didn't know what an architect was, actually. How was I to know, a farm boy? Of course I had seen the Kun House, which was a strange thing, and I was impressed by its unusual design quality. I had never seen a modern house before.

Mr. Neutra bought five copies of each photograph, and when we finished talking, he ordered others and said he was going to have me photograph more of his work. In the meantime he wanted me to meet Raphael Soriano, who used to be his apprentice.

I met Soriano the same day I met Neutra. After Neutra and I said good-bye, I drove up the hill to where Soriano was inside his Lipetz House, his very first commission. He was sitting on the carpeted floor, leaning back against the bookcase wall. I told him Mr. Neutra had sent me, we shook hands, and he asked me if I'd had lunch. When I said no, he shared a sandwich with me. I recall that so vividly. We sat and talked for maybe forty-five minutes.

He asked if I would come photograph the house when it was finished. I did, and from that day on I photographed almost all of his work. I met Rudolph Schindler, too, toward the end of 1936, and he immediately gave me some assignments.

Every photograph I ever took came out. I never had any second or third exposure or revisits to a site. In sixty-four years of photography, I've never had a remake. I never was told by an architect to go back and do it over again. Never. As a matter of fact, people began to call me "One-Shot Shulman," because I took one negative of each picture and that was enough. I knew it would come out.

I tell students today, "Don't make Mr. Eastman richer than he is. Don't shoot all that extra film and waste your money repeating your work. If you can't do it with one negative, you shouldn't be a photographer. If you have faith and trust in the material and in the film and processing you use, you don't have to be a gambler."

That's the story of my life, and that's why I'm so healthy at the age of eighty-nine. I haven't wasted my energy. When I was young I didn't chase the girls. I was a loner. Girls didn't enter my life until much later. Even then, when I met a young lady in 1930, we were friends for seven years before I decided to ask her to marry me. So everything was delayed in my life. I was never in a hurry, whether doing photography or hiking or whatever.

When I ran in track meets, my high school coach used to be so angry, he would shout at me. I'd be running twenty, thirty, forty, fifty yards behind the other racers. He would yell, "Get going, Shulman, you're way behind," and I would wave my hand at him. Then, as we came around the last bend of the track heading for home, I stepped on the gas. I invariably either won or got second or third place.

I got my letter in track at high school and at university too, mainly because I conserved my energy, which is the power of my life even today. When I go skiing I don't *shoosh-boom* down the slope. I'm not in a hurry, and my photography reflects that. When I make a composition of a building, I don't have to take alternate views here or there. They are not necessary.

When I give a lecture to architectural students, I try to imbue in their thoughts that if you're going to be a good architect, you have to be a good person. You have to have an ability to communicate with nature, with your friends, with architectural subjects, with your designs, and you also have to be able to communicate with yourself. And this is the story of my whole existence, always being able to imbue in my work the quality of architecture, but also the quality of a good life.

I have a built-in sense of observation, which I transfer to my camera. This has been my trademark, if you will, all my life. I could walk past a building and then stop and turn around, like I have eyes in the back of my head. Walking with an architect around his buildings, all of a sudden I would stop.

I was there from day one. No one is alive now among all those people—Neutra, Schindler, van der Rohe, Gropius, Stone. They were the giants of the architectural profession, and I knew them all personally.

I was blessed that I was in my profession during the postwar years, when everyone was busy and thriving and doing a lot of work all over the country. There weren't many architectural photographers that specialized as I did. I was at the right place at the right time.

morton SUBOTNICK

Born in Los Angeles in 1933, Morton Subotnick was a musical prodigy at the time Southern California concerts were introducing new works of both Stravinsky and Schoenberg. Hollywood studio musicians taught him and played his music, and well-timed study with distinguished composers Leon Kirchner and Darius Milhaud at Oakland's Mills College reinforced his leanings toward avant-garde, twelve-tone, and, later, electronic and computer music. The much-honored composer and performer cofounded and directed the San Francisco Tape Music Center. He was the first music director of the Vivian Beaumont Theater at New York's Lincoln Center and music director of the Electric Circus, and in 1969 he returned to Southern California to help launch the California Institute of the Arts. Many of his large-scale compositions were written for his wife, composer/singer Joan La Barbara, with whom he lives in Santa Fe, New Mexico, and New York.

When I was around six or seven, I had a bronchial condition, and the doctor recommended a wind instrument to help strengthen my lungs. I had seen a Tommy Dorsey movie, and I wanted the instrument that Tommy Dorsey played, and I made the motions of what it was. My parents got a list from the school library of all the musical instruments, but it had no pictures. I picked the clarinet, thinking that was the trombone. It came—a little metal clarinet—the wrong instrument. But I was very proud. I never told my mother. I wouldn't say that I made a mistake.

I started composing in junior high school, mostly for woodwinds, but I wrote for strings, I wrote for everything. I'd get up in the morning early and do counterpoint and theory, and in the afternoon I'd practice the clarinet. My parents moved all the time. I went to three or four elementary schools, two junior highs, two high schools. My friends were all in music, and that was basically it. I never got too involved in school activities. I was never there long enough.

So probably by the time I was in high school, I was putting in six or seven hours a day on music and nothing in homework. Then, my junior year at North Hollywood High School, I had a harmony class with Joel Harry, who said I already knew everything he was going to teach us, and he gave me special things to learn. He took me to Peter Yates's "Evenings on the Roof," the Monday Evening Concerts, where I heard Stravinsky and Schoenberg for the first time. That changed my life and wouldn't have happened anywhere else in the world then.

At that time Los Angeles split down the middle between Schoenberg and Stravinsky. You could walk down the aisle during the intermission and it was like Moses walking through the sea, because on one side would be the Stravinsky people and on the other, the Schoenberg people. It became pretty clear that my fascination, even that early, was more toward Schoenberg. There was something wonderfully mysterious about it.

I got a scholarship to USC—I had a great time taking classes, but I was out of school half the time playing concerts. I played with a lot of the studio musicians in their chamber work, and if they'd get called out to do a studio job, I'd come in and sub for them. They sort of took me under their wing, and they played my music, which was nice. I could hear my music played for the first time by the top musicians in Los Angeles.

I went to work at the Denver Symphony when I was only eighteen, and I already knew I didn't want to be a clarinetist. It was boring to me. It was no real challenge. I really wanted to be a composer. What attracted me to electronic music was the ability to not just be the composer who writes music that someone else plays. I could create something and be the person who makes it come to life at the same time. Of course we had to create the technology that allowed you to be flexible enough to do that, and that's something else we did in California with Donald Buchla, the electronic-instrument builder, and the early synthesizers.

After the army I finished my degree and was offered a fellowship at Mills. Everyone was in the Bay Area then—Harry Partch, La Monte Young, Pauline Oliveros, Terry Riley. I also played clarinet at the Composers Forum in San Francisco, and I'd meet all these people, because I'd be playing their music and we'd all get together.

While I was at Mills, I spent a year on and off working on the music for the Actor's Workshop production of *King Lear.* Herbert Blau wanted a far-out young composer, and we hit it off. I knew about electronic music and that people were working in studios with tape recorders, and I decided to try it. I got some money in advance, bought a tape recorder, and recorded a Wurlitzer electric piano, French horn, and cello playing every single note. I took the pizzicato of the cello and spliced it to the sound of the French horn. Then I recorded noises and altered the actor's voice, playing it backwards and forwards. It was a very successful production, and led to my becoming director of music for the Actor's Workshop. It was also the beginning of my addiction to technology.

At Mills I also studied with Darius Milhaud. He didn't like my music—it was too off the deep end in a dark way, and he liked sunnier music—but we got along as people very well. He wanted me to have a chance to just write some music in Aspen one summer, but he knew I couldn't afford it. So one night when I was conducting a concert of his music, he put my hand between his two hands and when I pulled my hand away, there was a check for the money I was going to need.

So I ended up in Aspen, where I wrote my piece *Sonata for Piano, Four Hands*. It was my first big public performance, and I walked into that tent and thought, This is miraculous. These people are going to hear this piece, and it's so fresh and so new, they're going to stand up and say, "Wow! This is incredible that someone thought of this." I couldn't eat for days before the performance.

There were some wacky, very loud notes that would happen every so often in the first movement, and when the performance began, people started to laugh. There was a dog bark, and everything became part of this piece, and people were laughing. Before the last movement, there was so much noise that the two pianists just stared the audience down until everyone got quiet enough for them to play. At the end people were running up onto the stage pounding on the piano, and the two pianists were in tears and ran off the stage. There was no applause, just this chaotic moment. I walked over to Milhaud, who was sitting in his wheelchair. He pulled me down—I think he had a little tear in his eye, but I may have projected that—and he said, "Thank you, my dear. It reminds me of the old days."

It was at that moment that I realized if I was to continue to compose—because I could always play, I could always teach, I could do all sorts of things—I would have to contribute something that had a uniqueness. Whether the audience liked it or they didn't like it, it just didn't make any sense for me to continue just writing music. I loved music. I just didn't want to write another *piece*. I wanted to find a place for myself, and if I couldn't find it, I was willing to say it was not for me and I'll do something else.

There was another personal moment. I was in New York a few years later, and inadvertently I wound up doing commercials. I was also doing a concert at Colgate, two nights for $500, and my associate and I had to pay for our own hotel room and borrow a car, a very old car. The first night not only did the audience boo, but a person came up onto the stage and threatened to kill me. He was so angry. People were holding him back. We get back to the hotel the first night and there was a message for me—"Morty, we've got a Dream Whip commercial." I called back, and the pay was $4,500 to compose a twenty-second commercial and another $4,500 if they used it. But they needed it right away, and since I had a concert, I had to turn it down.

The next night when we went onstage, nobody threatened to kill me, but they booed again. Then, driving back to New York, after I'd just given up $9,000 and people hate me, all the car's forward gears go out five miles outside Colgate. We had to put it in reverse, and we drove on the side of the road, backwards, into Colgate, and back down the main street and into a garage. When I got out of the car, I started laughing and couldn't stop. It was like what happened in Aspen. The two experiences together set me totally clear. I felt my whole life was like that— going this way while everybody else is going that way.

It was easier to go my own way in California. If you did a concert in New York, you got written up, or word-of-mouth happened, and information was everywhere. That puts a lot of pressure on experimentation; you can't afford to fail. It never occurred to any of us that we had to succeed in what we were doing in San Francisco—that we had to be successful. I remember a "smell opera" we did at the San Francisco Conservatory of Music. The headline the next day was CONCERT LITERALLY STINKS and the critic threatened to sue us because he couldn't get the smell out of his suit. We laughed. It didn't hurt us in any way. But I don't know how we would have felt to have gotten that notice in New York.

For some people it may have been the weather or the light of

California. For me it was the people. "Evenings on the Roof" and that whole crowd represented the last of the expatriates, and as that group began to go out, I never found a comparable group. It seemed to me that Hollywood had taken over the general culture in Los Angeles.

In the mid-eighties, I wasn't teaching full-time anymore, and we moved to Santa Fe. I'm back at CalArts every fall, and I still love CalArts, and I have a nostalgia for Los Angeles from having grown up there, but it eventually didn't hold me.

Part III

Golden West

david **HOCKNEY**

He may have been born in Bradford, England, in 1937, but David Hockney has captured a sun-drenched, multicolored Los Angeles recognizable around the world. After study at the Bradford School of Art and London's Royal College of Art, Hockney visited Los Angeles on and off, then settled there permanently in 1978. A painter, photographer, and stage designer, he works in a Hollywood Hills setting as colorful as his canvases. The sprawling studio is built on a former paddle-tennis court and generally houses not just his work in progress but a set model for his newest opera, chairs for portrait sitters (often his two dachshunds, Stanley and Boodgie), Xerox and assorted high-tech machines for his experimental artworks.

⌒

I must admit I think of myself as an English Los Angelino. I'm an English person—you can't be anything else really—but I feel this is my home.

I always used to say I came to LA because it was sexy, but I have no doubt at all the climate attracted me. I come from a cold, dark, Gothic gloom place, the North of England, so the climate of Southern California is very attractive. I love the great big spaces of the West. I'm a bit claustrophobic, and I now realize I probably sensed that a long time ago and wanted to be in great big spaces. Well, this is the most spacy city there is, isn't it really?

My knowledge of California was from movies, naturally. I used to say I was brought up in Bradford and Hollywood, because Hollywood was at the end of the street, in the cinema. In the Laurel and Hardy movies that my father used to take me to see, I always noticed the strong shadows, meaning that wherever they were it was very sunny. They didn't particularly say they were in Los Angeles, but they were and I noticed the strong shadows. You don't get strong shadows in Bradford.

Sun was very rare in Bradford. Very rare. You can have, of course, glorious days, but there are days you don't see the sun. In the winter you're lucky if you get five hours of daylight. It's a long way north. I must admit I am attracted to the light. I've no doubt that's an enormous pull for me in LA.

I painted Bradford when I was an art student, but everything was gray. It was hard to see any color. You got the green of nature, but it seemed to be dominated by gray.

I grew up in a little terrace house, basically two rooms on the downstairs floor, which meant one room was a living room/kitchen, and the other room was only used on a Sunday. Everybody—seven of us—was in the one room, simply because you couldn't afford to heat the other room in those days.

I started painting when I was about nine or ten. I slept in the attic, and I painted in the attic. My first oil paintings were done there. I went to the art school in Bradford at sixteen.

Frankly, I was a person brought up in terrible austerity. I was eight years old at the end of the Second World War. There was not much in shops. Toy shops were practically nonexistent. You only saw those in movies.

In American movies there were two or three things I noticed that I thought were very unrealistic. One of them was you would see people light a cigarette, take one puff, and throw it away. Never, ever, in Bradford would you have seen anybody do that. They'd put it out and put it behind their ear then. The other thing I would notice was people might be in a restaurant and they'd never eat the food. When you're young and there's not much food around, you notice—"A plate of food, and I didn't really see her eat much, just two forkfuls or something."

Everything was rationed. Even sweets did not come off ration until about 1954. You couldn't just go buy a bar of chocolate. You needed a ration book. So in a way I have known shops empty in my life.

No one in California has known going to a supermarket and seeing an empty shelf. That would be unheard of here, wouldn't it?

I was eighteen years old when I first visited London, two hundred miles from Bradford. My mother was sixty-three years old when she first went there, and she went there only to see me. She wouldn't have bothered going. In those days, you see, you didn't travel. Nobody traveled, really. In fact, I remember the big wartime posters that used to be around: "Is your journey really necessary?"

When I was young we didn't really know anybody who'd been to London. My father had been once, in 1926, in a general strike. It is a provincial life, a very provincial life. London was as far away as New York to us. It was another world.

I first came here on a hunch, really. I'd been to New York City, but somehow or other I got it into my head that California would be very good for me, and arrived here in January 1964. I didn't know anybody. I couldn't drive. But I did have a bit of money. I'd sold some pictures in London, and I thought I had enough money to paint here for six months, which I did. I quickly got a driving license, found an apartment, and began to paint. My first show in New York was all painted here in California.

I did the first swimming pool pictures in 1965. I never did that many pictures with swimming pools; I think at the most seven or eight. People think I did hundreds. The subject was sunlight on water, really, and how do you find a graphic method to describe transparency. Things like that are interesting problems you set yourself.

I painted my own swimming pool. I just emptied it and painted wiggly lines on it, and it made it look much more amusing, I thought. Then I did one for the Hollywood Roosevelt Hotel, although I did point out it would only last about five years in California because of the strong light.

I didn't really move here until about 1978. Before that I was always just coming and then going back. I've been in this house for nineteen years now. I like it because you can live very privately here. I've always understood that in California the private spaces are better than the public places.

Los Angeles has changed, but I've also changed. For instance, I'm seriously losing my hearing, and therefore I'm not very social. I'm just unsocial, meaning I avoid crowds, anything with quite a lot of people and so on. LA is a good city for that. You can just stay at home, as I do.

I like driving. I drive up in the mountains a great deal now. I go in the San Gabriel Mountains probably more than I go down to West Hollywood. I like the mountains. I like the deserts. I like the big spaces, and I do like driving in them. For instance, the Grand Canyon—whenever I go, I drive there. I wouldn't dream of flying there. I plan music to listen to; the only place I listen to music anymore is in the car.

I realized my hearing was getting bad, and I wasn't listening to music in the car, so I had a new stereo system put in it. It was just at the time I got a little house in Malibu on the beach, and so at the same time I was exploring the Santa Monica Mountains, I was listening to music again in the car. I then realized that some music fit the mountain drive very well indeed, and I slowly choreographed two drives through the Santa Monica Mountains, one of about half an hour and one of about an hour and twenty minutes. That hour and twenty minutes was mostly the music from Wagner's *Parsifal*. I matched the crescendos with landscape crescendos and it worked very well. I mean, I even took children on it who sat in silence and said to me later, "Well, it's like a movie," meaning what they saw and what they heard combined into something.

I've just done a new one now for the San Gabriel Mountains from this house, again timed with the sun—nature does the lighting. I'm into Schumann symphonies at the moment; they sound marvelous in the mountains. I take people up there, and most say they've never been up there, even people who've lived in LA for a long time. There's nobody up there. The roads are empty, and of course I like it. I'm very attracted to places where there don't seem to be many people.

I must admit that still the thrill in California is driving, actually, around through the spaces. It's strange. After all, virtually everybody in LA has a car, so they can go anywhere. The only reason they don't go in the mountains is lack of desire, I suppose.

For many years I used to live in what we call the flatlands in LA. And if you do, the right angle, the horizontal, the vertical, the cube, the square, seem to dominate, in a sense. Then I came to live up here on top of the hills, and when I did, driving up and down, suddenly wiggly lines become a part of Los Angeles. They're not if you live down in the flatlands.

So the wiggly lines started appearing then in the paintings. I think the first one was of Nichols Canyon. My studio then was down on Santa Monica Boulevard, and so the view of Nichols Canyon is really from the bottom looking up, because I painted it down there. So is *Mulholland Drive,* in a way. I was driving up and down it and realized that, yes, it's a wonderful wiggly road, with a marvelous view of the San Fernando Valley.

LA is a very bright city at night. You get spectacular views when you look down on the city. The reason is the streetlights are twice as tall as the buildings in most parts of LA, if you think about it. That's what you're seeing. If they weren't, it wouldn't be as bright. Look down on London or Paris. The buildings are twice as tall as the streetlights, so you don't see them. Most of LA is actually one story, maybe two. It makes it very beautiful, doesn't it, flying in at night? Fly over London or Paris at night. They don't look the same. They don't shine and sparkle.

This house is right on the top of the Hollywood Hills overlooking Universal Studios, if I look down into the Valley. I painted the outside of the house, which isn't visible from the street, deep blue and red, to go with the green of nature. The colors, of course, are taken from a great Matisse painting, which I used when we did Ravel's *L'Enfant et les Sortilèges* in New York in 1980 for the Met.

I've also altered the space inside, which I do slowly. I like to be able to put my feet on the furniture. I'm a bit un-California in that I like it if it's worn a bit. That's my Englishness probably. You know the lines in Robert Herrick's poem, "Delight in Disorder":

> *A careless shoestring in whose tie*
> *I see a wild civility:*
> *Do more bewitch me, than when Art*
> *Is too precise in every part.*

Do I think place has anything to do with creativity? Well, of course it does. Los Angeles is also a very active city. It's full of active people, creative people. I can live anywhere. I want to live in an interesting place for me, I do.

I'm going to paint Monument Valley. That's what I'm planning. I'm finding ways to deal with the great big spaces of the American West. You can paint them again, though you need different new ways to do it, as I've found for the Grand Canyon. That's exciting, actually. No camera could see it like that. Only painting can do it that way.

It never occurred to me to be anything but an artist. I never, ever thought about anything else. Going all the way back. That's what I'm interested in—pictures and images. So is Hollywood.

I went to a discussion at the Getty on the conservation of art, and what they were really discussing is, Who should decide what to conserve? How is this decision made? I listened to them all, but then I pointed out that it is only what someone loves that is preserved. Most things will disappear, quite likely, otherwise we'd be up to our necks in rubbish, wouldn't we?

In Hollywood they're not necessarily respecters of their own past. For instance, they've just done a remake of *Psycho*. Somebody like me thinks, Well, why remake *Psycho*? Can you improve it? But Hollywood knows that for a mass audience everything has to be "now" in films. Only the movie buff goes to see *Psycho*. In fact now you have to be a movie buff to have heard of Alfred Hitchcock. Movies are always about now.

The moment I've done that painting, the painting stays that way. You bring your time to a painting. Video and film bring their time to you, and it's a profound difference. I'm involved with one, not the other, and I'm aware of that. I once joked that Vermeer's color will last longer than MGM's.

larry GELBART

Since he first began writing for radio at the age of sixteen, Larry Gelbart has made America laugh. Born in Chicago in 1928, Gelbart has written over the years for everyone from Danny Thomas to Sid Caesar to Bob Hope. He was nominated for Oscars for *Tootsie* and for *Oh, God!* and won Emmy Awards for both *M*A*S*H**, which he developed for TV and which ran for eleven seasons, and HBO's *Barbarians at the Gate*. The author of *Sly Fox* and *Mastergate*, he won his first Tony for coauthoring *A Funny Thing Happened on the Way to the Forum* and another for his book for the musical *City of Angels*. The man Neil Simon has called "the wittiest man in the entire world" works in an office above and behind his Beverly Hills house and pool.

⌐⌐

Writing the musical *City of Angels* was a wonderful job I gave myself. I returned to my loves of swing music and black-and-white movies and to the Los Angeles of my boyhood. It was a chance to write about the Los Angeles that was, the one I first knew and not the one I know now.

I came to California from Chicago in 1943 when I was fifteen years old. My uncle Max, my mother's brother, had come here first. He was a housepainter who dabbled in real estate and did well, and I think he encouraged my mother to come out. It was the Golden West and a new start. My dad, who had been a barber in Chicago, went on to become one of the haircutting stars of Hollywood.

I was encouraged to tell jokes when I was five, a kind of midget emcee, because jokes are the currency in a barbershop. It was very cute, I suppose, that a five-year-old could tell these jokes with the odd off-color punch line. My mother was a very humorous woman, so I was around laughter a lot. Some of it was what the Jews call *shayneh gelechter,* meaning things that aren't really funny but you laugh at them because it's better than crying.

In grammar school I was a serial show-off. In high school I spent half days working at the Ace Slipcover Factory—Fairfax High School gave credit in those days for outside jobs—but I was also involved with talent shows that kids put on. I really only wanted to be Donald O'Connor, who could do it all—he danced, he sang, he was funny.

For a long time I did want to be a performer. I had a couple screen tests. But writing professionally really satisfied the show-off part of me. Writing is the perfect medium for shy extroverts, getting out whatever's in there, and that suited me. If I could have acted, I probably wouldn't have written at all. Or written for myself, but I don't think I could afford me.

Saturday I was very religious. I was an orthodox cinemagoer. I lived for Saturdays to go to the movies, and without question, the comedians were the chief draw. The Ritz Brothers. The Marx Brothers. The Three Stooges. Laurel and Hardy. There are a few people who just stay in your ear and in your hard drive your whole life, and Groucho's got a guest room in my head. Or maybe just an audiotape. But I can hear his rhythm; I know the influence he had on me.

W. C. Fields is another one. Of all the people we're talking about, he was the most extreme in terms of irreverence. Fields sent up family values. I always think of a scene where he's leaving this little boy in a hotel room, second floor up, and he says to the kid, "Stay in this room until I get back and do not fall out of the window unless it's absolutely necessary."

All those wonderful movies—what we now call screwball come-dies—with their fast-talking, wisecracking character actors. Jimmy Gleason, whose house this was. And Franklin Pangborn. An endless parade of people who were like your family, whom you'd go to visit every Saturday, only they were very tall and flat, and most of them, for some reason, were just black-and-white. They were my other life, and I would come back and do whole sections of movies for my friends.

A lot of my tastes were first set in Chicago. Besides movies and filmed performances, I would see live comics because the major theaters in Chicago had stage shows. When the movie was over, Benny Goodman or Tommy Dorsey and their bands would rise from the pit or come forward on risers and play swing. I also studied clarinet, so I was wildly interested in music. There would invariably be a comedian on the bill and, for sure, I would come home and do all his routines.

When I moved out west, one of the nice things about living where I lived was that I was right around the corner from the silent movie house on Fairfax, and so I was forever dropping in there and watching the old masters. Then I would go to where my dad was working, and there would be my boyhood heroes sitting in his barber chair: Edward G. Robinson, Edward Arnold, George Raft, Kirk Douglas, Gregory Peck. It was unreal.

I didn't want to be *in* the movies, really, except for half a second. I just wanted to enjoy them. I never dreamed I could write for anybody other than myself. And I had a band: "The Esquires. Sophisticated Rhythm. Call Wyoming 5443. Jimmy Drake, manager."

I think my dad was a cross between Mama Rose and Sweeney Todd. He was very ambitious for his kids. My sister was quite beautiful, Elizabeth Taylor–beautiful, and I think he envisioned that maybe down the line she'd be a movie star. I think he saw my potential, and I think he saw his potential, too, being the creator. I remember my father and I were chatting with Jay Burton, a comedy writer, in the doorway of Nate 'n Al's deli and somebody came up and Jay said, "This is Larry

Gelbart, and this is Harry Gelbart, who invented Larry Gelbart." I think my dad felt that way. And why not? He did. He saw the potential for getting me an opportunity to work in show business. He said on a number of occasions, What a funny kid, or that the shows I wrote in school were wonderful and terrific and I could probably become a writer.

The notion of my entertaining his customers was not a new one. Back in Chicago, my dad worked three jobs—on the West Side, downtown in a much more prestigious barbershop, and very often in our apartment. He'd cut people's hair in the bathroom. Or shave them. I would sit on the edge of the tub and play clarinet for them while they were having their hair cut.

He was proud of his kids. He was an immigrant, and he saw us as more than people who would be in the service business. He was ambitious for me, far more than I was for myself. I thought I'd be a first- or second-rate musician. You can see—I was working in a slipcover factory.

One of his clients was Danny Thomas. He would go to Danny's dressing room at the studio every Sunday and shave him. He kept singing what was praiseworthy about me to Thomas, and Thomas one day said, "All right, have the kid write something." Thomas did a spot on *Maxwell House Coffee Time* about a Walter Mitty kind of character, Walter Dingle, the mailman. He would deliver mail to someone different every week, that person would insult him, and he'd go off and say he could be a better whatever than the guy was—whether a restaurateur, tailor, or policeman—and he would have this fantasy. So I had the character fantasize that he was a barber. Thomas liked it enough to show it to Mac Benoff, the head writer, and Mac said, "Why don't you come by my house, where I write the show, sit with me, and think up some jokes?" So I did.

I did that for a few weeks. I was finishing my last class at school. I was in show but not biz yet. I would sit with him, there'd be a premise, and he used a few of the lines I threw. Then the show was going off the air for the summer, and Mac gave me a check for forty dollars and said, "Buy yourself a sport jacket." That many years ago I could have bought myself a car.

It's hard to recapture that state of mind, but I just remember that it felt very natural to sit there and do what I was doing. I don't know that I made this connection then, but it was the same as when I was writing for high school. I wasn't writing up, down, or sideways. There would be another adult or two around, the grown-ups would be doing their stuff, and I had my situations as a kid. I just tried to say things that were funny and germane for this set of characters. I felt I was doing something I instinctively knew how to do.

I think my parents had to drive me to Mac's, but on my next job, writing for *Duffy's Tavern,* I was seventeen and could have driven. But I would walk on Genesee to Fuller Avenue, seven or eight blocks, in my ROTC uniform and sit there like a little soldier. It's crazy, isn't it? But I didn't think it was strange.

I got out here when I was so young. When I moved to Beverly Hills many years later, I was moving west, not up. This was just another part of town for me.

The most emblematic symbol of this industry is the nails that the construction people use to secure a set. The nail doesn't go all the way down into the floor. It has a collar that's the same width as the nailhead, so they're easy to remove. I always feel that anybody can come out at any time and say, "Let's strike this town."

It's the make-believe of the movies. People have forever built their homes to look like what they saw in the movies, dressed like what they saw in the movies. You can't indulge your fantasies anywhere else the way you can here. This is where you come to be who you really should have been, to live the life you should have lived. It's much more open here—people see what other people have and how other people live. In New York or any other big city, it's all behind big buildings or in the suburbs somewhere.

I think people come to California for the same reason my uncle Max did. California is like a reward. It's more comfortable here, but in a way it's not nurturing. You think you should be out by the pool. It's hard to work in a place that has a holiday atmosphere about it. Most comedy comes from friction, rubbing up against somebody, or against conflict. People live isolated lives here. You don't buy a paper from somebody. You don't mix with others who aren't in your economic or social orbit. I don't think this place is all that good for creativity, because it's pretty and I think a lot of art comes from conflict, from anger.

It's also a crap shoot. We don't know when the plates are going to shift, and the state is not going to leave a forwarding address. Other people live and watch history being made. We live and watch geography being made. We really do. I've written a piece I have yet to finish called *Shake, Slide, and Burn,* and that's what happens out here. It's very unstable, and the hubris is that we think we've conquered the hillside, the oceanfront, and the very land we're on, whereas we're very vulnerable. But we like our stuff, and we don't want to go someplace else where we can't take it with us.

I've watched this town go from *Andy Hardy* to *The Terminator.* This is not a rerun—it's a sequel. I was here in the forties for what was, for me, the original. I miss the old LA and the young me.

eleanor ANTIN

Bronx-born Eleanor Antin has been living in the San Diego area since 1968. Her first one-woman art show was at Long Island University in 1967, and a year later she and her husband, the poet, critic, and performance artist David Antin, were headed for San Diego, where they have lived ever since. A writer, performer, and filmmaker as well as a visual artist, she has long crafted videos, conceptual artworks, and room environments. Among her artfully documented "other selves" are the King of Solana Beach walking his oceanside Southern California community; nurse Eleanor ministering to Hollywood; and prima ballerina Eleanora Antinova, a dancer and film actor. She took one hundred black rubber boots around the state, then cross-country to end up at the Museum of Modern Art in New York, photographing them for postcards that chronicled the boots' adventures everywhere from a California meadow to Lincoln Center. **Her credits include MOMA and Whitney Museum exhibitions and a Los Angeles County Museum of Art retrospective.**

⌣

I lived in New York until I was in my early thirties, and we came here. Before that I'd been absolutely a New York street brat.

My mother owned hotels, and the one I remember most, the one that was the most interesting for me, was at the edge of the Catskills, near the Pennsylvania border. I worked summers there from the age of ten.

I was a counselor and took care of children who were three to almost my own age. In order to make them interested, I'd tell stories—scary stories, continuing stories—and make faces.

I think telling those stories certainly had an effect on me later. The whole ambiance of the place did. My mother had been with the Yiddish theater in Poland, and she loved running the hotel—it was after her own heart. The place had great charm and warmth. There was a Gypsy orchestra, and we always had an opera singer who could sing opera arias as well as Russian folk songs. The old Cossack sword swallower would turn and tumble and then swallow swords; he was going on eighty or something, and he was fabulous. It was a wonderful bunch of crazy characters.

I was always writing, painting, and drawing. I knew I was an artist. I just didn't know which kind. When I was in sixth grade, my principal wrote in my autograph book that my talent for art—dramatics, she called it—writing, dance, I don't know what else, would ensure a successful future. Of course it was the opposite, because in those days, everything was compartmentalized. If I had any criticism in one area, I'd just run to the other. So I used it rather neurotically. It was only later when I could pull it all together that it turned out to be something that was a great pleasure for me and very important for my particular vision.

But in the early days, until I matured sufficiently as an artist and until the art world opened up, I didn't realize it was possible to be a mixed-media artist. They didn't have a word for that, although there were people doing "happenings" and that sort of thing in the late fifties and sixties. But basically they considered themselves painters, and were doing it because they had to somehow get off the wall; they were doing something that was secondary to their main thing. For me it became my whole way of working, just moving freely, in whatever domain I needed.

We came to California in 1968 for a specific reason. UC San Diego was a young school, and Paul Brach, who started the Art Department, invited David out to run the gallery and teach art history. I was delighted to go, because it was like a magic place. It felt like we were going in the gold rush. Not only was the New York art scene in the last gasp of minimalism, but it was getting rather tedious. It got boring. We wanted to leave, and I wanted to see the world.

California, you've got to understand, was the West. We came by car like a bunch of Okies. It was an old, ancient car, filled with our little baby, who was a year old, and all our books. As soon as we got here, we looked at the books and said we don't want most of these, so we brought them to the Salvation Army or one of those places so they could sell them there. We had to bring the books to feel like we weren't totally isolated and alienated in this big scary world. At least that was my feeling.

We got to San Diego, and our little boy was sick. He had a 103-degree fever, and he was throwing up. We arrived at this place Paul had gotten for us—this charming little house with an orange tree. An orange tree! You've got to believe what that meant. So we immediately started squeezing oranges for the baby, and he got better in a day.

I think that in New York, where everyone is looking over everybody's shoulder, and you're centrally located within the art world as I had been for a long time, you kind of know what everyone's doing, what's the new thing, what's the way it's going to be tomorrow, who's already passing over the hill, what's old hat. I didn't have that trouble here. I had total freedom. But the flip side was that my connections were *only* New York. I didn't know anyone here.

The first thing I discovered here was a Sears catalog. That was a knock-out thing to see. I knew department stores—you got on the train and went to Macy's—and I saw a whole world in the Sears catalog. They had hunting clothes and all sorts of things. It was hardly chic, but I didn't care. I didn't want it to wear. I wanted it to invent people, to imagine the lives of people I saw around me in Solana Beach. I did a first show, *California Lives,* literally out of the Sears catalog (except when I needed something like a peace sign, and I went to a head shop). It was the funniest thing when I had to take it off my taxes as art supplies.

The *100 Boots* came out of work with consumer goods. I shlepped the boots all over Southern California, then took them to New York to all my old haunts in the Bronx and Manhattan. But they didn't fit into the landscape in the same way in New York. Maybe it was the grayness of everything; I don't know.

The *King of Solana Beach* came after the boots. I wanted to see what my male self would be like. I found out I looked like a portrait of Charles I, and I started reading about Charlie. I thought this neurotic nudnik is a lot like me. Very romantic. Stubborn. Persistent. A real drag. He did not have to have his head cut off—Cromwell didn't want to do it—but he was such a nuisance.

When I realized I was a king, I realized I needed a kingdom. You see how my work unpacks with possibility, from the germ or kernel of the idea? So Solana Beach became his kingdom, and he walked around, talking to people once every three weeks or so for about a two-year period. It was fun. What would sometimes stop me is that I had to put on the beard hair by hair, so it took me two hours to do it. I had to have a good chunk of time.

So I would walk down the hill from where we lived, maybe into the market or to the beach. Sometimes my little red dog would follow me but I wouldn't let him do that very often, little Clarkie, because people would know him. Once I went into the library as the king, and Clarkie followed me in, and I remember the librarian looked at Clarkie, then at me, and said, "Eleanor?" I kissed her hand. I didn't say yes or no, but she knew it was me.

There's a strong sense of community in New York, but you lose a sense of confidence to try things. In California I could do what I wanted to do and explore what I wanted to explore. I'm not glamorizing the place—it's not like you're coming into a utopian situation—but I could walk around town as the king. What would happen if I did it in New York? I'd meet some guy who would sock me in the eye.

I used to get up in the morning and look out at the Pacific Ocean. I heard it at night. I smelled it. A couple of steps, and I'd be down at the beach. Every time I looked at that water, I saw an old Greek boat. I would say every day the same stupid, corny thing—that this is the same water that was lapping the shores of ancient Greece. Of course that's in the Mediterranean, but it's all right. I knew what I meant. Those are the colors you associated with ancient Greece. The light sky with the light blue sea. The Atlantic is steely blue. It's very different.

I don't live by the ocean anymore. We live now in an unpaved, rural area north of San Diego, and when I'm away, I miss the isolation. I'm kind of a hermit. I live in my dreams. I travel so much and meet so many people. I'm intensely interested in them, but as soon as I come home, I forget.

fay KANIN

Few writers have spent as much time at lecterns as Fay Mitchell Kanin, four-time president of the Academy of Motion Picture Arts and Sciences. Only the second woman to hold that job— Bette Davis was president briefly in 1941—she has long been the role model to other women that Eleanor Roosevelt and Margaret Mead were to her. Enamored of film while still in high school in upstate Elmira, New York, she arrived in Los Angeles as a college student in 1937 and was working at RKO within three months of graduation. Leaving RKO in 1940 to marry writer Michael Kanin, she wrote many films with him, including *Teacher's Pet* in 1958, and several plays, including *Rashomon*. On her own she wrote the Broadway hit *Goodbye, My Fancy* and such landmark television films as *Hustling, Tell Me Where It Hurts, Heartsounds,* and *Friendly Fire,* which won her an Emmy. She first met Eleanor and then-governor Franklin Delano Roosevelt as the thirteen-year-old winner of the New York State Spelling Contest and launched an acquaintance with them that later resulted in her first invitation to the Oval Office. She lives in Santa Monica.

⌒

I first realized you could get paid for writing when I was about twelve years old. There was a column in the *Elmira Star Gazette* called "My Most Embarrassing Moment," and anyone who wrote a letter that was

accepted got a dollar. I thought, "A dollar is pretty damn good," so I figured out an embarrassing moment and wrote it up. It got published, so
next time I asked a friend if I could use her name, and I wrote two
embarrassing moments. I got two dollars, and a couple of weeks later, I
had all three letters in the column.

When I was growing up, we went to the movies, my girlfriends and
I, every Saturday like clockwork. It didn't matter what the movie was.
We just went to The Movies. Hollywood represented for everyone in
the East, and probably in the world, this golden city where you would
rub elbows with movie stars.

I'm sure part of my desire to go to Los Angeles was that I loved the
movies, and Los Angeles was next to Hollywood, but the University of
Southern California football team was also big news then. I don't know
why that recommended the college to me, because I certainly was not a
football player. But I said to my folks, "I would love to do my final year
of college at USC." I was an only child, and now that I think back on it,
I just can't get over it. My father decided to give up his job and move us
to California.

My mother had been in vaudeville—I think she sang a little bit and
was part of a sketch or something—and she was one of the swimming
Annette Kellerman girls, so she had this kind of show business background. My father managed a clothing store and was just a sweet, quiet
man. He went to Los Angeles a month or so ahead of us and looked for
a position. He found a store he could manage there, so my mother and
I packed up everything and we got on the train to California.

The train porter knew we were going to Los Angeles, and he knew
how excited I was. I was a college girl, but I was like a kid with the
excitement. He said to me, "Little Miss, when you wake up in the
morning, you raise your window shade, and you will be in California."
So when I woke up, just a little after daybreak, I climbed down from
my upper berth and woke up my mother, because her berth had the
window.

I raised the window shade. We were going through an orange grove, and when we went through the orange grove, I saw palm trees. I just fell in love. That's the only way I can describe it. I had never seen a palm tree. I had never seen oranges growing. It wouldn't have mattered if we had to sleep on the street, because here I was in California.

After college I told my uncle, a businessman who had many friends in the movie industry, that I wanted to get a job as a writer. Today being what we call "mature" is a liability, but in those days, if you were young they'd pat you on the head and say, "Get more experience and then come back." Nobody hired young people.

My uncle arranged for me to meet with story editors of various studios, and I would bring my writings from school—my themes and my stories. When Sam Marx, story editor at MGM, looked at them and said they were very nice, I said, "You know, Mr. Marx, I know you own *Gone With the Wind*. I read it, and I would be a wonderful writer for it." I can almost see now the way he had to keep himself from smiling, and I still remember his response. He said, "I think they have in mind a more expensive writer." I loved the word "expensive." He didn't say "talented."

I went then to RKO. The story editor was Robert Sparks, and he read my themes, too, and he said—I'll never forget this—"There's one producer on this lot who might take a chance with a young writer, and I'm going to talk to him." So he arranged a meeting for me with Al Lewis, to show him my stories, and Al Lewis put me on as what they called a "junior writer."

I was in heaven for about two or three weeks, and then the studio changed hands. Just as they do today, they swept out all the executives, including my producer, and I was swept out, naturally, as his employee. I went over to Bob Sparks and thanked him and said, "It was wonderful. But it's over, I guess." And he said, "Wait. If you want to join the reading department, I can get you in as a reader. You read scripts for the executives, write a synopsis of what you've read, and make recommendations. You'll learn more about writing when you start reading what's submitted." The pay was twenty-five dollars a week, and I thought, I would pay *them,* if I had the money, to be inside the studio. I said, "I'll take it."

There were three women and a couple of men in the reading department, and we all had desks in one big room, about as big as my living room. We read, and everybody typed, and it was almost like working at a newspaper. Nobody bothered anyone else, but we had this nice communal feeling.

Since I was inside the studio, I decided that I would give myself a film education. At the time there were no film departments in the colleges. So every noon hour, when the movie company broke for lunch and people went off to the commissary, I went on the set. No one stopped me then, because there was nothing shooting, and I walked around and saw everything. I made friends with every department that I could and constantly asked questions.

Garson Kanin had done two movies at RKO and sent for his brother Michael, a writer and artist who supported his family during the Depression and put Gar through school by such things as painting scenery for Minsky's burlesque. Michael had just arrived at RKO when I appeared in a little theater group we had at the studio. He saw me and asked this mutual friend to introduce us. He did, and Michael said, "How do you do? Will you marry me?" which was his idea of being cute. But a year and a half later we were married.

I wasn't looking to get married—I was working in a studio, I was making a little money—and I must say for my parents, they never pushed me. I remember asking myself if I wanted to get married, and decided I did. So we got married and decided we'd write together. We bought a story from *The New Yorker* about a boardinghouse for fighters and wrote the screenplay for *Sunday Punch* on our honeymoon. We rented a house in Malibu and worked there. We decided we couldn't afford the luxury of going away somewhere and the nonsense of it. We both were workers.

The war was on, and I decided that just as important as writing for movies was communicating with women who were being asked to take part in the war effort. Men were going off to war, and women were taking their places, and it was a whole new day for women. So I produced and hosted a radio show called *The Woman's Angle* at NBC Radio. I interviewed Lucy Ball and took Charles Laughton with me to talk with women who were on the assembly lines building planes.

Michael and I also wrote together for a while until he got involved with Ring Lardner Jr. to do *Woman of the Year,* and we put our collaboration on hold. I had written alone in the past—a story for *Liberty* magazine, a one-act play for the RKO theater group—and I decided to write another play, *Goodbye, My Fancy.* It was autobiographical in a way, about a woman going back to her college to get an honorary degree, which I had done.

I showed the play to Garson who said he liked it and would show it to Max Gordon, the producer with whom he had done *Born Yesterday.* Gar said, "Now, I don't know if Max is going to buy it or want to do it or anything. But it can only be to the good, because whatever he tells you will be very valuable."

So I got on the train and went to New York. Max Gordon read the play and called me over to his office. "It's very good," he said. "I liked it, but I'm not going to do it. Let me explain. I can do one more play this season. I have on my desk a play by George S. Kaufman and Edna Ferber. And I have here a play by Fay Kanin. Now if you were me, which play would you do?" So dummy me, I said, "Well, of course, I'd do the Kaufman and Ferber play." He said, "But yours is very good, and maybe you'll get a production of it somewhere else. You just hang in there."

I took my play and went back to Los Angeles. Michael said, "I think I'm going to try to produce this myself. We're going to put a bigger mortgage on our house." So we did. We opened in Canada, and then we went from there to Toledo, Ohio. In Toledo we knew we had a hit—we could tell by the audience reaction—and we opened in New York to the most glowing reviews. Michael and I went to New York for the opening, and we stayed for about ten days. I would go stand in the back of the theater, because I just loved seeing the audience, and at that first matinee, who came walking up the aisle but Max Gordon. The Kaufman and Ferber play that had been on his desk had opened and closed, and he came up to me and said, "Why did you have to give me such lousy advice?"

The play's success both encouraged and excited me. I was on the cover of *Writer's Digest,* the leading writers' magazine of the time, and to have your first play be on Broadway *and* be a hit *and* run six or eight months *and* go on the road was very heady and very exciting. It committed me to writing both alone and, later, together again with Michael.

When I was in high school, my mother and I would come in from Elmira to visit my grandmother in the Bronx, and I would take the subway into New York to see plays. After we were married, Michael and I also went to New York to see plays, and I loved the theater. But I loved the movies more. Michael and I wrote many movies together, and I got involved first with the Writers' Guild board and later the motion picture academy board. I thought the Academy was a terrific institution, and my mission in the four years that I was president was to spread the message of what movies were and what the Academy represented.

When I'm away I always miss Los Angeles. To this day when I drive along and I see the bougainvillea and the jacarandas and the green lawns, I love the look of it. The great German writers and musicians and other artists came here to live in this warm, delicious climate, lured by the idea of living in a golden countryside with its sunshine and ocean and all the things that California promised. It was really a mythical city to people. It still is to me. I always say the best part of my traveling is coming home.

john **OUTTERBRIDGE**

Artist, teacher, and community leader John Outterbridge was born in Greenville, North Carolina, in 1933, the second oldest of eight children. His father was a recycler before it was fashionable, and he became one himself. From his first paintings on used window shades to his assemblage art pieces, Outterbridge has used familiar things in unfamiliar ways. Always working as a child, he was a delivery boy, short-order cook, waiter, and dishwasher, and in his early years as an artist supported himself as a city bus driver. Cofounder of Compton's Communicative Arts Academy in the early seventies, he was director of the Watts Towers Arts Center from 1975 to 1992. Even during those years of full-time jobs, he was working nights and weekends in the studio. In addition to other shows in California, New York, and elsewhere, he was the subject of a 1994 retrospective exhibition at the California Afro-American Museum.

⌐⌐

I grew up in Greenville, North Carolina, in a row house, one in a series of tiny houses, all painted the same. They had great tin roofs that made music when the rains came.

My house was tiny and painted gray, and across the street was this big two-story house, painted yellow, with pear trees and a great magnolia tree out front. An old couple lived there, and I used to draw that particular homestead a lot. The old man had white, white hair, and he used to sit out on the grass. I thought it was just a beautiful setting when I was a kid.

That was one of the first paintings that I did on window shades. When they wore out I would always save them, and I'd paint on them. It was this unique material that would take paint, and I knew that instinctively.

I started to draw very early in my life, simply because there were people around me who drew, and there were always things that I wanted to record. My mother drew some and wrote poetry, and I remember her playing piano and clarinet. Relatives were blues singers and harmonica and guitar players, and there was that kind of sensibility around.

My father, John Ivory Outterbridge, was a man who hesitated to work for anyone other than himself. He had big trucks and he hauled and moved, hauled and moved. I worked with my father very early on. When the circus would come to town, he was a magic man who got to haul sawdust for the big tent. We were the lucky kids who got to hang out at the circus before anybody would get there.

Our backyard too was a highlight, in that my father salvaged a lot of things that he would haul. Many times he would move very wealthy families, and when there would be big boxes and trunks of toys left in the attic for years, they'd always come to us. Some were like new and well preserved. Others needed repair and painting and that kind of thing, and that was always an enjoyable task for us. And he always saved some of those toys for families that did not have any.

My father was a volunteer fireman during those years. The black firemen were volunteers who had the training and uniforms and did the same chores. They were firefighters, but they were not accommodated by the civil service system. Once, when I was around twelve, I built a fire engine out of scrap material—wood and old wheels and that kind of thing. They kept it on display for some time.

I was really interested in what was in the backyard. Old metal pieces, bicycle parts, old washing machines, and furniture. Things that were used. Things that simply sat.

It was the greatest playground in the world. Across the street at my school there were swings and basketball courts, but there was nothing like the backyard because it had so many possibilities that you could fashion yourself. Play became a way to escape into other worlds.

I think what I do today is greatly attached to that period because I'm really doing the same thing. I feel very strongly that I practice my life by doing art. How to be a better person. How to keep investigating. It really has not changed that much for me.

I went to an all-black school in North Carolina and during that time I lived a few blocks from East Carolina University. We were not allowed to go on that campus, but I had a job delivering prescriptions for the drugstore. I got on campus a few times, momentarily, and I saw my first art studio, a really well-facilitated work environment for artists. One day I'd like to show in my hometown.

I first went to college to become a mechanical engineer, but I thought of myself, and was referred to, as an artist all through school. I was the kid in junior high who got to get out of class to do a backdrop for the Drama Department. And when holidays came, I was the kid who went around from classroom to classroom illustrating images related to Thanksgiving and Easter and Christmas. Everybody knew me: "There's John. He's an artist."

I moved to Chicago after my military service, where I studied at the American Academy of Art and was in a co-op gallery situation. I always believed that artists had more strength in numbers than as isolated individuals in their studios. You have to be with yourself and with your work, but at times it takes collaborating with other people to pull it together. Music is that way—you play in bands and orchestras—and I guess I have that nature.

I came to Los Angeles in 1963 after marrying a very beautiful woman. I had never been west before, nor had she. An artist friend had relatives here, and he was always coming back to Chicago in the dead of winter. We'd have on so many overcoats and galoshes, we'd be looking like bears. He'd say, "You guys have to go to California. They have lemon trees in their yards. Oranges lying on the grass. We were on the beach on Christmas Day, man."

I simply couldn't fathom that. I worked for the city of Chicago as a Transit Authority operator, and my new wife and I decided that we were going to pack up and start our new life in California.

One of the first jobs that I got in Los Angeles was in a studio that made props for the movie industry. But eventually I got a part-time job working at the old Pasadena Art Museum in installation and teaching classes. I enjoyed that very much because the museum had such a great relationship with the surrounding community. And it was a world-class museum.

When Andy Warhol's soup cans were exhibited, I hung all sixty pieces in the gallery. I worked with sculptors like Richard Serra and Mark di Suvero, who became a good friend. He was traveling a lot to carry out commissions, and he used to leave all of his tools with me.

I was working in the same vein as the artists that I assisted, but I have to say that as African American artists we had no inroads into the art world's social arenas. We barely had galleries, except the galleries that we formulated ourselves. We're talking about the sixties and the seventies, when the streets were active and when the civil rights movement was in full gear. Many of us were part of the demonstrations of that era. We felt that we had a responsibility to our communities.

We didn't have galleries. We weren't showing in museums. We confronted a lot of the major institutions. I was on staff at the Pasadena Art Museum, and many times I'd end up after work fighting the board of trustees. It was kind of insane. You worked at an institution, and still you opposed a lot of its viewpoints and posturing. Fortunately I didn't get fired.

I did my own work, and I exhibited it as best I could, like all of us did at that time. But we were about the business of not just making art but building institutional attitudes that were not there for us.

My piece *Together Let Us Break Bread* grows out of the sixties, when I was at the Communicative Arts Academy, the Pasadena Art Museum, and being an activist artist in the streets, just thinking and feeling and holding on to the notion of human potential in whatever the political or social arena was. It grows out of the title of an old black spiritual, and its title was also influenced by the social collaboration of the sixties, when we were saying, Let us find a way to create tapestry that brings us together. Let us look for possibility.

I always had a sense of assemblage, even when I made toys as a kid. I didn't know what they were at times, but there were certain elements, materials, and textures that I simply related to: an old post out in the countryside that had its own kind of dignity.

I loved to draw those kinds of things, but I started to get fascinated with material and surface. Old paint. Rusted metal. That had a lot of appeal to me, and I saw that as art. So I started to collect that kind of stuff and just hang it about.

I enjoy painting very much, and I might do that again in my life. But when I came to California, I started to combine the painted surface with objects. I met Noah Purifoy around 1964, who became a mentor. He corralled debris and whatnot from the 1965 revolt in Watts, using things he could find in the burned-out buildings that were relevant to the revolt—bedsprings, neon signs, old burned-out toys, anything that he got his hands on.

I found how similar our approaches were, although I don't think I was as free and fluid in my selection of materials as he was. But it was much more reasonable for me to use discarded materials than it was for me to buy paint and canvas and stretcher bars and frames.

Psychologically and socially at that time, during the sixties, I started to disassociate myself from things that were framed anyway. I started to see the frame as another fence, another corral, and I wanted to break past that. In my mind a frame was another way to fence my thinking in.

I bought materials from junkyards where it didn't cost me as much. I found in a junkyard on Alameda Street years ago quite a bit of stainless steel, and I did a whole series of work with that metal.

One thing that I was influenced by when I came to California was almost an assembled kind of culture. It was innovative. It was daring at times. It was damn near backward at times. But it was uniquely progressive. There was the aerospace industry. There was the phenomenon of Hollywood. I started to make car sculptures, partly because I was really impressed by the homeboy and Latino influences—the very colorful kind of shimmering vehicles.

I began to think that maybe assemblage was a discipline that had as much to do with the way one assembles one's life and vision as with the material that you use. It seems that we all assemble notions, directives, disciplines, disappointments. We put all these things together as we seek a mode of expression and a way to live.

California taught me that. There might be the practitioner who builds something that hangs on the wall or that we might refer to as sculpture or as an installation. But there is also a little old lady who has the greatest flower garden in the world, and if you could steal it away from her and take it to an art museum, it would be a hit.

june WAYNE

Largely responsible for the resurgence of lithography in the United States, artist June Wayne is also well known as a writer, feminist, and social activist. Born in Chicago in 1918, she dropped out of high school at fifteen to work, and after several years in Chicago and New York as a jewelry designer, moved to Los Angeles in the forties. Besides founding the groundbreaking Tamarind Lithography Workshop in 1959, she has created at least three hundred lithographic editions herself, as well as hundreds of paintings, drawings, collages, and tapestries. There have been more than seventy solo exhibitions of her work here and abroad, and she is represented in such major museum collections as New York's Whitney Museum of American Art and Museum of Modern Art and the Los Angeles County Museum of Art. The subject of 1998 retrospectives at both the Neuberger Museum in Purchase, New York, and the Los Angeles County Museum of Art, she lives in Hollywood.

⌣

When I was four or five, I fell upon the dots that made up color in the Katzenjammer Kids comic strip. I was nearsighted, and I noticed how the green dots were a mixture of blue and yellow, and the orange a mixture of yellow and red. That was very exciting to me, and I promptly began making drawings that were made up of colored dots.

My parents were separated when I was an infant, and ours was a household of women—my mother, my grandmother, and myself. I was a chronic truant and dropped out of high school at fifteen to support myself. I worked in a liquor-bottling plant and an auto parts plant, but I was painting all the time. When I was seventeen, I had a solo show of my watercolors. The next year I was invited to Mexico City by the Mexican government, and my paintings were exhibited at the Palacio de Bellas Artes there.

I became a designer of ornaments for the garment industry, first in Chicago and then in New York, but my job was wiped out by the war. The war effort had commandeered all the factories in New England, which had been the center of costume jewelry manufacturing, and converted them to the production of bits and pieces that went into guns, tanks, who knows what.

The winter of 1941 was miserable in New York, I just couldn't shake this sore throat, and I needed to go to a more forgiving climate. I had the classic California dream of rolling green hills, oranges on every bush, wide streets, sunshine, cleanliness, opportunity. That's what I expected to find, and in many ways I did. There was no smog. There were no flies, no mosquitoes. It was just delicious.

My link was a distant uncle, but unfortunately, while I was on the train, I was incubating rheumatic fever. The day I stepped off the train, the symptoms arrived full-blown, so my next housing was a sanatorium in Montebello.

I had weeks of bed rest, during which I got to read all the books I never would have had time for, especially Proust, and to write. I might have made a few sketches, but in my mind to be an artist was a vertical, active thing. You walked around. You had supplies, easels, the appurtenances of your trade. To be in bed is an introspective thing.

When I left the sanatorium, I got an apartment in Los Angeles and began painting again. I also enrolled in a course in production illustration. There was a great expansion of the aircraft industry, and aircraft factories out here were hiring a lot of unskilled people. Artists were brought in to project blueprints into 3-D drawings, in perspective, to help the workers understand what they were building.

I also began writing radio scripts for the war effort, and I decided that whichever field I got a job in first, that's what I would do. Before I could connect in the aircraft industry, I received an offer from WGN Radio in Chicago to join their writing staff.

It seems my life was always this series of opportunities or accidents. You go through this door and not that one, and it takes you somewhere where you would have arrived anyway because it's very hard to get out of your own way.

Why did I come back to California when I was writing for radio in Chicago? I was married to an air force captain, and when he came back from overseas in late '43, I became a traveling army wife who trailed after the man in uniform. He was sent to Southern California, so I left WGN and followed him out here.

One was starting one's life over, as it were, after the war, so why not in a more felicitous place? And for me it also meant more space, light, and opportunity for a decent studio.

I first became interested in lithography quite by accident. It was the happy coincidence of propinquity, serendipity, and need. Around 1946 I had a problem that was just not working out in oil paint. I was trying to paint things that had a special op-art quality about them, and I thought that it might help to change mediums.

As it happened, I was only six blocks away from the only hand-printer of lithography east of the Rocky Mountains, Lynton Kistler. If he had printed etchings or silk screens, I might have taken off in those media.

I dropped in on him and sniffed around. I persuaded him to let me take home a stone, began experimenting with it, and got hooked. It was very useful for the resolution of the technical problems I was having.

Also, I could see that the medium itself had enormous potential that had not yet been tapped.

Lithography in the United States at that time was very nineteenth century. George Bellows and many other artists of that period had made lithographs, but it was not lithography as we understand it now, and it was hemmed in by the technical limits of what the printers could do and what the conventions were at the time. Eventually I abandoned Kistler and began going to Europe to work with European printers. But even they were not nearly adventuresome enough for me and what I needed for my art.

In a way I was then and still am a kind of free-floating radical. I am willing to go wherever I need to go to realize the images in my head.

In 1960 Los Angeles happened to be an ideal place to open Tamarind. First of all it was not New York. It was not the heart of the art market. There was not an ant run of kibitzers to annoy us or carry tales—"Oh, Sam Francis is there," "Louise Nevelson is there," or, "I didn't like what I saw," or, "The print was a failure," or, "Do you know so-and-so was there and got drunk?"

As a matter of fact, W. McNeil Lowry, the head of arts and humanities at the Ford Foundation, would have liked for me to open Tamarind in New York because a lot of New York honchos wanted it there, not here in LA. I said, No, we need the privacy to fail. I don't want everybody to know what we're doing.

One has to remember that when I opened Tamarind, printmaking was low on the totem pole. You were either a printmaker or you were an artist. American artists, unlike Europeans, did not have a tradition of moving from painting into printmaking and back again. So in the beginning, artists were not too eager to announce that they were going to be making prints. Then suddenly it became the in thing. Tamarind paid their fare, gave artists a stipend, and the association with the Ford Foundation was kind of sexy. Artists could come here, then go back and say, "Oh, I've been in California making prints, you know."

All that glitter made us the thing to do. But the most important draw for the artists was the creative opportunity to do something new. Artists always respond to that, and that was our bait.

People who were here later carried the word elsewhere. Many of them established workshops or became museum curators or dealers. There had been no standards that were generally accepted, so one post in the desert is really a landmark.

Then, after ten years, there had been significant changes in the outside world. We had created a number of master printers and established the significance of lithographs. Changes in the tax laws, beginning in '68, meant that the means by which we were funded had to change. The third factor, and it was a big factor, was that I myself felt that I had done what I said I would do, and I wanted to go back to the studio and my own work. So I sent Tamarind to the University of New Mexico in 1970.

I came to California for the quite mechanical reasons that I described. But the reasons why I stayed—while not enunciated as such to myself at the time—included the quiet. This is a silent place as compared with other cities, and I love silence. When I hear something, I really hear it in its own full dimension.

The sense of isolation here is important to me. One has to deliberately make an appointment to see somebody. In many a city just going to the grocery store announces your presence to a lot of people. Your propinquity may cause them to ring your doorbell. Here they have to drive to ring your doorbell.

The space and light of this area is also of a quality and scale that's very hard to find in other places. For one thing, because our streets are wide and our buildings low, we don't have many shadows cast. At the end of the day, the lighting comes down the way it does in a theater.

Cal Tech and the Jet Propulsion Lab are here, and my work has always somehow occupied the dual territory between the arts and science. One can see very frequently the vapor trails not only of planes but of missiles. Those damn things go off and write themselves across the sky in a kind of portentous longhand, and where else can you see that? You might get a little piece of it between two skyscrapers if you happen to look up at a propitious moment somewhere. But here it's in your plate. It appears in my art. You can see it in my uses of inking and in my images.

There were other inducements. Aldous Huxley was living here. Bruno Walter, Alma Mahler and her daughter Anna, and that whole troupe of people. Dorothy Parker. On the Sunset Strip, I would run into Oskar Fischinger, the painter and abstract filmmaker, and Max Yavno was there taking these great photographs. I played charades with Jascha Heifetz.

The German refugee colony here was very special in itself. Salka Viertel's house is now occupied by Gordon and Judi Davidson. All these mythical characters—people like Heinrich and Thomas Mann and Garbo—used to gather in that house, and just the other night I was having dinner there. Where do you draw the line with this? Walter Arensberg lived near here with that fabulous collection of seminal modern art. We even had the same property-tax collector who came by my place, saw all these paintings on the walls, and said, "I've got another nut like you in my territory who's got all this crap on the walls too."

Just up my block is the Hollywood sign. I can look at it and remember that such and such an artist lives under the H and such and such an actress friend lives just down the hill from the W. And I'm across the street from the tombs of Rudolph Valentino and Tyrone Power.

All around here, for several miles in every direction, there are all kinds of little shops of craftspeople who can do just about anything. It's like being in the Sixth Arrondissement in Paris. Even if you never have to use it, you know it's there.

My studio, now in the heart of a huge film industry, has double walls to keep out noise and double fences to keep out people. Every kind of data I need for my work comes to me through the computer, but I still prefer reality to virtual reality.

don **HENLEY**

Born in 1947, musician Don Henley grew up in Linden, Texas. He moved to Los Angeles in 1970 with his band, Shiloh, and in fall 1971, joined Glenn Frey in forming the Eagles. Cocreator of such Eagles hits as "Desperado," "Hotel California," and "Lyin' Eyes," the Grammy-winning singer, songwriter, and drummer in 1982 launched a successful solo career as well and has since recorded such hits as "Dirty Laundry," "The Boys of Summer," "All She Wants to Do Is Dance," and "The End of the Innocence." Founder in 1990 of the Walden Woods Project, a nonprofit effort to protect Henry David Thoreau's historic woods in Massachusetts, environmentalist Henley is also a cofounder of the Los Angeles conservation group Mulholland Tomorrow. Henley was inducted into the Rock and Roll Hall of Fame in 1998, and in 1999 *The Eagles, Their Greatest Hits 1971–1975* was honored by the Recording Industry Association of America as the top-selling album of the century. Henley lives with his family in Dallas.

There was always music in our house. I have memories very early on of being in my crib and hearing my mother sing while she was ironing, and she also played piano a bit in a rough gospel style. My dad liked to sing around the house or in the car, and Julie, who worked for us, would sing spirituals. My parents were also avid watchers of Lawrence Welk, and once, when he came to Shreveport on tour, they

took me with them. For some reason I went backstage and got the drummer's autograph. I was only in elementary school, so I guess I had an interest in drums even back then. You don't realize these things until so much later in life, but when you put it all together, there's a pattern.

Some friends of mine recruited me into the high school marching band. My original instrument was trombone, and I learned to play fairly badly. But I was always sitting in class doing cadences on my books, tapping them, and I drove my classmates and teachers crazy until one day, somebody—I don't know who it was—asked, "Why don't you put down the trombone, which you don't play very well anyway, and try your hand at drumming?" The band was apparently in need of drummers at that time, and I guess I had a natural ability for playing the drums. I would practice at home—I still have the red sparkle drums my mom bought me—and listen to Beatles records, playing along with Ringo.

Cars were a big thing in my family. When my dad came home from World War II, he went into the auto parts business with two other gentlemen. I remember going shopping for cars with my dad to all the dealerships in all the little towns in East Texas. I remember the smells of the interiors—that "new" smell. I loved cars from the time I was a kid. I got my first one when I was fifteen or sixteen. It was a '48 Dodge and had belonged to my grandfather. I lived in that thing. I slept in it, drove it all over northeast Texas. I was under the hood constantly tinkering with it.

I believe that the first place I became exposed to California culture, even before the music, was the hot-rod magazines I started to read after I got into junior high. All those magazines came from California, and there were pictures of hot rods and customized cars and souped-up roadsters and drag racers. When I became interested in go-carts, I ordered one from Azusa, California, and I used to order those airbrushed T-shirts that were made in California by this guy Big Daddy Roth.

The Beach Boys were really important to me and merged with the car culture. When I was in high school, as I was just beginning to drive, the Beach Boys were having hits like "I Get Around," which was our anthem. Me and my buddies would go from one neighboring town to another, cruising for girls because we were tired of all the girls in our hometown and they were tired of us.

We all worked on our cars back then. We changed our own oil and spark plugs. We flushed the radiator. We tinkered with the carburetor. The Beach Boys songs had these lines in them about souped-up cars and fuel injection and stick shift. It was real guy stuff. It was the stuff of every young man's dreams. They would talk about pistons and camshafts and other car terms that I suppose had subconscious sexual connotations. But we weren't aware of it then, and the Beach Boys probably weren't either.

I guess the first time I realized music could be associated with California was the Beach Boys and all the spinoffs—Jan and Dean, Dick Dale, the Ventures. I was in a rock band since high school, and we went through various incarnations. When we were an instrumental group, we played a lot of Ventures music because you didn't have to sing. It was all instrumental. "Walk—Don't Run" had a drum break, and I could sort of show off. The big [Surfaris] hit, "Wipe Out," had a drum solo.

I was with my band, Shiloh, playing at some club in Dallas when we met Kenny Rogers in '69. He was passing through on tour with the First Edition, and he was looking for groups to produce. We chatted with him, and he came to see us play. I guess he thought we had some potential, because he said, "Come on out, we're going to produce a single for you."

I'm forgetting the music magazines, which also sparked my dreams of California. In the late sixties, I read about the Byrds and the Flying Burrito Brothers and Linda Ronstadt and the folk scene at the Troubadour, which became the seminal spot, really, for so much of what happened in the seventies. I saw Elton John's first American performance there—his American debut.

So we packed up our things and came out here. We arrived in Los Angeles at night—and I've recounted this many times—and I remember the first recognizable thing I saw was the Capitol Records Building, because it's right there by the Hollywood Freeway and it was all lit up. Then, stretching below that building was the Los Angeles basin and all the twinkling lights of Hollywood.

I remember being very very excited and hopeful and feeling like a whole world of opportunity lay before me. I literally felt that I had arrived in the promised land. It was both frightening and welcoming. I felt optimistic, but it was a cautious optimism. I was still deeply attached to Texas, and I had modest goals at that time. I felt that I would be satisfied if I could just make one album, and then I'd go home and buy a farm. I was so naive; as if I was going to make enough money to buy a farm with one album. It was also very intimidating at first. I had cultivated an attitude before I arrived here that this was someplace that I didn't want to stay. The people were different, and I think we all felt a little out of place for being country boys from Texas. Even then we were smart enough to be wary of the record industry.

Kenny signed us to Amos Records for our first album and also signed to that label was a duo called Longbranch Pennywhistle, which consisted of a fellow Texan named John David Souther and Glenn Frey. I ran into them at the Amos offices, and also in the Troubadour bar, and we were all languishing in obscurity. It was spring 1971, and Glenn was going on the road with Linda Ronstadt. He asked me if I wanted to come and be the drummer. I had been in LA about a year at that time and nothing had happened. I was beginning to realize that perhaps my future lay elsewhere. So I went on the road with Linda Ronstadt with Glenn, and by September of 1971 we had formed the Eagles.

We all converged here as so many young people did in the sixties, looking for that dream—whether it be music or acting or just a lifestyle. California was being packaged and sold by the media as ground zero for the counterculture, and LA and San Francisco were where it was all happening. An entire generation was coming of age and going through a period of self-discovery. California during that time represented a place where one could reinvent oneself and leave behind all the negative aspects of home.

That, of course, turned out to be both a good thing and a bad thing. While this culture gave rise to the Beach Boys and the Byrds and the Mamas and the Papas, it also gave rise to Charles Manson. A lot of the kids that came west didn't have enough stability in their backgrounds to be discerning about who they spent time with and what they did. So a lot of them got lost in the shuffle, and their dreams got lost with them.

I would say that we're lucky to be here right now. But Glenn and I never lost sight of the goal, and we both possessed the drive and the work ethic and even, in a strange way, the discipline to carry it through. This is not to say that we didn't get sidetracked or that we didn't waste a great deal of time that could have been used more productively. But in the end we somehow remained focused and did what we had to do. We had a great support group that consisted of Jackson Browne and John David Souther and John Boylan and Linda Ronstadt. So we formed kind of a loose-knit family. We were all going in the same direction, and it was important, so far from home, to have a sense of family.

The first song that Glenn and I collaborated on was "Desperado." I had begun writing it back in 1968 when I was still in Shiloh. Musically that song is very southern in its influences, which range from Stephen Foster to Ray Charles. So it's really a Southern song that sort of evolved into a Western song on its way. It traveled with me from East Texas, which is really part of the South, all the way across Texas, New Mexico, and Arizona into California, and got completed almost five years after it had begun. So the song itself is a journey that parallels mine in a way.

The afternoon I showed "Desperado" to Glenn for the first time—and I think we finished it maybe that day or the next day—I was living in a house up at the top of Laurel Canyon. It was one of those houses on stilts, and I had moved into it not knowing who the previous occupants had been; later I found out that Roger McGuinn of the Byrds had lived in that house.

Glenn and I both lived in other houses in Laurel Canyon, and I still have a great deal of feeling about that area. When my original band, Shiloh, moved out here, the first place we lived was on Skyline Drive. We could afford a couple of months' rent but we couldn't afford any furniture, so we slept on the floor. Laurel Canyon was the heart of the music scene and every well-known musician had lived there at one time or another; I make an effort to drive through there every so often just to remind myself of that time. It's sort of a marker for me. There are certain places in this town that hold creative and spiritual meaning for me, and Laurel Canyon is one of them. My first audition for Linda Ronstadt's band was in Laurel Canyon. A great many significant, life-changing things happened up there, not just to me but to a lot of other people.

Pacific Coast Highway between Santa Monica and Malibu is another spot for me that's very powerful. I would say I've written the majority of the lyrics and melodies for all of my solo work driving on Pacific Coast Highway or sitting on Zuma Beach. Zuma Beach is a place of contemplation for me, where I can make the world—or at least half of it—go away. It's a good place to think about the pilgrimage that many of us make at some point in our lives. When I'm out there I think about the fact that it's about as far west as you can go in the continental United States. Even though I wasn't raised near the ocean, I find that it has become a very important part of my life and that I miss it when I'm not near it.

Mulholland Drive is another area where I've written a great many lyrics. It's a wonderful vantage point because you can see in several different directions. You can see the Santa Monica Bay to the south. If it's clear enough, perhaps in the wintertime, you can look in the other direction and see snowcapped mountains.

All that brings up a lot of questions about what this place must have looked like before all these people got here, and, back in 1976, it led me to think about not only Los Angeles but all desirable places. Places like Aspen, Colorado, and the Hawaiian Islands and how, by our mere presence, we ultimately spoil wonderful places because too many of us want to live there.

I wrote a song called "The Last Resort," the last line of which is: "You call some place paradise. Kiss it goodbye." That has been one of the major themes running through our music and my music as a solo artist. Civilization has migrated all the way around the globe and ended up here. We're all sort of huddled together, too many of us. This is a place where nature's work is unfinished. You have all this geological upheaval, as if to say, "Go away! There are too many of you."

I got engaged in 1994, and my wife and I decided to move back to Texas to raise the children that we have subsequently brought into the world. That move was also precipitated by the earthquake of January 1994. The earthquake destroyed my home on Mulholland Drive. It had to be demolished, and I took that as a sign that it was time to move on, to go back to Texas and reconnect with my roots there.

But after I was back there for a little over three years, I realized that I had put down roots here that were in some ways just as deep, if not deeper, than the ones I had in Texas. I'm fifty-two years old now, and I have lived just about half of my life in each place. I am deeply attached to both of them, and in some ways it's troublesome because it doesn't allow me to fully exist in or to fully partake of either place. On the other hand, it fills my life with an interesting kind of duality.

Part IV

Community

buddy COLLETTE

Los Angeles–born composer, arranger, and instrumentalist Buddy Collette had his first band at the age of twelve. At home on alto and tenor sax as well as clarinet and flute, he played with the Chico Hamilton Quintet as well as for Lili St. Cyr, Frank Sinatra, and Ella Fitzgerald. Born in 1921, Collette was among the first black musicians to play for TV and film, and he both founded a groundbreaking interracial symphony and was instrumental in promoting the amalgamation of then-segregated Musicians Local 47 and Local 767, the black musicians' union. The versatile wind player helped immortalize the midcentury jazz scene along Los Angeles's Central Avenue, a place *West Coast Jazz* author Ted Gioia calls "an elongated Harlem set down by the Pacific," which was at its heyday in the twenties, thirties, and forties. Honored with a Buddy Collette Day in 1990, he was named by the Los Angeles Central City Association as a local "treasure."

I grew up in Watts. There was plenty of land at a reasonable price, and many people went out and bought land. People kind of helped each other build their homes, and my father built our house with a bunch of friends.

The greatest thing was the different kinds of people—Mexican, Chinese, Japanese, black, Italian, what have you. We all went to the same school, and everybody got along quite well. It wasn't like you hear about now, where somebody gets beat up because of his race. We didn't know what that was about. It was a great way to grow up because your favorite friend could be just anybody that you chose. Everybody was accepting, and everybody was respected.

I went to Jordan High School. Joseph Lippi, who was a music teacher there, loved music. He liked to have a band—not a jazz band, we had a jazz band on our own—and he was really enthusiastic about being a musician and playing everything right. He influenced a lot of us.

There were pianos probably in every home. Walking down the street, you'd hear saxophones and trumpets. Maybe a saxophone player would stand on one corner, and then if I heard him, I'd get my horn and stand out in front of the house, like talking on the horn. There wasn't much traffic, and sound travels.

At my house we had a piano and record players. Movies were popular, but you didn't go more than maybe once every two or three weeks, and there was no television of course. But my mother and dad loved music. We listened to the radio, and there was a lot of jazz on the radio.

The big bands were very popular too. Count Basie or Duke Ellington would come to town, maybe play the Elks Hall. I forget what club it was, but my sister and I went along with our parents to hear Louis Armstrong. It was great because the band was so entertaining; the way they dressed and their personalities, and everything was just outstanding. I was taken with how they seemed to enjoy themselves so much, and how people were reacting to them.

My mother and dad knew this gentleman who was a fine musician at the time, Dootsie Williams, who lived four or five blocks from where we lived. Once they were at his house and began to talk about me, saying "Our son is twelve and plays saxophone." Dootsie Williams said, "Well, I have a lot of music. I can send you some music home for him." He pointed to a trunk and said, "Take that to him."

When I woke up the next morning, there was this trunk full of music from Dootsie Williams. I don't know how great it was, but it was great for me. Any music at all was a beginning for me. I had a few friends who were playing, and this music was already laid out—first saxophone, second saxophone, third and fourth, and then trumpet and trombone. I had my saxophone and was playing pretty well, and I had the music, so I got a bunch of my friends to come over and fill those parts. And that's how I got the band started.

I met up with Charles Mingus about that time, a month or so one way or the other. We had never had a string bass in any of our orchestras then. We had just broken up with a band—the Bledsoe Brothers—and they had a tuba that played the bass parts. There was a song called "Slap That Bass," and I thought, Well, why not use the string bass?

Charles actually was playing cello with a trio I think he had with his sisters, and when I met him I said, "Well, if you had a bass, I could hire you in my band." That excited him, so we talked about it, and he said maybe his father could trade the cello in for a bass. He did that, and after a couple of weeks I saw him and he said, "I've got the bass now." So I hired him in the band, which made him very happy.

We played in the school band and with the Woodman brothers. They inspired us because they were playing so great when they were just kids. They were only about fourteen or fifteen themselves, but their father had spent a lot of time with them studying and having them practice every day after school. They were very professional, and they used to have a studio and dances where we'd go hear them. They would play little jobs two or three nights a week, and since they liked me and my playing, they took me on some of the jobs. They were excellent players, so you had to play well if you wanted to be in there with them.

When I'd go to visit Charles or the Woodman brothers or the McNeely brothers, I'd have to go by the Watts Towers. I'd see this gentleman, Simon Rodia, who wore old clothes and an old hat, and it seemed like he didn't know what he was doing. We thought maybe he was building a wall because then it was only six feet high, and he used shells and rocks and glass, anything he could find. It didn't look like anything. He'd be busy working with his catch of the day, and we'd be in his way, so he'd chase us away. It wasn't until years later, when I went back to see it, that I could really appreciate it.

Central Avenue was about ten miles from where I was living. We would go on the Red Car, which ran right through Watts, or by car. We met other people there who were musicians—Chico Hamilton, Jack Kelson, Ernie Royal, Marshal Royal, a bunch of people who were going to Jefferson High School. Everybody played dances at the Elks and in Watts, and you know how you hear about people and you find them?

My earliest memory of Central Avenue would be when I was about fifteen or sixteen years old. Charles Mingus and I used to go there and hang out and try to meet people who were in the business, and a lot of them would go to the after-hours spots. There was a place called the 54th Street Drugstore. They had food and soft drinks, malts and everything, and people would come there for a late-night snack.

If Duke Ellington or another big group was in town, they would come in and hang out. Celebrities like Jack Johnson, the fighter, and bands like Cee Pee Johnson's were the local hotshots. Everywhere they'd go, Cee Pee would talk to the owner of the club and say we've got to have radio, we've got to bring the people in, which was true. Cee Pee Johnson's was the first professional band I joined that paid money, and that was a good band to be with. They were on radio everywhere they played, and they always had steady work.

Central Avenue was a business area—barbershops, clubs, barbecue places. People would dress up and walk from spot to spot, showing off. If you had a new car, you'd bring it over and park it on the avenue. People would conk their hair, get their shoes shined. It was an interesting place, because everyone was out there. You'd go on over to the avenue to see what was going on. It was like your newspaper.

There was never a dull moment. There was always something going on that was worth your while, and it was much better than staying home. Bands might be rehearsing in some of the clubs like the Alabam.

Or I'd go over to the black union, Local 767, which was on Seventeenth and Central. You'd see famous musicians there who were in town or doing business or rehearsing at the union hall. Word gets around, and we'd go over to see how they rehearsed, what they looked like, how they read music.

We would just have a ball, going to hear the bands. We were going to school, too, but I also began to work at the Follies Theatre downtown with the Woodman brothers. It was a good little job. We'd work seven shows a week for people like Tempest Storm and Lili St. Cyr or with Joe Yule, Mickey Rooney's dad. They were big stars, and there we were, working with them, talking with them. What a way to spend a week.

After the service, I went to school for four years on the GI Bill. Later I met Barney Kessel, the guitarist, who was doing *The Jack Smith Show*. I went almost every day and watched them do those shows. They'd rehearse in the morning, then do the show in the evening. I was basically a jazz player, but I was studying flute and clarinet in order to be a studio musician. I was sort of preparing myself.

We started a symphony orchestra in the late forties. Mingus and I met guys who played in the symphony, and they'd heard about the amalgamation of the white and black unions that we were trying to get together. I thought it was a good idea for us to have that symphony training, so I got people together, mostly minorities, to play Brahms and other literature. We called ourselves the Humanist Symphony Orchestra because we met at the Humanist Hall. Our first conductor was Eisler Solomon, and we had Henry Lewis, then only nineteen and a great bass player, so there was a lot of press coverage. We got other conductors then, and we played every week. We had jam sessions and meetings to exchange information.

Once we invited Josephine Baker to come. She came between shows. The word got out that she was going to be there, and the place was packed. She got up and spoke. She said she saw no reason why there were two musicians' unions, and asked why we couldn't all get together like we were that day. Before she finished, she looked down at a couple of little girls in the audience, a white girl and a black girl, and had them come up onstage. She whispered in their ears, and they began to hug each other. She said, "I think you can learn a lot from these youngsters," and walked out.

Jerry Fielding, who was then the conductor for *The Life of Riley* and Groucho Marx's show, *You Bet Your Life,* heard about the symphony and came to a rehearsal one night. We were playing *Carmen,* and the conductor asked me to play the flute solo. After the rehearsal, Jerry and I started talking. He didn't know me, but he liked what I'd done. He asked if I knew Marshal Royal, and I said I knew him, but he'd just left town with Count Basie's orchestra. Jerry said, "That's too bad, because I need a saxophone player on the Groucho Marx show. Too bad you don't play saxophone." I said, "That's what I *do* play. I'm just learning the flute." And he sort of hired me on the spot.

I stayed with the Groucho show about ten years. Then, after Groucho, I began to meet other people, and my work expanded. I used to look at all the things I'd done, and I couldn't believe I'd done all that—played with Sinatra, with Ella Fitzgerald. I've been getting a lot of awards lately, which is great. People say, "You were a part of that, weren't you?" And I can say, "Yeah, I was there."

peter **SELLARS**

Peter Sellars was raised in Pittsburgh, where he was born in 1957, and traveled extensively before he was twenty. Today directing theater, opera, and arts festivals around the world, he remembers directing about forty productions in high school at Philips Academy, Andover, then another forty when he was at Harvard University. He has headed the Boston Shakespeare Co., the Kennedy Center's American National Theater, and the Los Angeles Festival, and in 1991 made his film-directing debut with *The Cabinet of Dr. Ramirez*. Much as he set operas in New York when he lived on the East Coast, so he brought California prisons, riots, and earthquakes to the musical stage upon moving to Los Angeles in 1987. He lives in Venice, California, in a house where visitors may arrive to the sounds of Indian music and the smells of incense.

⌒

When I was in fifth grade, I started apprenticing at Lovelace Marionettes. The theater was a little garage, painted fuchsia inside. The walls were covered with masks and puppets from all over the planet. Javanese shadow puppets. Masks from Bali, Africa, the Yucatán, Osaka.

It was this amazing universe, inside that garage. Everything was magical, incantatory. You felt a spell being cast, and it was an amazing way into the arts.

It was only much later in life that I began working in theaters where people were actually sitting down. I grew up performing in department store windows; shopping malls; on the street; in libraries, schools, and parks; off the back of pickup trucks, and really engaging an audience of whoever is there.

While puppetry and masks are all about hidden and invisible worlds, they're also popular art forms. You grow up learning that if people don't like it, they can just walk away. And if they walk away, they won't put money in the hat at the end, and you won't eat that night.

I used to spend weekends at the Carnegie Institute, which had in a single building a concert hall, an art gallery, an architecture museum, a science museum, a natural history museum, and a library. Painting, music, books, and nature were all wired to each other, which was really pretty fabulous. Everything connected.

At the marionette theater, everything was also interrelated, interdisciplinary, and inseparable. You learned how to paint and sculpt. You were carving puppets, sewing costumes, painting backdrops, lighting the shows. You were doing the music, text, acting, and movement.

I did not learn the way you learn in art school. You watch like a hawk everything going on around you and say to yourself, Okay, when I grow up I'm going to do it differently. And then, of course, you don't. You copy it exactly, until, as Balanchine says, "One day without realizing it, your imitation has become your own voice."

When I was in the seventh grade, in 1969, my mother, who is a teacher, worked on a curriculum project in Palo Alto, California. I went from Pittsburgh, which is the middle of nowhere in a certain sense, to being every weekend in Berkeley, with the moratoriums and large demonstrations. There was a sense of national destiny, that we were going to change the country, that there was a real people's movement, that the people's voices mattered.

I grew my hair all the way down my back. I wore bell-bottom pants. It was just liberation itself. And that really did deeply, deeply, deeply resound through my whole life. I'm still living in that year in lots of ways. When I went back to Pittsburgh, I could no longer fit. It was like putting on a pair of shoes that you've outgrown: You can't walk in them anymore.

I directed about forty productions in high school, then went with my mother and sister to Paris for a year. It was 1976, the American Bicentennial, and there were all these American artists there. I connected deeply to John Cage and a whole kind of American avant-garde tradition. I spent days in museums, walking Paris, writing, reading, going to concerts, theater, operas, and living in the Cinemathèque.

At the end of the year in Paris, I went to Russia as a member of the French delegation to the Union Internationale de la Marionnette. The great avant-garde theater traditions in the last fifty years have been in Poland, Czechoslovakia, and Romania, so my first taste of that was shocking and really thrilling.

The Russians had invited puppeteers from all of the republics, particularly the Asian and Central Asian republics. In those days, which were really the darkest years of the Cold War, basically Russian was the only acceptable language in theaters in those countries, but the puppets could speak in their native tongues and get away with the wildest things.

Those shows were red-hot and filled with this fierce commitment, vision, and hope. It was intoxicating to see this larger mission and sense the importance theater could take on when the issues were not merely aesthetic.

The shows I went on to direct at Harvard ranged from Chekhov, Shakespeare, Mozart, and Monteverdi to Gertrude Stein, Beckett, and Slavomir Mrozek, the great Polish playwright. I had seen my first Javanese and Cambodian theater during my year in France, and when I graduated I got a fellowship to travel and study in Asia. My mother by then was living in Japan, so it was an amazing opportunity to experience the performing arts there firsthand, on location, and with a sense of the cultural surround.

When I was back on American soil, I directed the first production of the reopened La Jolla Playhouse. Brecht's *The Visions of Simone Machard* was one of the most beautiful productions of my life. The images still linger. I was too young then to know that you don't do those things, so I just did them. Now I would never hire my young self. I can't imagine how people gave me jobs then. I got to do work that was daring just because it didn't know not to be.

Jack Kroll in *Newsweek* said, "Well, this is the new Orson Welles." So of course there were calls from Hollywood, and I came out here, stayed in the Château Marmont, and took meetings. But that was not exactly my world.

I was head of the Boston Shakespeare Company for a year, then was invited to run the American National Theater at the Kennedy Center. I was very busy staging a lot of work, and when I finished in Washington after three years, I was invited here to run the 1987 Los Angeles Festival.

The thing to learn about Los Angeles is that basically it's a desert ecology. If you don't know deserts, and if you're looking for a rain forest, your first experience is shocking. A lot of people spend a lot of time talking about what isn't here. They don't notice what *is* here.

If you know how to look at a desert, you realize it is a rich, densely layered ecology. Everything in LA is hidden. Everything important about LA is not on the surface. There are a lot of secret places, and you have to know where the special trails are.

Knowing your way around the Cambodian refugee community or finding a great restaurant in East LA is just like getting a film made in Hollywood. You have to know who to talk to, and if you're talking to the wrong people, you miss the entire scene.

LA is completely about who the people are you're in contact with. Because of the geography, and how spread out it is, the layout of the city actually enforces a very profound racial and cultural segregation. Most people visit the same three places every day, and are actively frightened to visit most of the rest of the city. They don't know how to participate in its larger culture.

As I began to experience this, I realized what I was missing from East Coast culture. When you walk down the street in New York, almost no one is like you. The widest range of people are rubbing shoulders and crossing paths constantly in New York, and that's what creates this cultural friction and vibrancy.

In LA, people just didn't know one another. They didn't have one another's phone numbers. People didn't know what was going on one or two neighborhoods over.

You and I are listening now to Subramaniam, the great South Indian classical violinist. He lives in the middle of the San Fernando Valley. I've just finished doing a production of *The Peony Pavilion* with the greatest living Chinese classical actress, Hua Wen-Yi. She lives in Arcadia. Who had any idea that living national treasures of world culture are in this city?

For me the shock was realizing how much culture here doesn't happen in a museum, concert hall, or other usual venue. A lot of Pacific and Latin American culture is not about going inside. Those of us who were raised on East Coast culture go indoors because it's cold in New York, Paris, and Moscow. But it's warm in Rio, Mexico City, and Jakarta.

I moved here at the end of 1987, and my cultural experiences here were so eye-opening, they changed all of my work and practice. They changed all of what I thought theater was for and all of what I thought music was about.

My *Mozart Trilogy* was set in the eighties in New York—Trump Tower and East Harlem—and in Greenwich, Connecticut. As soon as I moved here, all of my work has been focused on and about Los

Angeles, starting with Mozart's *The Magic Flute,* which I did at Glyndebourne, but which was entirely set in Los Angeles. *Pelléas et Mélisande* played here during the final phase of the OJ trial, which was happening five hundred feet away from the concert hall.

New York dominated cultural life in this country for a century, because a century ago it was the center of immigration. The largest single performing-arts institution in the United States is the Metropolitan Opera, and that's because a hundred years ago the immigrants were from Germany, France, Russia, and Italy. Chinese opera was performed before Western opera. That's what people don't know in the historical amnesia around here. They don't realize that white culture is the recent arrival.

Most people in Los Angeles have never been to South Central and have no intention of going there. They know what it looks like, because they've seen it on the news and on crime shows. People think that's the reality, and then they start voting that way. A series of destructive and mean-spirited laws the last ten years in California have come from voter initiatives that attacked immigrants and removed basic civil rights. English is now the official language in the state of California, when in fact large sections of the state have Spanish-speaking majority populations.

The arts communicate through humor, outrage, surprise, and a kind of acknowledgment of the real sadness and strange loneliness that is on the other side of the California dream. People came out here to live in their dream castles and tell the rest of the world to go away.

I think now we're in a very interesting situation in Los Angeles. The Chinese community long since outgrew "Chinatown," and Monterey Park is the first Chinese city in America.

We have the largest population of Native Americans in America living *here*. We have the largest population of Iranians outside of Iran living here. The largest population of Filipinos outside the Philippines. Koreans outside Korea. You can go down the list. Cambodians outside Cambodia. Vietnamese outside Vietnam. Salvadorans outside El Salvador.

The Western tradition arrived by the nineteenth century to the cult of the genius artist: the loner, the weirdo, the guy sitting in the corner of the bar drunk, who thinks he's better than the rest of us. You can't find that model in Pacific Island, Native American, or Mexican culture, because the cultural forms are all collective. They take the form of a whole neighborhood or village.

Of course there *are* extraordinary individual artists, but the art forms themselves are not for private ownership. Everybody owns the mural. Nobody can own the performance. It is art that was created not as something to own or sell but as a way in which a community is held together.

On Monday I go to Amsterdam and begin rehearsals of music Stravinsky wrote in Hollywood the last ten years of his life. It was written in a culture of exile, this last music. No one here knew how to listen to it, because it didn't fit in the pantheon of modern art, where modernism was defined as nonethnic. After all my experiences with the Cambodian community, I'm suddenly looking back at Stravinsky as an exile and saying, Maybe the reason this work never took, and the Museum of Modern Art crowd didn't know what to do with it, was because it's from somewhere else.

One side of California is xenophobia and paranoia, and the other side is *Brave New World.* This is the place where people have come in order to try new things. It's the newest edge of America, whatever that's going to be. New York and Chicago remind you of what America was. In California the question is, What will America be?

Every kid in America is wearing something today based on what LA teenagers decided to wear ten years ago. It is phenomenal that teenagers in this city have the power to decide what will be sold in a strip mall in

Kansas. Every teenager in the country, Europe, and Africa is wearing baggy pants now.

If you're interested in the future of this country, you have to deal with LA. Everything is going on here for better and for worse, and the way that balance is maintained is up to us.

judith **BACA**

Judith Baca has made or supervised hundreds of public murals throughout Los Angeles since the seventies, and for her the steps leading up to and around the mural are as important as the mural itself. More than artworks, they are instruments of social and individual change. The city's Social and Public Art Resource Center, which she cofounded in 1976, documents and nourishes the city's mural arts. Born in Los Angeles in 1946, Baca spent ten years supervising *The Great Wall of Los Angeles* mural in the Tujunga Wash Flood Control Channel, which documents the history of California and, in many ways, the struggle of the artist and her community to be counted. Today a professor at both UCLA's César Chávez Center for Chicana and Chicano Studies and its World Arts and Cultures Department, Baca has taught and supervised hundreds of people as they immortalized their culture on the walls of a long-disinterested Los Angeles. She lives in Venice, California.

M y grandmother always thought of California as *Mexico en El Norte:* "Mexico of the North." It was her mother's memory, and it was passed to her. My great-grandfather brought mules to the missions of California, and that was as natural as going south. People had been moving back and forth across the border freely for thousands of years.

When I started school I didn't speak at all. My mother had married a man who wanted me to speak English, and Spanish was the household language. We moved from the Watts area to Pacoima; I started school, and she married him almost simultaneously, so I had this catastrophic language thing between home and school. It created a really introverted child—one who didn't speak in school, didn't raise her hand, and was terrified.

That was why, I believe, my teachers gave me special lessons in painting. They gave me paper, paintbrushes, and shiny tin cans filled with paint. I distinctly remember moving that yellow brush across newsprint, and the smell of it. The whole experience was very vivid. I painted and painted.

Although today that school is 99.9 percent Spanish-speaking children, there were not that many then. I was of that generation of pre-bilingual-education-trauma children, and what I think happened was that the visual arts became a method of communication for me.

There was a Judy Baca Day at Haddon Avenue Elementary School, and my kindergarten teacher was there. She talked about how she had a particular love of the arts and how she used the arts for students she couldn't reach in other ways.

In Pacoima our schools would close every year because of the warfare between blacks and Chicanos. It was a few really wonderful teachers, I think, who kept me from being a delinquent child.

I was the first of the Bacas to get a college education, and I chose art as my field. By that time I had been through high school, and I had distinguished myself as an artist. People had begun to recognize me as a person who could draw.

My mother was very upset that I was going to do something that would make me totally useless. I should be a translator or an attorney or something that would get me a really good job. But the basic underpinning was that I should never rely on anyone to take care of me and that I should be independent, which I think she did instill in me very well.

I got an education degree, but I was clear that I wanted to be an artist who taught. I loved adolescent kids, and I thought that I particularly could understand them. I became a teacher at the same Catholic high school I'd attended myself, with the Sisters of Saint Joseph of Carondolet.

I came to murals through graffiti and through collaborative projects with youth. I didn't come to them from an educated point of view. I actually came to them by accident.

I needed to find ways to engage young people to work together. They were separated into racial and neighborhood factions, and the idea occurred to me that if you made something too big for one person to do, or too difficult for one person, it would force cooperation. I was interested in all the underlying social architecture, where you really try to build something between people.

I also was looking at what was written on the walls. There was a revolution going on when I stepped out of the university in the mid-sixties. "I would rather live one year as a lion than a hundred years as a lamb" was in four-foot letters at the end of one street. It always struck me as amazing that people were saying, *"Yo soy,"* "I am." It was like this assertion of self, of presence, in a city that makes them invisible and disappears them.

You can recall in the late sixties and early seventies that although there were large populations of various cultures, they weren't visually present. Politically I was motivated by the idea that those who could take up the most space had the most power. If you could take a little space back, you could assert that presence.

About that time a big conservative element of the Catholic Church came in, and those of us who were doing this progressive teaching, including the Sisters, were kicked out. I probably would still be a high school teacher if I hadn't been fired.

As my mom said, "God closes a door and opens a window," and God clearly had another idea for me. I was to go somewhere else, and I ended up in East LA within minutes, organizing gang members and working on the first mural.

I painted a 350-foot-long piece at Mott and Second Street at the Little Sisters of the Poor Convalescent Home. It's such a prevalent theme: The Sisters lived among the poor in the middle of the inner city. I created a project that brought the young people from the community together with the convalescent older people and the Sisters.

I hired gang members and all these kids from different neighborhoods. I actually have on my desk an invitation from a kid who worked on that project who has been a police officer for twenty years. He just finished his own mural and was inviting me to this event where he was being honored.

Murals, you know, are not easel paintings. For one, the scale is integral to the work. It is about space and the occupation of space. It's integrated architecturally to the physicality of a site. Third, it's integrated socially into the locale. It has a relationship to who lives there, who sees it, and why. I don't think this is true for all muralists, but for me muralism is a participatory process in which observers can sometimes also be participants.

Los Angeles has a year-round painting season. Eastern murals basically are closed down for half the year. It gets pretty hard to work even in San Francisco at certain times. Also, we did a tremendous job of concreting up everything. Los Angeles became this sort of giant concrete monster. We concreted our rivers. We created freeway systems with tremendous numbers of walls.

We divided up communities with endless acres of walls, and there was a lot of healing that needed to be done. The city was a city divided geographically, culturally, economically. And the murals actually became a really interesting method of stitching it up. They were cheap and available.

I think Los Angeles is also a particularly nourishing place for murals because of its Mexican roots. And maybe for me and many other Latino muralists, the omnipresence of Siqueiros's mural on Olvera Street, *América Tropical,* the central image of which was a crucified *campesino*-type figure. It was whited out in 1932, and in the late sixties and early seventies, the sun started to burn off the whiteout, and it became a reappearing apparition. As our population grew and as our political strength and assertion of our civil rights appeared more, that image resurrected. It's an interesting parallel for me.

Most important was that we didn't have other options then. We were not in the galleries, and we were not in the museums. In those years—around 1970—there weren't other spaces in which these artists could show. So we worked in our communities. We saw the art as daily life activity anyway.

Much of the early work was done without even signature. I didn't sign my first murals. It was a joyful activity of reclamation of one's culture and one's life. It's hard to imagine today, but it was an absolutely revolutionary act to put any brown face on any wall in LA. It was even more revolutionary to put a woman's face on a wall. It just wasn't done. So we broke a lot of barriers with that work. We began to make it clear who lived there and what they thought about.

I think of them as sites of public memory, and that's why I don't think they're temporary. I'm thinking about pieces in Sylmar, in which parents cooperated with muralists to talk about children who had been killed in gang warfare by mistake. Little babies, kids four and five years old.

It basically was about healing for those families, and it brought the whole community together. I feel very strongly that that piece shouldn't be disappeared by every developer who comes through with a new mall.

If the land has memory, and indeed I think it does on some level, we wouldn't put a shopping mall on top of a burial site. We would understand a reverence for all those things that preceded us. We would perhaps move a little bit more sensitively.

The LA River was concreted in as the first sort of developer's notion of Los Angeles. The river didn't behave, so we concreted it. We essentially hardened the arteries that run through the land.

When the Army Corps of Engineers approached me about creating a mural for the flood control district site, it was a pretty interesting opportunity. Look at it. It's only three miles from Pacoima, where I grew up. It's in a middle-class community. No drive-by shootings. It's not in the inner city. I could stop preaching to the converted.

By that time, 1976, I'd been organizing in every part of the city. And I thought, Wow! What a great opportunity to pull everybody together and make one piece that looks at the connections between us. I was creating a monument to interracial harmony.

Then I thought, Let's tell our stories. Little did I know it was going to become this incredibly giant research project and that I would end up with a family of hundreds of children I'd never get rid of.

I wanted to do a narrative, and California was so rich as source material. We were this immigrant state and exemplified, more than any other state in the country, a very rich story of race relations and the intersecting of cultures.

This young kid who had worked with me in East LA became an organizer with me and was speaking very eloquently against gang warfare. He had a wound on his stomach and he was very embarrassed by it when he'd take his shirt off, so he had a tattoo put over the scar. I thought that's what we're doing. Our mural, *The Great Wall*, would be a tattoo on the scar where the river once ran.

We weren't exactly welcome. The neighbors didn't exactly think it was a great idea that I was going to bring a hundred adolescents of color to that site. But I have to say they more than got used to it. They really, at the end, were marvelous. They brought us fruit from their trees and big vats of lemonade. And it helped because we returned. We came every other summer for five summers. It took us a year in between each time to raise the money. So we're talking ten years.

It's not over. I've got a big proposal in for a repaint and restoration this summer, and I'm hoping we get money to design the last segments, the sixties, seventies, eighties, and nineties.

My great dream is to stand on the side and watch it in production with children of the children of my first pieces. The children who began it could now lead it entirely—raise the money, put it together, and run it. I think it's more possible now than it ever has been.

It's the basis of democracy, what we're doing here. We're including different cultures and experiences and celebrating in some artistic way. I think that's what my work is about. I try to bring gang members and neighborhood kids to see themselves as valuable participants in the changing of their community.

gordon DAVIDSON

Gordon Davidson has been artistic director of Los Angeles's Mark Taper Forum since its inception in 1967 and artistic director/producer for the city's Ahmanson Theatre since 1989. Born in Brooklyn in 1933, Davidson won a Tony Award for directing *The Shadow Box*, Obies for directing *The Trial of the Catonsville Nine* and *Savages*, and staged Leonard Bernstein's *Mass* to open the Kennedy Center in Washington, D.C. In 1993 the late *Time* magazine theater critic William A. Henry III called him "reigning godfather of the American regional theater movement," and under his leadership, the Taper has launched such groundbreaking plays as *Zoot Suit, Children of a Lesser God,* and *Twilight: Los Angeles, 1992* and developed the Pulitzer Prize–winning *Angels in America* and *The Kentucky Cycle.* Davidson lives in Santa Monica Canyon with his wife, the publicist Judi Davidson, in the former home of John Houseman and, earlier, of the émigrés Salka and Berthold Viertel.

M y dad, Skipper Jo Davidson, taught theater at Brooklyn College for forty-three years. It was his first and primary adult job. He was an extremely popular teacher, and among his students were people like Alfred Drake, Sam Levenson, Paul Mazursky, and Michael Lerner. My dad was great at taking me to the theater, and it was wonderful exposure.

I tried to hang out and watch rehearsals, and I also acted in a couple of plays. In Lillian Hellman's *Watch on the Rhine,* I played the part of Bodo Muller who was a smart-ass kid. I made myself thoroughly obnoxious by learning not only my own part but everybody else's parts, and correcting them.

It was fun and exhilarating, but I thought my career work would be in science and engineering. I was in a work-study program at Cornell, and one summer I went to Pittsfield, Massachusetts, to work at a naval ordnance plant designing guided missile systems. I arrived in Pittsfield, rented an apartment, and checked in at the plant. Then I saw something in the local paper about ushers wanted for Tanglewood, and I thought, Gee, that's a good way to earn some extra money.

My mom aspired to be a pianist. She did some piano teaching, but I stopped studying piano when I was fourteen or fifteen. Standing in the back at Tanglewood, listening to Koussevitzky conduct, I just knew right away that I had come home to something. It was such a sharp contrast from the kind of dreary predictable atmosphere of naval ordnance. I asked myself, Why am I having more fun at night than during the day? I decided to switch to liberal arts, and when I made that decision, I knew it was going to be the theater.

While I was in the army, I wrote to theaters throughout the country, which at the time you could count on one hand: The Arena Stage in Washington, D.C.; the Alley Theater in Houston; the Actor's Workshop in San Francisco; the Cleveland Playhouse; maybe a few others. I asked for a job, and they all said, "Sorry, we don't have any, but if you're ever in town, please come by and say hello." I found myself a number of years later writing the same kind of letter to people.

There was nothing available outside New York, but the American Shakespeare Festival was in New York rehearsing before they went to Stratford, Connecticut, and I had a friend who was working in the press office. I got a job there as an apprentice stage manager, and that changed my life.

Although it isn't the case anymore, stage-managing then was the route to directing. Now there are directing internships and directing programs. The stage manager is a stage manager. But in those days that was the way you began. It was a hell of a way to learn about production.

When I talk to young people today, I always say, "Don't be afraid of negative learning. You can sit in a room and watch a director screwing up a play and say, 'I will never do it that way.' It's more likely you'll be in that situation than moments of inspiration." I was lucky. I met the great lighting designer Jean Rosenthal, who then introduced me to the Dallas Civic Opera, where I stage-managed for a few seasons, and, of course, Martha Graham. I like to say that I learned more about the theater from Martha than I did from most teachers of theater, just because she *was* theater.

I also met John Houseman at the American Shakespeare Festival, and one day in '64 I was guest-directing back at Western Reserve, where I got my M.A. in theater, when Houseman called. He wanted to know if I would come out to California. He was running the Theater Group at UCLA. It was not a permanent company, but it was a professional theater with an emphasis on the classics.

John was doing a production of *King Lear* with Morris Carnovsky, whom I got to know at Stratford, and asked if I would assist him. He also said he needed someone to stage-manage its move to the outdoor Pilgrimage Theater. So I said, "Sure."

At that time Judi was pregnant with our firstborn, Adam. I had some directing work lined up for the fall, but summer was clear. I came out in May, and we rehearsed in an empty Ralph's supermarket. I thought I'd come for one assignment for *King Lear,* move it to the Pilgrimage, then go back east and we'd have the baby.

But that didn't happen. Instead I got a call asking if I would come talk to the Theater Group people about the possibility of staying on. John Houseman was leaving Los Angeles after *King Lear* to go write what turned out to be the first volume of his memoirs. Going to Paris— lock, stock, and barrel.

They wanted me to run the Theater Group and my first thought was, I don't want to run a theater. I'm a director. I'm going to go out and direct. Then I said, Wait a minute. Somebody just offered you a theater. You'd better think twice about that. And I asked Judi, "What do you think?" She said, "Well, let's try it."

One of the attractive things was that the job probably wouldn't last more than two years, because the university was going on the quarter system. So I thought, Okay, two years, and we'll go back to New York. For me the theater business operated on what I called the rubber-band theory. You left New York to do a job and you snapped back as fast as you could, because that's where "The Theater" was.

American theater was just starting to decentralize then. In fact the Theater Group at UCLA was a pioneer, because of the concentration of acting talent here. Around the same time, the Guthrie opened in Minnesota, Lincoln Center in New York, and South Coast Repertory here in Costa Mesa. It was starting to really happen.

The first show I did was *The Deputy,* a play about silence in the face of responsibility. It was the summer of '65, the time of the Watts riots. I'm still new to Los Angeles, opening a play, and somewhere in the city, a place called Watts is going up in smoke. I didn't know the city yet, and in a certain sense that began my journey to know it better.

A year later, I did the first fully staged revival of *Candide* since it played on Broadway. Dorothy Chandler, who was the principal force behind the creation of the Music Center here, came to see the production and came back to our house afterward. We had coffee and pastry, and she in effect offered me the job of running the Music Center's theater, the Mark Taper Forum. I came down and had brunch with her here, sitting up in the pavilion and looking at the Taper's round building, which was still being completed. They hired me in the fall of '66, and I opened the theater in April of '67.

Right from the beginning, when I did the *Lear* at UCLA, I found audiences here totally recognizable, which was a way of saying they all looked like they came from the Upper West Side—predominantly Jewish, middle-class people who were theatergoers and were now living in Los Angeles, whether they were transplants or homegrown. I found them very lively, well educated, engaged, caring, and an audience that seemed to want to go to the theater. It was a wonderful introduction.

When I moved downtown, I brought most of those people with me. The Theater Group was alive eight years, and we're starting our thirty-third season at the Taper. So somewhere in there is forty-one years of regular theatergoing, and I don't think too many places can claim that. The excitement of coming downtown is that it broadened the audience to include Pasadena, the Valley, and points to the south, plus ethnic communities, specifically Latino, Asian, and African American, that could be drawn upon. I felt that challenge right from the beginning, and I still feel it.

I found the atmosphere open, informed, and loyal. Its roots are in some way back to the East, which also means way back to Europe, but the introduction of the Pacific Rim and our friends to the south made it alive with possibilities. I still feel that to a great extent. But to quote a well-worn cliché, it ain't no bed of roses. Someone asked me then what's it like living in Los Angeles, and I quipped back very quickly, "Why, it's just like living in New York without Manhattan," meaning, it's the equivalent of Long Island and New Jersey and Westchester and Connecticut. But there is no center. Regrettably I still feel that way, although I could add that New York has gone through so many ups and downs that I'm not so sure what New York is anymore either.

My biggest problem is getting my arms around this city. It's still hard to feel the heartbeat. You feel it more in cities like Seattle and San Francisco and Prague, and that's troubling because there's a part of me that says I don't know how to beat that. The geography works against it.

What's indigenous to Los Angeles? What makes this a place? John Dennis, a writer-director who was head of our Improvisational Theater Project, tried in the mid-seventies to imagine what it would be like to literally do an archaeological dig here. They looked at a freeway interchange and the land underneath it in the way that archaeologists might have in order to trace the origins of life here before—in the time of settlers, then back to American Indians, then back to Hispanic culture. You keep peeling back layers.

Some of the audience is older and it's harder to replace them with the next age group. They can go to England. They don't have to wait for a show to come over. When I started there were three television networks and one public television station. Now there are so many channels you don't know what to do with them. There's the Internet. There are other forms of diversion, excitement, entertainment, or what have you.

Southern California is extremely complex, but I still feel more than anywhere else in the art of the possible here. Audiences are not so blasé that they've seen everything—"Ho hum. Robert Wilson again." If you present it well enough and are daring enough, you can find an audience.

There are 750 seats at the Taper, and it's an intimate space where the audience surrounds the stage on three sides. After thirty-two years, it's still an ideal place to bring a group of people together around a campfire.

robbert **FLICK**

Born in Amersfoort, Holland, in 1939, Robbert Flick moved with his family to Vancouver in 1958. A teenage birdwatcher with dreams of becoming a wildlife photographer, he first wrote to Disney and later got a government grant to study photography in Los Angeles. He never went home. He has been teaching at the University of Southern California since 1976 and established USC's Matrix digital photo lab in 1991. Creating visual "diaries," first of the Midwestern landscape and, since the seventies, of Los Angeles, he documents his adopted city on foot as well as with a Hi-8 video camera set to shoot out the window of his moving Isuzu Trooper. He lives in Los Angeles with his wife, the artist Susan Rankaitis.

⸺

I wanted to come to Los Angeles almost from the moment that I started hearing about it. When I got here in the sixties, it was vast and fast. Going across an overpass was a sensual experience, and for a while, driving east on the Santa Monica Freeway and looking toward Westwood was in a sense looking at Tokyo. One of my motivations for photographing Los Angeles was the changes that were happening. It seemed to be dealing with the present and embodying the future.

I grew up mostly in Holland. Amersfoort. Mondrian's birthplace. My father was an accountant, and my mother is a weaver. She basically supported us during the war, trading woven craft for food and things, and immediately after the war, we left for the Dutch West Indies, where she started a weaving school. I was seven years old when I left, and I returned when I was about eleven years old.

I had always been deeply involved in nature, looking at plants and birds, and so my initial experiences in the West Indies had to do with explorations of the natural countryside, the Kunuku cactus wilderness. I would roam around there basically by myself, and commune with the wild goats and donkeys and have a hell of a time exploring and spelunking. That carried over into the Netherlands when I returned, where my favorite pastimes were looking at birds and tracing the movements of deer in the woods near Amersfoort.

The first time I saw a photographic print being processed was when I was around seven. A friend of my parents had taken pictures of me and my brother, and after she developed the film we were invited into the darkroom. She set up a little stepstool so that I could look into the developer, and as I was looking at this blank, submerged piece of white paper in yellow-greenish light, my own face started to appear. It was magic, and it really hooked me.

My parents gave me a camera when I was about eight years old. I would sit by myself for hours in a one-yard cube of jute that I'd built, and wait until the birds came back to their nests. It was a wonderful introduction to observing and being part of something while also being separate from it.

I saw some Disney films, especially *The Living Desert,* and had read an article about another Dutchman whose name I've forgotten but who basically was a Disney photographer. I thought, My God, this is what I want to do. It's a combination of the act of photographing and living in nature.

In the meantime our family moved to Vancouver when I was in high school. I put myself through college by working in the Canadian woods as a logger, and my first serious photography dealt with rocks, water, grasses, and ferns.

I had been dreaming about coming to Los Angeles, and I got a Canada Council Grant to study photography here. I drove here in a VW that I had bought for $125 and that never went faster than forty-five miles per hour.

There was something about Los Angeles—just a promise, I think. Besides studying I also wanted to create a documentary, a set of photographs about the city. To me Los Angeles was the future.

While I was doing graduate work at UCLA in the late sixties, I began photographing the city in layers. I was incredibly poor, so I had only a limited amount of film, and I would shoot the same eighty or so rolls over and over again. Images of personally relevant moments would layer on top of one another, and out of that came a layered look at Los Angeles.

Seven years later we were living in Santa Monica, and I would walk the alleys. I liked the way the light would penetrate spaces and how the backs of apartment buildings had these curious garages with stilted support structures. Graffiti were beginning to appear in silver paint, so one moment you'd see it, the next moment you wouldn't. In the mornings, especially if it's foggy, there's a wet, blanketing light which would break and make shadows. The shadows become crisp, and you'd begin to see very subtle colors, really wonderfully pastel-like colors.

In 1979 I was invited to become part of the Documentary Project for the Los Angeles Bicentennial, and that is when I began to shoot specific neighborhoods. Now I can identify at least sixty visually distinct areas in Los Angeles.

In each area I would select one street, then the next, and photograph at every street corner or from the middle of the street. I tried to get a set of images that might function like a medieval map.

I chose where to photograph based on familiarity and accessibility. When you photograph like this, you are consistently accosted. You are perceived as an intruder with questionable motives. Almost always when I would be in the middle of a block, especially when there was a NEIGHBORHOOD WATCH sign somewhere, suddenly people would come out or the police would come by, and I would have to explain what it was that I was doing.

When I started out, LA was flat. It allowed one to photograph consecutively without having to deal with interruptions of that flatness. And what really motivated me to continue intensely with this documentarylike process was that the city was changing.

Suddenly the flat skyline I was used to was being interrupted by tall buildings that created canyons. At the same time the freedom of movement that had existed in the late sixties was also being changed. Flowing across freeway overpasses at seventy miles an hour and drinking in the city as you go no longer was possible. This sort of gorgeous scan across the cityscape was no longer there.

I began to photograph from my car, but when I tried using a still camera and motor drive, it was too random and I didn't have enough control. Then, in the late eighties, I discovered how incredibly accurate a Hi-8 video recording could be, especially in conjunction with digital-image capture. I could photograph blades of grass at sixty-five miles per hour and freeze them.

Photographing in this way is a little bit like playing basketball, since you've got to maneuver back and forth between cars so that the camera can usually have an uninterrupted view. You can't stop. You go until you're at the end of your trajectory or until the battery or tape runs out.

I found obvious rhythmic flows that have to do with traffic and time of day. People go sixty, seventy miles an hour to their jobs, creating a sound that is like the sea. When they get to the areas where the jobs are, there's yet another rhythm.

I think every city has its rhythms, but the nature of this city's rhythms are a little bit more particular. I'm thinking for instance of how a congregation of Russian Orthodox people may gather from all over to go to one particular church on Sunday, then disperse again. There are hidden patterns that have to do with the extraordinary richness of origins here.

If I were working somewhere else, it would be different, because the method of movement in this city is the car. One forms one's experience through driving, and the driving process defines both the terror and joy of Los Angeles. When people come here who don't know how to drive, there is an extraordinary sense of pride at learning how to get around. I used to think of those freeways like being in a glider, just flowing movements. They were fluid. Then. Not anymore.

rupert **GARCÍA**

Born in French Camp, California, in 1941, artist Rupert García was raised in nearby Stockton. He attended San Francisco State College on the GI Bill just in time for the 1968 student strike there, which profoundly affected his artwork as well as his politics. The silk-screen posters he first learned how to make for the strike led to the colorful, strong portraits of such figures as Orozco, Kahlo, and Picasso, which are among his best-known work. Also an activist and writer, the painter was a member of the Artes 6 co-op gallery and helped establish the Galería de la Raza in San Francisco's Mission District. He formerly taught art at San Francisco State and has been on the art faculty of San Jose State University since 1988. The subject of retrospectives at San Francisco's Mexican Museum in 1986 and the city's Palace of the Legion of Honor in 1990, he lives in Oakland, California.

I have fond memories of being raised in Stockton. There seemed to be a lot of fields to run in. I remember the sky being so blue and the sun so bright. Color was always so important to me, and the sunlight that I experienced as a child in Stockton just enhanced the color.

Stockton was divided into areas by race and money. I knew that even

as a kid. Where we lived was primarily a mixture of working-class
Mexicanos, Filipinos, Chinese, Japanese, and whites. Maxine Hong
Kingston, whom I went to school with, and I have talked about this,
about hanging around with a variety of ethnicities and races and how
we got along well. We trusted each other. There was never an idea
about being with a different race.

Now I don't mean to suggest that there was no consciousness about
racism. I knew about racism for a long, long, long time, just from my
own family being Mexicanos. I also knew about class. We always
noticed that if we were to go into another part of Stockton we would see
beautiful houses, sidewalks, street lamps, unbroken bulbs. In our neighborhood, not so.

In the third and fourth grade, I saw friends make these incredible
drawings of cowboys and musclemen, which I guess were based on
comic books. I would stare at that and think, My, how in the heck did
they do that? I can't say I thought about being an artist, but I knew
what I saw them do was fantastic.

What my grandmother used to do was also fantastic, which was to
pull Kleenex tissue out from under her long sleeves. With her hands
and fingers, she would roll the tissue and magically, so it seems, produce
a chorus of people and animals on the floor of our living room.

My mother had always wanted to be an artist, and she used to help
me make drawings. I had aunts and uncles who would sing and dance,
and my aunt Mary made hats out of feathers. My grandmother would
design and produce the dance costumes for the local Ballet Folklórico in
Stockton, and I remember going to where she made them. The range of
color was amazing: rows of sequined blouses and dresses in reds, blues,
yellows, and greens. When my aunt, who is about my age, would dance
in the costumes, seeing the color move around and the sequins was so
exciting.

Cousins were musicians, and others wanted to be actors, so in my
family, being creative seemed natural. I always had the feeling that

making objects or drawings was the right thing to do. It smelled correct. My fingers touching a crayon or a pencil seemed correct.

Even when I would take pieces of my mother's old jewelry apart and recombine them to make something new, I always got a pat on the head. In retrospect I know my mother would think, What is this young fellow doing? But I don't recall her ever scolding me, and I love her for that.

I got a very strong foundation in the technique of art making at Stockton College, and in 1962, I went to San Francisco to become "an artiste." I say it that way because that's the image I had. You're supposed to make drawings, somehow get discovered, have a show, and become rich and famous. That's the way it goes.

Well, that was certainly a myth. I went to San Francisco, and I became a dishwasher at a restaurant in the Mission District. My roommates were going to San Francisco State. They had money to do that. I didn't have any money whatsoever, so going to school was out of the question. I made drawings and paintings in our apartment, and I had no idea what you're supposed to do to get representation. I didn't even know you're supposed to get representation. I just thought you go to San Francisco and things fall from the sky.

Nothing fell from the sky, except once. There was a pizza parlor, Papa's Pizza, near where we lived that showed my drawings and a few paintings. To me that was arriving onto the art scene. It could have been the Met in New York or the Louvre in Paris.

That's as far as it went for trying to become "an artiste" in San Francisco. I went back home and stayed with my brother for a little while. I went job searching, and I wound up joining the air force to get a job. I spent four years in the military, three years in Montana and a year in Southeast Asia.

I was in Southeast Asia in '65–'66 and got out in May of '66. I went home to Stockton. My mom had worked as a meat packer to support me and my two brothers when I was a kid, and I promised myself I would never, never work in a can plant. But I did.

At the plant I swept the floor at first. Then I used to move cans off a conveyor belt onto these big flats. That's all I did, and I hated every second. I felt like I was out of my body, disconnected. All I thought about was getting paid on Friday and going to school in San Francisco when summer was over. That—and that I was alive and didn't die in Indochina—kept me going.

When I got to San Francisco State, I only knew two people out of thousands of kids. I felt lost anyway, because the antiwar movement was developing, and no one knew I was a vet from the Vietnam War. I didn't tell anybody, because I knew it was bad karma, and antiwar sentiments were so strong. I kept my mouth shut.

The student strike there in fall '68 raised all kinds of ethical and soulful questions for me, questions of politics and everyday life, questions about being a student, questions about art history and philosophy, questions about all aspects of society. I was trying to answer my own questions about being involved in the Vietnam War as well as becoming a part of the art-student-faculty-poster-making brigade.

Like I mentioned earlier, I thought you leave a small city, go to the big city, and become an art star. You don't question anything. You are just supposed to be as unique and original as possible at any stake, no ethics involved.

Now I wanted to know how an artist is supposed to act, think, and feel. I began to question my previous romantic and distorted comprehension of artists like Vincent van Gogh or Pablo Picasso.

What ultimately grounded me was that I did have a real grasp of being an artist from my own family members. And I was getting more involved with the developing Chicano, African American, Native American, and Asian American movements in the United States that were both political and cultural.

When the strike occurred we had a big meeting with art faculty and students to discuss what we could do to support the strike, which was going on as we were meeting. Somebody had come back recently from Europe, and he had heard about all the students making posters during the student/worker strike in Paris the previous May.

Posters seemed to be the visual answer for us. So our print teachers taught us how to silk-screen. My first few were very tentative works, but they got my feet wet. If the strike hadn't occurred, I would not have made silkscreens.

Some of us got involved in it very seriously, and I became an unofficial liaison between our poster-making workshop and the Third World Liberation Front. I stopped making easel paintings, because it didn't feel connected to what was happening on and off campus. I became a full-time screen printer.

I did a poster of Ruben Salazar after he was killed in 1970 by a sheriff's tear gas canister shot into an East LA bar following an antiwar rally. He was really becoming a very important writer on behalf of the Chicano movement, and when he died, it was a very powerful moment for many of us. Out of respect to him, we had this homage at the Galería de la Raza here, and I did a very simple silkscreen.

The poster was based upon a photograph I got from the Los Angeles magazine *La Raza,* an important source of material for me. I've used photographs as a frame of reference since the late fifties, coming out of my experience with my mother's Hollywood film magazines. I would make drawings of movie stars based on photographs in these magazines.

It seemed as natural to use the magazine to make a drawing of a movie star as to use a tree outside to make a drawing of a tree. It was a frame of reference. I liked that the photograph was immobile, and the gray tones and high contrast defined the shapes. I think my exposure to those Hollywood magazine photographs is where I began to really get a deep sense for simple shapes and high contrast.

I always felt color was life affirming. My attraction to color comes out of many sources. The animation of Walt Disney and Warner Brothers cartoons. Motion pictures in full color. Going to church and seeing the incredible stained-glass windows. The colors I would see in the Ballet Folklórico wardrobe that my grandmother designed. Going to fiestas on holy days. We played "breaking the piñatas," and there were these eggs that were filled with confetti that you would break on your friend's head and make a sparkle of color. Those things stick with me to this very day.

My first awareness of the Mexican muralists was at San Francisco State. I took a course in art appreciation, and at one point they talked about Diego Rivera. That pricked my ears up. I taught myself the history of art in Mexico, from the Olmecs to the twentieth century. It was very difficult. A lot of work.

I never made a choice politically that was not embraced personally. I just don't work that way. Some people can work by splitting the two. I can't do that. So all that I have done in terms of poster art, writing, and, more recently, my paintings and works on paper, come out of an individual necessity. I have to do it. Because of that I believe I have made posters and prints that aesthetically endure.

I remember folks making works of art that were politically on the mark but visually embarrassing. They haven't endured as artworks, and in some instances, that's okay because that was not what it was about. Some people made posters not because they were artists per se, but because it was a convenient way to get a message out. Not me.

One thing that's important for me when I talk about the sixties and seventies and my involvement in these various activities is that I myself have never limited my vision to merely being a political artist. That's been done to me, by the way. I've been categorized as a Chicano artist or an artist who does political themes, but that reduces who I am.

I am Chicano, no question about it, but I'm also that and more. I'm also an artist who's interested in politics, society, science, and astrophysics. I'm about a lot of things. All human beings are what they are and more. Being able to come from one point of view but also embrace more is the power of culture, the imagination, and the human mind.

alexis **SMITH**

Artist Alexis Smith was born Patricia Anne Smith in Santa Monica, California, and while in college changed her name from that of a rock music legend to that of a forties film star. While she is still best known for her conceptual art, collages, and assemblages, her work in the 1990s also comprises such larger-scale artwork as a mixed-media installation for the Getty Center restaurant, a six-hundred-foot-long garden path, and a 120,000-square-foot terrazzo floor at the Los Angeles Convention Center. After studying with Robert Irwin and other cutting-edge artists at the then-new University of California, Irvine, Art Department, she moved to Venice, California, where she has lived and worked since the early seventies. The subject of a 1991 Whitney Museum of American Art retrospective that traveled to Los Angeles's Museum of Contemporary Art in 1992, she has called working away from the New York art scene "a good thing in the guise of being a bad thing." An observer of Hollywood as both dream maker and metaphor, she is a fan of such California writers as Jack Kerouac, Joan Didion, and particularly Raymond Chandler, whose phrases have appeared on her answering machine for more than twenty years.

⌒

My father had been a medical resident at Cedars of Lebanon Hospital in the thirties, when there really were a lot of movie stars and film people around, and I think he's the one who subtly gave me the notion of LA as a paradise and Garden of Eden. He'd come out from Utah, where it was freezing cold and where the moral climate was pretty rigorous. I'm sure it seemed like heaven to him here—a heaven of possibilities.

When he came back from the war, my father didn't want to be a surgeon anymore and decided to be a psychiatrist. He took a job as assistant superintendent of Metropolitan State Hospital, which is a mental hospital in Norwalk, and we moved onto the hospital grounds.

I was probably about four or five, and I spent my formative childhood years on the hospital grounds. It was like a walled city, where the patients ran the laundries and worked in the cafeteria. They had bands and went to movies. It was like a city run for the pleasure of the patients, and the doctors and their families lived around the outside as a buffer.

Patients who worked in our house did things to remind you that they really were patients, like wax the cellar stairs or boil the poker chips in the coffee. But there wasn't as much difference between the doctors and the patients as you would expect. I think that had a long-term impact on me, in the sense that I have a really high tolerance for eccentricity, and I'm probably pretty eccentric myself.

I always made things. I had an electric train layout, which I was very fond of, and I used to pick up junk for it, mostly from construction sites. I made collages out of words that I cut out of magazines, and I was always trying to incite the kids on the hospital grounds into participating in extravaganzas and plays. I guess because I was an only child, I had to amuse myself. I had a lot of time to fill.

We moved off the hospital grounds when I was around eleven, and my mother got ill and died right after the move. It was a difficult and depressing time, so I was really anxious to go away to college. I made a very impulsive choice, based on absolutely nothing except that I knew

some people who were going there and that it was inexpensive, and I
went to the University of California, Irvine. And that turned out to be
one of the defining moments in my life.

I went to college as a French major but I was bored with it, and after
a summer in France, I could see that was not going anywhere. A friend
knew that I was making collages and stuff like that and talked me into
taking some art classes.

Irvine was brand new then. It only had about three buildings and no
tenured faculty. Its fledgling art department didn't have any facilities,
technical support, or equipment. They brought down working artists
from LA to teach, and it was really open ended. Students fraternized
with the artists, and it was like sitting under the tree with Socrates.
They didn't really have very many rules.

I had thought art was rigorous oil painting. Instead, I got this sense
from people like Bob Irwin, Vija Celmins, Ed Moses, and Bruce
Nauman that it was much more something that you could invent
yourself. Even though it had to fit into a little bit of a framework of
what had been done before, that framework in the sixties was really
loose.

You could invent your art, and when it stopped filling your needs you
could invent something else. You could set your own problems and
work on things that were of interest to you, and that could be a job. It
could be what you did with your life.

My name change was unpremeditated. My real name is Patricia Anne
Smith. I didn't really feel like a Patty, and I wanted to distance myself
as much as I possibly could from my unhappy adolescence. I can't imagine what possessed me, but I brazenly picked a name out of a movie. I
had some college friends, and we were thinking of nicknames for ourselves, and I picked Alex. Everybody else's nickname faded away, but
mine stuck. I found out that there was a movie star named Alexis

Smith, and there were some photos of her I started using in my work and just gradually I became Alexis.

The actress Alexis Smith was really generous about the whole thing. She bought one of my early works, and when I had my Whitney Museum retrospective she kindly gave me permission to use one of her movie stills as my poster. I called it *Queen for a Day,* and put a crown on her head.

The TV show *Queen for a Day,* where whoever had the most tragic story could win fur coats, Amana freezers, or whatever, was a very compelling image for people of my age. So was *Rocket to Stardom,* which was a local version of *Ted Mack's Original Amateur Hour,* promoted by car dealerships in Downey. It was a combination of car advertising and children who had aspirations to be musicians or actresses. All that desire and possibility was very influential on me and probably still is.

I think that my particular experience of the West came from my father and his leaving Utah to come to California. The inevitable loss of innocence that happens to people as they get older and the world doesn't live up to those desires and expectations are the basic themes of my work. My father's failed expectations in this paradise had a major impact on me and have to this day.

California is the farthest place west, and Americans as a group have this westward-ho mythology that you just keep going farther west to the next new place whenever you get tired of the old place. Then you can be what you want, get away from the people that you don't like, and basically have a new life.

The advent of Hollywood really crystallized that myth. The Hollywood of the mind is this place where any soda jerk can become Clark Gable, Rita Hayworth, or Lana Turner. If you're not brilliant or incredibly industrious, you can still have something wonderful happen to you. It's not the Horatio Alger myth, where you work your whole life and make a lot of money. It has to do with luck and magic and all these things that we want to believe in.

I did four or five years of work based on Jack Kerouac's *On the Road*. He's the person, I think, who best superimposed those two myths of manifest destiny—going across the country to find paradise and reinventing yourself—with the automobile as the focus for movement, desire, and change.

I got really fascinated with how pervasive the car image is in our culture and how much the car seems to be the symbol of freedom and mobility. I'm not all that superfascinated with my own personal cars, which are much more utilitarian objects. But I do think of cars as our own little personal environments and storage units that are like these little moving houses that we take around with us.

I'm one of those people who goes around as kind of a trash picker, and having a car is really indispensable. I just don't think I could do the kind of work I did if I didn't have some big moving storage unit. You can pick something out of the street or buy something at a thrift store or garage sale and throw it in the back.

In the last couple of years I've been traveling a lot. I didn't have any personal free time, and I started picking used, wrecked brooms out of trash cans. The more you start picking things up, the more they start coming your way, and I now have more than forty of them. They're all worn in different funny patterns and spawned *The Sorcerer's Apprentice,* a piece that I'm doing with my friend and longtime collaborator, the poet Amy Gerstler.

I would never in a million years do anything that had to do with storybook material if I hadn't picked up these brooms. But now that I have them, I can see definitely how all these kinds of storybook myths fit right into my childhood ideas and desires.

It's basically a kismet style of working. I free-associate, have these texts playing in my head and look for things that make sense with them.

If I lived in New York, maybe I'd pick wrecked umbrellas out of the street.

I'm a great believer in things that just sort of happen through serendipity. Over the years I took on more of a Buddhist approach of not trying to control so many things and just seeing what would turn up without my meddling too much.

I think that it was really important that I grew up in California, but I don't really think about myself that much as a California artist. I thought about myself more as a California artist when I was younger, because you couldn't live here in the seventies and even in the early eighties without having to justify why you weren't moving to New York. So I'm a California artist by default.

Actually the fact that California is so influenced by Asia and Mexico is one of the things that makes it interesting to me. The idea of going someplace else that's more white bread is not so compelling. I've lived in Venice for twenty-five years in a really diverse community, because I find all those differences between people to be interesting. I also find it easier to hone in on what things are common to everybody when everybody's not the same.

It's not like a political thing. It's just that when things or people start looking all the same it makes me uncomfortable. Homogeneity gets on my nerves. If I'm going somewhere, after a while I miss tolerance for extremes.

The public art, like everything in my life, came about in a real organic way. There was a time in the late seventies and early eighties that I was anxious to make my work more visually compelling. I started painting these big graphic images behind the collages, did some of that in museums and galleries, and gradually got some opportunities to do it in public places.

One thing leads to another. When you're not afraid to make them big, permanent, and expensive, and people are willing to go along with you, it works. Ever since I was five years old, I was always trying to get people to do stuff. I finally got myself in the position where I had the credibility to get people to provide me with financial, architectural, and social help.

My big public works are, first of all, for places that people don't necessarily choose to have an art experience. People come upon them unexpectedly and have to puzzle them out.

It's a balance in terms of my work. I do these small collages that I can control for a kind of elite audience of artists, museum people, and collectors. These large, common images are more or less meaningful to people no matter what culture they come from and whether or not they have an art background.

I think the public works tell them, Here's something that somebody really cared about and put a lot of effort and imagination into. They're like a gift. They're just there to be wonderful. They're free, they're for you, and there's no explanation.

Being a woman is kind of an asset in public art, mostly because women have a really high tolerance for aggravation and frustration. A lot of male sculptors don't really last very long as public artists because they get so pissed off at how complicated, stressful, and relentless it is. Men who have that kind of tolerance for frustration all become architects. Or movie directors.

For artists, at least early on, living here was kind of off the radar screen. One of the things that makes people creative is the ability to do the things that children do, which is to try options and have unstructured thought. It's hard to do that if you take yourself too seriously, if people pay too much attention to you, or if you're too busy. Even though I am, unfortunately, frequently too busy, I have to take big blocks of time and just have my life be unstructured or I can't keep doing stuff.

People don't realize how children, in order to grow up creative, need to be left alone a little bit to play. When we were kids, we didn't have so much stuff, and we made things. Our parents made things. Creativity would be better spawned in a looser environment than the one we live in.

Part V

Hollywood

carol **BURNETT**

Carol Burnett's story is very much one of hometown girl makes good. Born in San Antonio, Texas, in 1933, the actress grew up in Hollywood, where she was raised primarily by her grandmother, Mabel Eudora White. As she recounts in her bestselling memoir, *One More Time*, she finished Hollywood High and UCLA, then headed for New York, where she first supported herself as a hatcheck girl before going on to triumph on TV's *The Garry Moore Show* and Broadway's *Once Upon a Mattress*. She came back to California in the sixties and in 1967 launched *The Carol Burnett Show*, which won twenty-two Emmys before going off the air in 1978. Grand Marshal of Pasadena's 109th Rose Parade in 1997, she continues her award-winning performances on TV, stage, and screen.

N anny, my grandmother, kept talking about Hollywood. When I was seven, we got on the train in San Antonio to come here and to chase after Mama, who wanted to be a writer and interview movie stars.

Our room at Yucca and Wilcox was only a block north of Hollywood Boulevard, so whenever there was a premiere, Nanny and I wanted to get a gander of the movie star show. We'd get there at the last minute to hang over the ropes, on the side. Nanny would bull her way through to the front by saying she had to get up close because she had poor eyesight, and she had this little girl with her who couldn't see over their heads: me.

One time Linda Darnell got out of her car early and started to walk past the ropes to get to the red carpet. She didn't wait for the car to pull up, and we got a good look at her. Linda Darnell was my favorite. She was from Texas, and I thought she was just the most beautiful movie star there was.

As she walked by, my grandmother reached out and grabbed her by the sleeve, saying, "Give this little girl your autograph. She just loves you. She's got pictures of you all over the apartment." Nanny was so pushy, but Linda Darnell was very sweet, and she signed her name.

That was a thrill for me, and I swear that to this day I can duplicate her signature. I was a grown-up when she died, but I wept all day. I almost took to my bed, I was so depressed because of the impression that she made on me when I was little and how sweet she was in spite of my overeager grandmother.

I remember so vividly how, in the forties, I saw on an average about eight movies a week. Once movies left Grauman's Chinese, the Egyptian, or the Pantages, they would go to the second-run theaters and we could get a double feature. We would beat the prices if we got in before one o'clock on Saturday and Sunday. Nanny was a quarter and I was eleven cents. We'd see four over the weekend, then usually four more during the week.

My first recollection of seeing people on the screen was Bonita Granville and Joel McCrea—I think it was *These Three,* in the thirties, when I was in San Antonio. My dad was the manager of a movie house, so they used to take me there, and I'd just fall asleep in the seat.

My second recollection was *Blood and Sand,* with Linda Darnell, Tyrone Power, Rita Hayworth, and Anthony Quinn. That's when I fell in love with Linda Darnell. The thing that really impressed me was that she had been born in Texas and I thought, Oh, gosh. It can happen to me.

Daddy didn't work there very long before he and Mama came out to Hollywood. But I remember sitting in the theater and getting sleepy with some of these grown-up movies. I would wake up on the couch in his office, so evidently I just fell asleep and he'd pick me up and take me there.

I think I started "playing the movies" in Texas with my cousin Janice. When I was around six, we would do Nelson Eddy and Jeanette MacDonald and Tarzan and Jane. Because she was the pretty one, naturally she got to be Jeanette and Jane. So I was Nelson and Tarzan. That's when I started doing my Tarzan yell.

After we came out to Hollywood, my best girlfriend, Ilomay, who lived in the building next door with her grandmother, and I would go see Betty Grable movies and we'd play Betty Grable. We'd play Mickey and Judy.

Nanny and I had a little dressing area that was about the size of a postage stamp. It had a cracked mirror on the door, and I would do Betty Grable. I would just try to duplicate her songs "Coney Island" and "Down Argentine Way" and try to dance and sing like her. But I never let anybody see me do it. I was a closet performer.

Our friend Malcolm, who was very musical, could drum, and one time he set up cardboard boxes on the corner of Yucca and Wilcox. We put up the sign GENE KRUPA AND THE ANDREWS SISTERS. Ilomay, Norma, and I were Patty, Maxene, and LaVerne, and Malcolm was Gene Krupa. We had no music except for him banging on these cardboard boxes, and we'd be singing and hoping that somebody would discover us or at least give us a quarter. We gave up and tried to sell lemonade at one point, which didn't work either.

When Ilomay and I were maybe eleven, we would go up to the Hollywood sign. We'd climb behind it and hang over the letters. The o's for some reason were my favorite, and I'd stick my head out from the o. I would do a Tarzan yell. I'd overlook Hollywood, and [scream], We're gonna lick you yet, you're gonna be at our feet.

The roof was another escape. We'd go up there and play and sing down the airshafts. I remember it being such a beautiful blue, the sky. And the hills—you felt like you could just reach out and touch them.

The building at Yucca and Wilcox is still there. I still dream about it. I dream I want to redo it. I want to open it up. They were called apartments, but it was a room. I never measured it, but it was pretty small.

There was a Murphy pull-down bed, that would go up into the wall. But once we moved in, it never went back up into the wall because Nanny was a pack rat. There was stuff under the bed too. Sometimes she'd throw stuff on the couch where I slept, and it wouldn't be moved for three or four weeks. It could be a blouse, sweater, old scarf, or a newspaper or magazine.

My closet was the shower rack in the bathroom. She took the shower curtain down when we got there and hung my school clothes on the shower rack. My clothes were always kind of damp.

I never took a shower until I was twenty-one. I loved the bathtub, and Nanny couldn't understand why I loved to float in there for hours. But it was a great way to get away. I'd float and pretend I was a little mermaid. I loved fairy tales. And I drew. I would draw scenes from the fairy tales that I read in school.

Mama had stars in her eyes, and she did get a chance to interview some movie stars. She was freelancing for *Collier's* and *Pic,* and she interviewed Bob Hope, Rita Hayworth, George Montgomery, and Cesar Romero.

With Mama's zeal for all this, she said, "You know, baby, you can draw, too, but you should write." And one day I got the bright idea that I should interview famous people who went to Hollywood High for the school paper. Mama thought it was swell. I found out Joel McCrea had gone there, so we called the studio and set up an interview. The publicity department at the studio where he was working must have thought it was a cute idea for this high school kid to come in and interview Joel McCrea.

When I got there, we went into an office, and Joel McCrea sat behind the desk. He put his cowboy boots up on the desk, and he said, "Now, what do you want to know?" And I had no idea. "So, uh, how did you get your start?" I asked. I'm sure I asked really stupid questions, but he was very sweet. So I wrote the article, and that was cool.

Then I had an interview all lined up with Lana Turner, who I think went to Hollywood High for about ten minutes. But I was going to have to ditch school, and the principal found out about it and put a kibosh on it. I was devastated.

But listen—lap dissolves—years later she was a guest on my show. So was Betty Grable. So was Rita Hayworth.

I don't know that I would have been able to do what I did if I hadn't been in that era, because the movies were so innocent. When I went to New York and this agent said, "Go put on your own show," it never occurred to me I couldn't do it because Mickey and Judy did it. And so, by golly, we did—*The Rehearsal Club Revue*. We got agents out of it, and that got me started.

I never thought it was a foolish thing to do, and that came from the movies. They weren't cynical. They were so innocent, and a lot of fun. There was always hope. There wasn't anything you couldn't do if you set your mind to it.

New York gave me my identity, because I didn't have much of one out here. Things happened for me: You get your first job, you first get recognized for what you're doing, you first get paid. New York was so exciting for me those first ten years.

Then *The Garry Moore Show* was off the air, and I had closed in a Broadway show—I had been ill. We had a baby, and my husband, Joe, who was from California, felt that he had more opportunities out here. So we thought, Okay, we'll just come back.

The Carol Burnett Show was a whole new chapter for me, working in California and doing a television show. The fun of it was that our show most of the time relied heavily on doing movie takeoffs. So I was in hog heaven, just doing all of these movies that I used to do on Yucca and Wilcox, but now I had an orchestra and costumes. Lights. An audience.

I was a grown-up in a fairy-tale kind of a situation—"Okay, next week I'd love to be Mildred Pierce. How about in a couple of weeks we do *Gilda*?" It was just the most wonderful realization of what I used to do when I was a kid.

edward **RUSCHA**

Edward Ruscha was born in Omaha in 1937 and raised in Oklahoma City. Moving to Los Angeles in 1958, where he trained at
the Chouinard Art Institute, he put new spins on the everyday.
Service stations became subject matter; carrot juice, blood, and
gunpowder art materials; and the dictionary an unending source
of raw material. He painted the Los Angeles County Museum of
Art on fire and was the first, and surely the only, artist to use in
one painting both caviar and Pepto-Bismol. He works in many
media, from photography and film to drawings and paintings. His
artworks include fourteen books of photographs, often featuring such Los Angeles images as the Sunset Strip, palm trees, and
drab apartment houses, as well as hundreds of "word" and
other paintings. Between 1963 and 1999 he had 176 solo shows
worldwide. Based in Venice, California, he is also a film actor on
occasion.

When I was around thirteen, a friend up the street showed me a
paper replica he'd made of Williamsburg, Virginia, with painted
houses, streets, and all, and it just blew me away. I delivered the *Daily
Oklahoman* and the *Oklahoma City Times,* and I had a dream that some-
day I would make models of all the houses on my paper route. It would
have been very time consuming, but I always think of that as a way of
mapping your life and somehow documenting the way things are.

I see continually how my work is affected by that memory. Something connects with you and rings a bell. I'm ready to believe that anything I do today is going to be somehow relative to something that happened in my early life.

Being born and raised a Catholic and going to church in my early years was a profound, life-forming experience. I've made references to the ever after. Priests' vestments, colors, and sounds come out in my work unconsciously. I'm not trying to say, Look, I was a Catholic. It's that these things embed themselves in your life, and eventually they're going to creep out in your art.

When I was little I would make vacation trips to the West Coast. I had grandparents who lived outside of Santa Cruz. We would come through LA, and I remember liking it here. Early on I decided to go to art school in California.

I thought I wanted to be a cartoonist. I read funny papers and comics, and my first art was done with Speedball pens and Higgins india ink. I craved india ink. If I puddled it on paper, it would dry and crack. It was my love affair with the color black. And in the same sensual way that I might love to mix paints today, I was drawing cartoons when I was about eight. I didn't do narrative stories or cartoon strips. Just funny faces.

Animated cartoons had a powerful influence on me too, although being an animator seemed a little impractical. My dad didn't have much enthusiasm for me going to art school until he found out that Walt Disney financially supported the Chouinard Art Institute, where I studied.

At some point there, when I began making trips back and forth to Oklahoma from LA to see my folks and my friends, I began photographing things I saw on the highway, like gasoline stations. It was a little dialogue I had with myself about this subject. Gas stations were kind of mysterious to me even though buying gasoline, driving cars, and all that kind of thing are requirements in our lives.

It occurred to me to make a book out of this little study I was doing. This solitary subject of gasoline stations could be elevated to become art.

I started Heavy Industry publishing company. It was a hot duo of words that meant giant steel companies, drop forges, and huge machinery. Applying that name to something that's so tiny and frail, like a publishing company, had its attraction to me. There was no agenda to the whole thing, but it seemed to be on a cycle—almost every year I would come out with another book. The books sort of had the same format, size, and weight.

Ferus Gallery came along for me in the late fifties and was a crucial element in my life as an artist. It was deeply vital, and it had a very interesting array of artists. It was almost like a jazz catalog, where there are a lot of different voices under the same record label. All of them had very distinct voices, each in his own way. They all seemed to be friends with one another, yet they weren't necessarily influenced by each other's art. Each had a very distinctive take on the world and on his work, and so that made it a very vital place to aspire to and to be.

Ferus also introduced artists to this side of the world who were previously never seen out here. They showed Kurt Schwitters and Jasper Johns. They had Andy Warhol's first painting show. It was truly avant-garde. They were artists that I was aware of but had never really seen exhibits of, and that introduced me to another aspect of the art-making process, which is the showing of art rather than just the doing of art.

I settled on Western Avenue near Santa Monica Boulevard in Hollywood, and that was my official headquarters for years. From my studio I could see the Hollywood sign. I would look up there, and I began to use it as a smog indicator. If I could see that sign, I would figure that the smog was not so bad.

Looking at that sign every day, it eventually dawned on me that maybe I should do something with it, use it as subject matter. I began making drawings and paintings of it, and a silkscreen print of the image with sort of fictitious skies of my own design.

It was connected to my work in more ways than one, so it was likely subject matter for me. "Hollywood" is also a word, and I always liked the way it sort of rounded off in your speech. It had a perfect ring to it— not just from the pizzazz standpoint or from the cultural definition of it. I simply liked the word for its abstract self.

Then that led to other things in my art that involved words. I always looked at a word like it was a horizontal bunch of abstract shapes, which is really what it is. I liked that horizontalness, and I think it gets into other aspects of my work too.

What's always intrigued me is to take something as it is and not try to do too much to it. Just present it as information and let the art take its own course.

I did a series of paintings called Metro Plots that examines my feelings about the succession of streets that are in this big city. They look like maps in a way. They look like you're up in the air looking down, and they're reasonably correct. They represent my emotional attachment to this city. I might paint Wilshire Boulevard; someone else might paint a flower.

I think it's popular culture that motivates me as an artist. Popular culture to me is printed matter and sound matter, what comes in your ears and what your eyes perceive. It could be songs, music, anything that has a stylistic application. An automobile certainly does. It's a way of todayness as opposed to, let's say, "nature," which I've got a healthy respect for. And I'm influenced by it. It's the noise of this so-called popular culture that determines my drive and my work. I believe that if someone said, "Look, you can only make art out of the human figure," I would dry up and die.

judy DATER

Born in Hollywood in 1941, the photographer Judy Dater has lived in the San Francisco Bay Area most of her adult life and is a recipient of the Oakland Museum's Dorothea Lange Award. Befriended in her twenties by the photographer Imogen Cunningham, Dater wrote the 1979 oral history *Imogen Cunningham: A Portrait,* and shares with her mentor a keen eye for people and place. Usually working in black-and-white, she is perhaps best known for her portraits and has frequently turned her lens on herself. She had her first photography exhibition in 1964 and has since both traveled and exhibited extensively around the world, including trips to Egypt in 1979 on a Guggenheim grant. While she's also lived in both New Mexico and New York, she says, "I absolutely believe that my roots are here in California."

⌒⌒

My parents moved to California in the thirties, from Philadelphia. My dad was a lawyer, but he moved to California to not be a lawyer. He worked as an assistant director on B movies for a while, then bought a movie theater on Western Avenue. The Clinton Theater.

That theater is a constant memory I've had ever since I was a kid. It was a small neighborhood theater, 750 seats, and when I was twelve or thirteen, I had my first job there selling popcorn and candy. When I was a little bit older I was a cashier. I'd see absolutely everything, then often go to other theaters and see something else. I was a movie junkie. I still

am. I just don't get to go as often as I wish. I grew up on the movies and
in that theater.

When I was really young, I used to be scared to death of the dark. In
the morning before anything was going on there, the theater was a
huge, dark space. I would try to walk down the aisle and see how far I
could get before I got scared. My goal was always to see if I could get
myself all the way down to the front in this darkness. I would do it, but
I wouldn't do it all the time, and then I would go running out, as fast as
I could, because it was very scary.

I don't know how old I was when I did this, but it was a little game
I would play with myself. I have thought about the fact that my spending so much time in the dark in these theaters had something to do with
my liking the darkroom and my gravitating to photography. I was
watching these images projected in the dark, so large. I grew up on
black-and-white films, and I think I fell in love with black-and-white,
which is, I think, why I do that more than color. It was always the people and the movie stars that had the most presence for me. You don't go
to the movies to see landscape. You go to see people. I'm sure that also
had an influence on me.

The name I was born with, before I married my first husband,
Dennis Dater, was Judy Lichtenfeld. I wanted it to be more glamorous
because of Hollywood. So I was always trying to think up what would
be a perfect Hollywood name. My dream name was Gina Lester. I
thought that would just be a wonderful Hollywood movie star kind of
name. And I was always fooling around with the spelling of Judy.
Anything to change it and make it seem more glamorous than what it
was.

I thought about studying film and took some film classes, but to be a
filmmaker for me at that time, when I was maybe twenty, was really
very overwhelming. I think maybe if I had not been going to San
Francisco State, but instead gone somewhere with a bigger film program, maybe I could have felt more at ease with doing film. But it was

easier to be a photographer, because you didn't need to work with a crew and you didn't need to spend so much money. It was simpler, and it was something I could control and do every part of by myself.

I took my first photograph when I was six or seven with a little box Brownie. Later my father took family photographs and made a lot of home movies, and I used to talk him into letting me borrow the camera or shoot some film. I was interested in the idea of taking pictures, but I never thought about being a photographer. I wanted to be an artist, and my idea of being an artist was to be a painter. It really wasn't until I got into college that I realized what you could do with the camera.

I took beginning photography with Jack Welpott at San Francisco State, and it was love at first sight for photography—and also infatuation with Jack, whom I later married. I felt like I'd finally found something that I really connected with. Photography seemed magical for me. It opened up all kinds of worlds and possibilities in terms of communication and being able to express things that I felt were impossible for me to express verbally but that I could somehow express visually. Maybe part of it is that I started out with black-and-white and that in a way it abstracts and exaggerates things. I love the graphic qualities of it, the mystery and poetry. The black-and-white has an ability to romanticize things.

Jack would take his students on various field trips during the semester, and one of the places we went was a conference in Big Sur about the life and work of Edward Weston. Ansel Adams was there. Brett Weston. Cole Weston. Wynn Bullock. Imogen Cunningham and probably some other people that I can't remember. It was very informal— just old cronies kind of hanging out and reminiscing about Edward Weston in front of a small audience—and we were these very young, eager photographers who were there to listen to these grand masters talk.

That was where I first met Imogen Cunningham. She was this outspoken, funny, feisty eighty-year-old woman, in her little beanie cap, suspenders, peace symbol, and cape, and I had never seen anything like it in my life. I was speechless.

She was always very inquisitive about young people, asking, "What do you want to be a photographer for? You should get a real job." She also loved to photograph people. She did some portraits of me and said, "Well, now, when you get back to San Francisco, you come by and I'll give you a picture."

I was nervous about it but I did finally call. She invited me over for lunch and that was really the beginning of a friendship that I had with her for thirteen years, until she died at ninety-three. I think Imogen gave me permission—not by anything she said but just by the fact that she did what she did—to go ahead and photograph strangers. You didn't have to know who the people were in order to get a feeling from them. She tried to find that universal thread, and that's exactly what I try to do.

Her nudes of both men and women were also an inspiration. She took all those nude pictures of her husband on Mount Rainier, which didn't get exhibited for fifty years. I think that because I started doing photography when I was twenty, in San Francisco, in the sixties, that the atmosphere of the moment and the times allowed me to do photographs of the nude that maybe I wouldn't have done if I was somewhere else. There I was, living on Haight Street with the hippie movement and the flower children. Everybody was free and experimenting.

I took photographs of myself in the nude. I photographed all my friends in the nude. I photographed couples in the nude. Sometimes I would take people outside and try to incorporate nature. It seemed like in the sixties, and even early seventies, nobody thought anything about taking their clothes off, and sometimes they'd even suggest it if I didn't. In fact, if anything, it was politically correct. I don't know that it would have been politically correct in Kansas City, but it was in San Francisco and the Bay Area.

Imogen was also very interested in the fact that I liked to photograph people, because so many people from the Bay Area, particularly at that moment in time in the sixties, were doing landscapes in the Edward Weston/Ansel Adams/Brett Weston California landscape tradition. They wanted to do photography that was pure, not romantic, not using a soft-focus lens and to get things as sharply in focus as they could. It was something that only photography could do and had formed the basis for the Group *f*/64 photographers back in the thirties. We were all using large-format cameras and view cameras, and the f-64 was the smallest f-stop that you can get with that type of a camera; you could stop way down so that you could get a lot of detail and sharpness.

I think they were here because they were interested in photography as a fine art and not a commercial or journalistic medium. The grandeur and variety of the California landscape inspired a lot of these people to do the kinds of photography they did. It wasn't like they were in New York City photographing the grit and grime and urban landscape. They were photographing this beautiful, pristine, sublime, and varied California landscape.

The California landscape is unique, and that's probably what got a lot of these people. Ansel Adams was always going to Yosemite. Wynn Bullock lived on the coast and photographed the ocean and coast. Edward and Brett Weston spent a lot of time at Point Lobos, which inspired their work tremendously; I don't know anyplace else that looks quite like Point Lobos. The land had a very strong impact on the kinds of photography these people did.

Being able to look out at the ocean is incredibly important to me too. I like the desert. I like going to the mountains. I love the rolling hills of Marin County. People pay a lot of attention to what they eat and to drinking wine and to enjoying the sensual pleasure of eating and drinking. I think that it makes people relaxed in a certain way. I missed that when I wasn't living here.

john gregory **DUNNE**

In his 1967 book *Delano: The Story of the California Grape Strike,*
writer John Gregory Dunne notes he "married into [California's
Central] Valley." He was born in 1932 in Hartford, Connecticut,
the son of a prosperous surgeon who died when Dunne was only
thirteen. In 1964 he married the writer Joan Didion and moved
with her to Los Angeles. As a regular contributor to such publications as *The New Yorker* and the *New York Review of Books,* he has
covered such California phenomena as not just the grape strike
but also the trials of Rodney King and O. J. Simpson. He has
drawn on his Irish Catholic background in such bestselling novels as *True Confessions* and *Dutch Shea, Jr.,* as well as in his and Didion's extensive movie work. His 1969 book *The Studio* traced a
year in the life of Twentieth Century Fox while his 1997 book
Monster revisited Hollywood to recount the horrors of writing
the film *Up Close and Personal.* In 1988 Dunne and Didion left Los
Angeles for New York's Upper East Side.

I was just starting my novel *True Confessions* when I had dinner with
Matt Byrne, the judge. Matt and I got talking about growing up
Catholic and how you defined your life by your parish and your
Sundays by what mass you went to. He grew up in Los Angeles, a city
that I knew but where I never had realized there was this flourishing
Irish Catholic community.

Matt and I were hysterical. Your life was marked by your parish and by the mass and by being an altar boy and all that stuff. I had long since lapsed, but you're never really over it. It's always a part of you, and it was the same in Los Angeles as in West Hartford, Connecticut, where I grew up. That night, the more we talked, the more I realized I could set *True Confessions* in Los Angeles.

The most important formative experience I had, though, was my two years in the army. I was an upper-middle-class kid who went to Princeton and was supposed to go to Stanford Business School. Rather than do that I volunteered for the draft. I spent fifteen months in Germany in a line unit and—-I've said this many times—I think I've made my living off that two years.

Normally someone who went to a private boarding school and then to an Ivy League college did not spend time in the military as an enlisted man. I met people I never would have met, and I found them and their lives interesting.

I was living with hillbillies who, when you tried talking about the theory of evolution with them, would ask, "Are you saying my grand-daddy was a monkey?" They were people you don't meet at Princeton. I hated every second I was in the army, *and* I wouldn't have missed it for the world. I wouldn't be the person I am now. I wouldn't be the writer I am now.

It wasn't during wartime, but it was during the Cold War. You'd go out on maneuvers by the Czech border, and you could see tanks—I suppose they were Russian tanks—on the other side. If war had broken out, we would have lasted maybe ten minutes. So I had a sense of what real life was like.

I cannot say too strongly that it was the most important educational experience of my life. Maybe that's why I began writing about cops and stuff. Because of my army career, I think I understood the constituency of the dispossessed. The have-nots. The people from the redlined zones on the urban maps.

I got out of the army and moved to New York. I lived in a very fancy rooming house on Seventy-Fifth Street, where I shared a room and bathroom with three other people. When Joan and I first got married, we lived in the building right next door, in a fifth-floor walkup.

I worked for an advertising agency, which I hated, and eventually I got a job at *Time. Time* was wonderful because it taught me: one, to make a deadline; two, to write fast; three, to condense. It was a great professional learning experience. But at the end of five years, you've either got to fish or cut bait.

Joan and I got married in 1964, and I realized shortly after that I was going to become a chronic malcontent if I stayed at *Time.* So I went in to work one morning, called her on the phone, and asked, "Do you mind if I quit?" She said, "No," and I went over to the Chase Bank and got a three-thousand-dollar loan. That was a lot of money. You could live a long time on that.

We thought of the Caribbean, but we knew that we couldn't make a living. Then we thought we'd make a living writing television, ha-ha. So we moved to California and began freelancing. Joan was writing movie reviews for *Vogue*—she got three hundred dollars a month for that—and I was writing for *National Review, TV Guide,* and other places.

We lived on fifty-six acres on the oceanfront in Portuguese Bend. We would come in to Beverly Hills for dinner a couple nights a week. That's a forty-mile pop. Eighty miles round trip. We leased a poppy red Mustang convertible, and we'd always park the car so we didn't have to pay valet parking. We had a charge account at the fanciest restaurant in Beverly Hills, the Bistro, but we never had enough money to tip the valet, so we'd always park around the corner or down the street.

I loved the wide-open spaces. It was just less constricted than life in the East. It wasn't like my army days, which was a discrete experience, and it wasn't like the kind of faux Ivy-League-guy-in-New-York life I led with *Time.* It was nice.

What always got me about Los Angeles was how misunderstood it was by people who wrote about it. People who came in from the outside. They thought that Los Angeles radiated out from the Beverly Hills Hotel. They thought Los Angeles was Hollywood, and by that they meant the movie business, not Hollywood qua Hollywood. It would drive me around the bend. There's the movie business and there's Los Angeles, and it was Los Angeles that I found more interesting.

The first book I did was about César Chávez, and I got to know a great deal about East LA then because of the huge Hispanic presence. Most people on the west side of Los Angeles in those days didn't go east of Fairfax. They had no knowledge of the city. I learned a lot about the east side of LA and Hispanics when I did that book.

I decided on that book when we were going up to Sacramento to see Joan's family one Christmas. I had read about Chávez in the paper, and had no interest. Then we were driving up that highway that cuts right through the Central Valley, and there was some sort of march. I thought, This could be interesting. I worked on it, and then the editor Henry Robbins entered our life. We had dinner with him, and he offered me my first book contract. I got paid something like a three-thousand-dollar advance, and I thought I was in hog heaven.

I spent a lot of time up there, and I liked those growers, too. They were nice people. They were basically getting trampled by history, and they didn't know it. But I loved Chávez. I really loved him. He was devious but smart.

Then my second book was *The Studio*. I never wanted to write about the movie business, but when I got a chance to do *The Studio*, I thought, Why not? I never read the book. I hated it. Joan read the galleys and the manuscript. Years later I finally read it. I didn't like it because it was so easy. They gave me an office, a parking space. I always had my notebook out. Everyone always knew what I was doing. I'd write the stuff down, go type it up, and it was basically just figuring out the order to put the notes in. It didn't seem to be work. It was years before I picked it up to look something up, and I said, This isn't bad. This is okay.

We were not involved in the movie business in those days, and I understood the movie business as well as any outsider can understand it. But you don't really know anything about the movie business until you've worked in it. Then it's different. In the latest edition of *The Studio*, I wrote in the introduction that there have been only three good books by outsiders about the mechanics of the business: Lillian Ross's *Picture*, Julie Salamon's *The Devil's Candy*, and *The Studio*. These are as good as you can get by people who don't work in the business, and they were good because all three of us had total access. You can't do it unless you have the access.

Joan and I then got a column for the *Saturday Evening Post*. We got paid one thousand dollars a column, which was twenty-six thousand dollars a year. I thought I was Bill fucking Gates. That was a lot of money, and we lived in this big old house in Hollywood.

When the magazine business fell apart, we did our first movie. Writing is not writing screenplays. Tony Richardson, who was our dearest friend, said he could never understand why anyone only wrote screenplays and did not wish to direct. As I've said many a time, the best you can hope for being a screenwriter is being a copilot. You're never piloting the plane.

When you're writing a book, you're the pilot, the navigator, the engineer. You're in charge of everything. When you do a screenplay, even if your screenplay is shot without a change in it, what you're doing is ceding writerly functions like pace, mood, style, and point of view to the director in the cutting and filming process. You can *describe* a scene, but not how he shoots it and edits it and how the actors do it. In a book you're the director, cameraman, editor, soundman—you do everything.

One January, Joan and I were in the Newark airport. We had to wait seven hours to take off, and we just got talking. We had this small apartment here in New York which we bought and which was a mistake, because when you have a second place, you feel obligated. You spent all the money to buy the place, so you should spend time there. We thought why not put our Brentwood house up for sale and see what we could get for it.

So we went back to LA and called a real estate agent. She came by and wanted to have an open house that Saturday. We said sure. We went out for lunch, came back, and had three offers on the house. Then we were sort of stuck. We sold the house in one day, so we had to leave.

I think we both also felt tapped out. We weren't working productively. We weren't really satisfied with the work we were doing. I had done five, six, seven books about California. I didn't know what else I was going to do. That was 1988, and all these years later, I still miss Los Angeles every day. I don't think I'll ever like anyplace as much.

norman **LEAR**

Born in New Haven, Connecticut, in 1922, the writer, director, and producer Norman Lear changed the landscape of American television with the 1971 debut of *All in the Family*. Lear wrote for such people as Danny Thomas, Dean Martin and Jerry Lewis, and George Gobel before teaming up with Bud Yorkin to form Tandem Productions in 1959 and produce both television and film projects. Lear adapted the BBC's *Til Death Do Us Part* as the tale of the bigoted Archie Bunker, launching a television empire that soon swept in such shows as *The Jeffersons, Sanford and Son,* and *Maude*. The *New York Times* in early 2000 referred to such shows as "cultural touchstones" while Bill Moyers has commented that the award-winning innovator "broke the prime-time mold." In addition to producing such films as *Cold Turkey, The Princess Bride,* and *Fried Green Tomatoes,* social activist Lear founded People for the American Way and is a cofounder of the Business Enterprise Trust, an organization honoring courage in business.

In terms of my ambitions, I didn't have a mother or father who motivated me. They didn't ask me what I wanted to be and were indifferent to my schooling. But I had a typewriter in the cellar when I was in high school. I was the feature editor of the school newspaper—"Notes to You from King Lear" was my column—and my high school yearbook refers to me as Hartford's Walter Winchell. My senior year I won first prize in the American Legion Oratorical Contest for New England, talking about the Constitution, and a full scholarship to Emerson College in Boston.

I was a kid of the Depression, and my uncle Jack was a press agent. He had wingtip shoes and a tiepin, and he would flip me a quarter. Retrospectively I can see that there was a little too much shine in his suits, and he may not have been as expensively dressed as he seemed to be when I was ten, but then he looked expensively dressed. I thought that the greatest thing in the world would be if I could be an uncle who flipped a quarter to a nephew. That was everything I cared about. I was going to be my uncle Jack—a press agent.

After I got out of the service, Uncle Jack sent me the names of a half dozen press agents, and I got a job in New York at forty dollars a week with George and Dorothy Ross, who were Broadway press agents. After a year and a half, when my wife, Charlotte, was pregnant, I went in and asked for a five-dollar raise at a time George told me he was seriously considering asking me to take a five-dollar cut. I left, moved back to Hartford, and went into the manufacturing business with my dad.

I had an idea for a little ashtray. In those years, one of the rants of hostesses was the pesky idea of flipping ashes onto a coffee saucer. I thought that was a national problem, so I got a design patent on a demi-tray, an ashtray that clipped onto a coffee saucer. We had a good Christmas and made whatever a bunch of money was. So we added candle snuffers and silent butlers, but instead of making them cheaper than the next guy, we made them in sterling. We lost our asses the second year, and I decided to move to California.

I'd heard about California and Los Angeles a lot from my dad. The promise always hung in the air that we were going to move to California and live in a ranch house. That was a very special notion—a house with one floor. My mother would be able to lie in bed and reach out the window and pick an orange from a tree.

My dad told me to get a convertible because if I got a convertible in the East and sold it in the West, it would pay my expenses. So we drove—Charlotte; our baby daughter, Ellen; and I—across country in an Olds '98. I had it two or three months, then tried to sell it for two months. I got fifty dollars more or less than I paid for it.

After the war I was in Cairo with my air force buddies, and we stopped outside the pyramids. There was a guy holding on to three camels, and he spoke some Yiddish. My buddies went into the pyramid, getting all the facts and figures on it, and I stood outside talking to the guide because I was so much more interested in him.

I think of that because my first feelings about California when I got there in 1949 had more to do with people than with the geography or topography. I was fascinated by the Otto Preminger Building, the Abbott and Costello Building, the names-of-people buildings. They were always in the forefront of my mind. The landscape and the climate were the frame. The people and the stories were the picture.

We arrived on a Saturday, checked into a motel, and I went out to get the Sunday paper to look for a place for us to live. I was riding through Hollywood, and I came upon what appeared to be a theater with a marquee for George Bernard Shaw's *Major Barbara:* "Performance tonight, 8 o'clock." It was about 6:30 or so, and there was a guy sweeping out in front. He turns out to be George Boroff, who ran the Circle Theater. I got out of the car and said I'd never seen theater in the round. He asked what I was going to do here, and I said get a job in publicity. He said, "We could use some help. We can't pay anything." I asked if I could see the show that night. He said yes, and I went off to call my wife.

It was a small theater, and when the show was about to start, there were seats blocked off in the row in front of me. Just a little past curtain time, the lights were dimming, and in walk Charlie Chaplin and Robert Morley. Chaplin's son, Sidney Chaplin, is in the company along with William Shallert and Diana Douglas. When it was over, nobody moved. Everyone knew Mr. Chaplin was in the theater. Finally the cast comes out, and Mr. Chaplin gets up and says, "I can only express in one way my appreciation for the joy I felt at this performance. Let me do something for you." So the cast sat down on the stage, and he did a pantomime out on the floor.

This was my entry to California. Driving up Sunset Boulevard, I thought, What a night. But I know now that I took those things in stride. Of course it was a wonderful evening, but I did not think, What a beginning, the first night, it was an omen. I had none of those feelings; I just had a great story to tell. It's in *retrospect* that I realize so many different times in my life, my fates were so good. I had a goal if I started a script, but I never had a set path for myself. Maybe that's why I've made a number of changes in my life.

At that time my first cousin Elaine and her husband, Ed Simmons, were already living here. I wanted to be a press agent, he wanted to be a comedy writer, and we were working part-time selling home furnishings door-to-door. We would be driven out to a "territory"—suburban areas of tract homes—and take either a large lamp or clock with us. I'd walk down the street and offer a clock or lamp for free if they'd make an appointment with our Mr. Simmons. I wouldn't leave the clock or lamp; they'd get it later. Our Mr. Simmons would come by later to try to sell them a dining room set, living room couch, or whatever; and if they bought it, they got the lamp or clock.

I could have cried, I was so unhappy. Especially when we went into selling baby pictures. If there was a tricycle or scooter, we'd be knocking on the door. We took a free picture, of course, and we'd come by two days later with a whole set of them to sell the sweet woman lots of photographs she didn't need. Sometimes we'd have to come back in the evening, and I'd be scared to death. I hated it.

It was so painful that at night Eddie and I struggled to find something else we could do. One night, when our wives were at the movies, he had an idea for a risqué parody of the "Sheik of Araby," and we wrote it together. In those years there were lots of supper clubs. When the girls came home around ten, we got in the car and drove to the Bar of Music on Beverly Boulevard. Carol Richards was sitting at the piano singing risqué songs and joking with the patrons, and she bought the parody, just hot off the Simmons-Lear griddle, for forty dollars—five dollars a week for eight weeks.

If I made sixty dollars a week selling door-to-door, I was doing okay. We made twenty dollars each in one night. We could see a future, so we started to write together.

We wrote a piece for Danny Thomas about the slight difference in meaning of three Yiddish words—*tsemisht, tsetummelt,* and *farblondjet*—and he did it at a Friars' event at Ciro's. David Susskind, who was my first cousin, didn't know I was in California and couldn't believe it when he asked Danny Thomas who wrote the piece. He called me the next morning, and we were in New York three days later, writing for Jack Haley's *Ford Star Revue.* Jerry Lewis saw it, and he wanted us for *The Colgate Comedy Hour.*

We did two or three of those. Then they had laid the transcontinental coaxial cable, which meant that shows could be broadcast across the country. Since Jerry and Dean Martin now had a big film career, the logical place to do the shows would be Los Angeles. So we came back out here.

I've had any number of interviews over the years where people asked, "But how would you know that Ohio cares?" Or, "How would you know that Iowa gives a damn about this?" And I don't know how many times I've said that in terms of the subject matter we deal with, the whole country drinks out of the same trough. They're all reading AP stories, UPI stories. They're all looking at ABC, NBC, and CBS. Basically, the news I get in California doesn't disassociate me from anybody anywhere in the middle of the country or in the South or anywhere else. We're all getting the same news at the same moment, and we're all living with the same problems at the same moment.

A lot of people also would spend time here and say, "I can't stand it." My clearest image is David Susskind asking, "How do you people exist here?" I'd say, "What the hell are you talking about, David?" and he would go, "New York is, you know"—I can't snap my fingers the way he would, but he would snap his fingers very fast and then snap his fingers every two seconds to illustrate what the timing was in California.

I didn't think Susskind had it all wrong, but I thought it was an individual matter. You can't unilaterally say that all Southern Californians—most of whom are transplanted from other parts of the country—live by a slower tempo. I think a lot of people who get used to lazier days and more heat and so forth might slip into that, and perhaps their body clocks change. But then there are others who don't. I've always felt I'm among those who don't. My inner clock has moved at the same pace in Hartford, New York, and California.

bruce and norman **YONEMOTO**

Brothers Bruce and Norman Yonemoto grew up in the Santa Clara Valley, an agricultural paradise that was largely lost to Silicon Valley. Their art of memory sweeps in that changed landscape, along with the experience of their grandparents and mother during the wartime internment of Japanese Americans, their father's love of the California outdoors, and their exposure to Hollywood films, TV, and Disneyland. Each pursued his own art separately at first. Norman, born in Chicago in 1946, studied film, while Bruce, born in 1949 in San Jose, studied fine art in both the United States and Japan. They collaborated in 1976 on the film *Garage Sale,* and have since worked together creating objects, videos, films, and other installations. Their work has been shown at museums, galleries, and other sites in the United States, Japan, and Europe, and was the inaugural exhibition in 1999 for Los Angeles's new Japanese American National Museum. They live in Los Angeles.

B ruce: Our grandfather settled in Sunnyvale, in the Santa Clara Valley, at the turn of the century, in one of the major emigrations from Japan. He eventually started a nursery, where he cultivated the Simm variety of carnation, which was a relatively new hybrid flower at that time.

Norman: Our grandfather was a leader of the community. Both our grandfathers were. Our mother's father owned men's clothing stores in Sacramento, and both of our grandfathers were taken away to the internment camps. In the middle of the night. Nobody knew for weeks where they were.

We use the Japanese American experience in the camps in our art. It's there, but at a distance because we don't have firsthand knowledge of it. It's always far away. In our video installation piece *Framed,* you have to look at it through scrims, windows, and mirrors, and you don't have the luxury of seeing things without something in front of them. The image is never totally clear. It is silent and meditative, and the last thing that happens is when the light comes on, you have forgotten that it was a mirror and you see yourself.

The reason I was born in Chicago is that my uncle was murdered in the camps, and when my father heard about that, he came and got Mother out, and they were married immediately. There was family who lived in Chicago, and she was able to leave as long as she settled away from the West Coast. But three months after I was born, as soon as they could do it, they drove back to California with me.

Bruce: Some of our earliest memories were of cherries blossoming every spring. The street would be covered with white, like snow.

Norman: The Santa Clara Valley was called "the Valley of the Heart's Delight." There were orchards and fruit trees. When the trees blossomed in the spring, people would come and ride buses from down in the valley. It was a very bucolic, beautiful environment. We'd drive by these businesses called Hewlett-Packard and IBM, but we didn't really take much notice of them then.

I think our father truly loved California very deeply, and he was dedicated to the outdoors. He'd take us to Yosemite once a year on a big family outing. We'd go to Death Valley, to all the national parks, to see the redwoods. I don't know if it's a tangible thing, but he passed the love on to us. Somewhere in our work—I don't know where—I think there is evidence of our love for place. California is in our blood, and I think that we owe most of that to my father.

I always loved Los Angeles, even when I was a kid. They'd take us to Disneyland once a year, which was our introduction to simulated reality. Now you see Disneyland everywhere: Look at Las Vegas. But we had that exposure as children, and subconsciously or consciously, we understood the concept of simulation very quickly.

Bruce: We would also go to the state fair in Sacramento every year, where my parents would display flowers. The county building was a really wonderful sort of fantasy place, much before Disneyland, where they had dancing plums and strawberries and mechanized displays.

Norman: My earliest memory, when I was three years old, was when Bruce came back from the hospital with my mother. We always used to come into the house through the back door. We hardly ever used the front door, and I remember they came in that way because it was easier to come up the stairs.

I have another strong memory of when they brought the television inside the house. I remember that very vividly. Turning it on and trying to get it adjusted; it was like magic. My family loved technology. We had TV long before the other kids. We had the first color TV.

I think the television set had a lot to do with my getting interested in films because there was a station that played a lot of old MGM movies from the thirties, and I loved them. They made me feel something—I didn't know quite what it was—but I'd stay up late at night when everybody else was asleep, and I'd watch them. I wanted to know how they worked. I wondered, Why does this thing make me feel this way, and how do they do it?

I went to Berkeley, and I was there in 1964. One day I was walking back from class, and there was a commotion going on around a police car. The police were putting some guy—a student, obviously—in hand-cuffs, and somebody climbed on top of the police car, and it was Mario Savio. It was the beginning of the Free Speech Movement.

That was not what I expected from college. There were strikes and walkouts, and there weren't really any classes. I was totally confused, so I left and went back home and to Santa Clara University, a small Jesuit college near us.

I decided to enroll at the Film School at UCLA, and my partner, Nikolai Ursin, and I shot a documentary about the People's Park rebel-lion at Berkeley. We called it *Second Campaign,* and as far as I'm con-cerned that's my yearbook, because that's what going to school was like back then.

I went to the American Film Institute next, and after that I tried my hand in Hollywood. I wrote a couple of produced scripts. On one of them I met a producer who said, "Think of a title." I spent a day or two thinking of titles, called him back, and said, *Savage Streets* and he said, "Write the script." I wrote the script, and he paid me. I was getting dis-illusioned with this Hollywood scene, trying to find something else, but I still wanted to make movies.

Bruce: While Norman studied film, I studied fine arts. I always liked art, and when I went to Berkeley I continued, even though I studied botany and other subjects. In 1968, because of the extreme political unrest at Berkeley, I decided to transfer to Colorado State University in Fort Collins, which is where my father went. I tried studying horticulture for a year, and I enjoyed it, but it wasn't expansive enough. I decided to become an artist and to continue art studies.

After that I went to Japan and did graduate studies in photography and printmaking. When I went to Europe, everywhere I went, people would ask me what I was and I would say, "American." And they would say, "No, you're not American; where were your parents from?" And so I'd say, "The United States." And they would say, "Well, where are your grandparents from?" So I said, "Japan." And so they'd go, "Oh, so you're Japanese." Then and there I knew that I would never be perceived as anything else, so I decided to find out about Japan. After I got my degree from Berkeley, I lived in Japan for approximately three years.

When I got back from Japan, I moved to LA. I was taking video classes at Santa Monica City College, and this drag queen, Goldie Glitters, who used to be part of the Cockettes troupe, was running for homecoming queen. I decided to make a documentary about it, and that became the seed for this midnight movie feature, *Garage Sale,* that Norman and I made. We were later able to open it at the Fox Venice, which was a center of the community at that time.

I went back to graduate school and started to find out more about video art. I also became interested in examining art structures. I was thinking about architecture, art, and what has power for me when I enter a room, and if the television set is on, I'm drawn to that. So I started to look at television as a site of behavior.

I wanted to make a series of soap operas that would show stereotypes of love and things like that. But I wanted the material not to be like artist's material, not like a collection of appropriated material. I wanted to create something that actually looked like a real soap opera or a real "home drama," as they call them in Japan, and I asked Norman to help me.

Norman: Let's talk about what I was doing at the time. I was making pornography, which I did for a couple of reasons. One is, you can't lose your money. You're going to make the money back. Also it was a way to practice and hone your craft. The first one I did was called *Brothers,* and it was a melodrama and narrative. So when Bruce was talking about melodrama, and making it look like a real soap opera, I was able to do it.

Bruce: That's where the collaboration comes in.

Norman: There's a shot in one of our films where they go to the mountains and see the big trees. Our father took us to all those places, and the wonder and awe that we felt as children comes through in the film.

Our coming from Northern California to Southern California has partly to do with our parents bringing us to LA when we were young. We always thought it was beautiful down here. Southern California offered distance from Northern California, and I had to get away. Also I had to build my own life as a gay man. This was the perfect place to come for that and to learn about film.

Bruce: I also think that one of the reasons why our work looks the way it does is because there are so many artists in Southern California who are involved in filmmaking. They are very eager and anxious to work on projects that they find interesting and different.

I think that when people come to California, it all feels very familiar because they have seen the streets before. They've seen the bridges and the skies. Artist Gary Lloyd, who's worked with us on some of our videos, talks about how people don't want beautiful skies from New Mexico or something like that; they want the really cloudy, hazy, polluted skies of LA because that's what they've seen in movies.

I think that is very much a part of our work. What we're trying to show is that these images are generated here, and that they've created a virtual environment for the world. In that way, California exists in Cologne or Madrid or wherever.

Norman: The big example right now is *Baywatch,* the most-watched television program in the world. Venice Beach is the number one tourist attraction in Los Angeles, and the reason why is they want to come and see *Baywatch.* They go home satisfied.

Bruce: It's a tradition. I was talking to this Japanese curator who told me that as a child he used to watch *Lassie,* which was shot somewhere in the San Fernando Valley, I'm sure. When they were sitting in their crowded three-room apartment in Tokyo, it was like a dream to have a house like that.

Norman: That's become the reality of Los Angeles. When visitors come from all around the world, the cast is in place and the sets are up. They see what they wanted to see.

randy **NEWMAN**

Musician Randy Newman has been writing songs since he was a teenager and singing them himself since 1968. Called a "superb pop craftsman and wickedly funny satirist" by *Los Angeles Times* pop music critic Robert Hilburn, the witty observer with the raspy voice has recorded eleven solo albums of such legendary songs as "Short People," "It's Money That I Love," "Sail Away," and, of course, "I Love LA." Born in Los Angeles in 1943, he also works in the family film-composing business, honoring the legacy of his uncles Alfred, Lionel, and Emil and followed by his cousins, composers Thomas and David Newman. His scores for such films as *Ragtime, The Natural,* and *Toy Story* have received thirteen Oscar nominations, and in 1999 the Grammy- and Emmy-award-winning musician was nominated for Oscars for three different films. The first recipient of ASCAP's Henry Mancini Award for lifetime achievement in film composing, he also wrote the 1995 musical *Faust.* Sitting at the piano in his studio by the backyard pool, playing a song his physician father wrote and Bing Crosby recorded, the singer-songwriter worries about indulging in "old crock-ery."

⌐⌐

My father grew up in New Haven, Connecticut, in a family of seven boys and three girls. He was a doctor, but he loved writing songs all his life. Now only my brother and I know his songs, and when we go they'll disappear. Most of them weren't put down or published, but some were. Bing Crosby recorded his song "Who Gave You the Roses?" I think that my dad liked show business better than any of them because he wasn't in it.

My uncle Alfred was a musical prodigy and was essentially supporting the family from the time he was about fifteen. He conducted on Broadway and came to LA in 1929 to work on *Whoopee!* with Eddie Cantor. A couple of years later they all followed him out.

Lionel was also musical, very much so, and was the head of the Twentieth Century Fox music department for forty-five years. When he was fifteen years old he went on the road with Mae West, playing the piano, and he did the Marilyn Monroe movies. Emil did the Danny Kaye pictures at Goldwyn and stayed there awhile.

Alfred was the father figure for the rest of the boys and the girls. He was essentially a serious man who worked very hard, and Lionel joked around and got away with things that you just wouldn't believe anyone could get away with. They were a lively bunch, and I don't think they make them exactly like that anymore.

I remember Uncle Alfred doing the music on *All About Eve* in 1950. *How the West Was Won*—he did that. And I think I remember seeing *The Gunfighter* at Fox. His last picture was *Airport,* and he won nine Academy Awards.

I was there when he did *The Robe* in '54. There wasn't a big recording booth like now. You'd sit on the stage and have to stay real quiet during the take. I was always worried the chair would creak or something.

To be onstage and hear a live orchestra, particularly one of the caliber they had in those days, is quite a thrill. And to see your uncle conducting it and telling the musicians what to do and having it be his music, I think it impressed me.

At a very early age I thought that's what *I* would do and that I had some talent for music. My father wanted me to be a composer for films, and to do what they did, even though it didn't seem to make them particularly happy. But he thought it was the greatest art form that ever was, and because his brothers did it, that it was a great thing.

I started piano lessons when I was six or seven. I never practiced much, and I've felt it ever since. There were inadequacies technically, which I've overcome and which aren't too important in the nature of the stuff I play. But I really didn't take my education seriously until I was older. Just by experience I've overcome a bit of it, but it still slows me down in terms of writing.

I studied theory and harmony, privately and at UCLA. All of which did me good, very much so. I wrote little things when I was eleven or twelve, little pieces for my grandma. I started writing songs when I was about sixteen and then signed with a publisher about the same time.

I listened to classical music from a very young age, then rock 'n' roll when it started. I always watched *Your Hit Parade*. My uncle had a hit song called "Again," and any Fox movie you see, they'll put it in there. It could be *Lost in Space,* and spacemen are playing it. Any chance for the performance money. If you hear "Again," you know it's a Fox movie.

Then came "Shaboom" and all that stuff. I liked Fats Domino very much, and Ray Charles is probably the love of my life. I don't think I ever liked anything better.

I had a job at Fox in the music library, running a Thermofax machine, making copies of music, and I saw the TV music at the time: *Peyton Place,* Arthur Morton; *Lost in Space,* Johnny Williams. Nelson Riddle was doing *Batman* when I worked there. I'd see the scores, and I learned a lot.

Pat Boone was one of my dad's patients, and he heard demos of my songs. He liked my voice and coproduced a football song that I had written at my friend [now record producer and executive] Lenny Waronker's suggestion.

There were always other people pulling me and pushing me each step of the way, which I'm very grateful for because I was a timid kid. At first I didn't play on my own demos. Leon Russell was there, just out from Oklahoma, and I heard him play and I said, "Oh my God, I can't do that." Jackie De Shannon would sing on them and PJ Proby. Now I'm overconfident, but then I just didn't think much of my abilities. I'd know when I wrote something that I liked, but it still made me nervous.

The first score I ever wrote was for Norman Lear's film *Cold Turkey*. I conducted for *Performance,* but I didn't write it. Norman Lear had heard the albums, and he asked me to do the picture for him.

I used to get very scared writing for orchestra. It would make me sick because it was where I lived. There was the weight of the family. I don't know how my cousins feel about having grown up with Alfred and Lionel and Emil as part of history and also me—I'm older than they by ten or fifteen years. Even though Alfred was never anything but encouraging, I think it maybe made things a little harder in some ways.

I wrote a couple of songs in New York, and I've written one or two on the road. I think I was in San Diego or Chicago for some of the scores, but 99 percent of what I've written has been in LA. I don't know what geographically being here has done, but it's probably slowed me down some. I think had I been in New York, I might have written more.

It seems like every time I go there, I'm a little bit energized, but I would not want to give any ammunition to those who say this is an intellectual wasteland. That isn't true anymore, if it ever was. I found that when I went to New York, my metabolism would sort of increase and I'd bop around a little quicker. I'd be walking in the street, and old ladies would be passing me, and six-year-olds would be passing me. But it picks you up.

Here I always tended toward indolence, watching television. For too many years I didn't have a schedule or anything and just flowed. Still do. I'm fifty-six now, and I still need a movie assignment. I did the new album without it, but basically I spend a lot of time watching television and worrying about not doing my work.

No one ever told me, This is the time you do your homework, and I wasn't able to inculcate it in any of my kids either. It wasn't like I was just grooving and enjoying and watching *My Friend Flicka*. I was worried, but I just couldn't make myself work.

The Industry has created creativity by consuming a lot of it. People have assignments and do them. You have a job, so you have to come up with a story. TV eats up tons of stuff. It's remarkable they put *Frasier* on every week, or *The Simpsons,* absolutely remarkable.

We're going through a golden age of comedy and not noticing it. It's like *Sergeant Bilko,* it's that good. As a matter of fact, as much as I regret the time I've wasted watching it, I think that television basically is doing better than any other mass art form right now. There's better stuff on it.

I've never had an idea when I wasn't trying to have one. Maybe a couple of times, but I'd have to sit down and think about it. Or maybe I get them and reject them and don't know it. I don't think, Oh, look at that. That would be a good idea for a song.

"I Love LA" really came as sort of a direct suggestion from Don Henley. He said, "Why don't you write a song about LA? Everyone else has written one, and you actually are *from* here." So I wrote one, and that's how it turned out. There's a degree of sort of benign ignorance to it: "and all the people dressed like monkeys" is such a stupid lyric, but I like that kind of stupid. I like Beach Boy kind of stupid. I like that about LA. There's something I like about aggressive ignorance.

That's why the guy in the song is not me, and it's certainly not a chamber of commerce guy. The streets I picked are not Fifth Avenue or Michigan Avenue, or the Champs-Élysées. Victory Boulevard and Santa Monica Boulevard are ugly. Imperial Highway has got nothing taller than I am, and it goes for seventy miles. And yet, the idea of riding around in a convertible with a big redhead and listening to the Beach Boys appeals to me tremendously. I love it.

Sometimes I think that while I don't have much of an aesthetic sense visually, this town's kind of ugly. Not from the air; at night it's phenomenal. But there are stretches, coming back from the airport or something, that might depress you.

There never was much glamor to the glamorous side of Hollywood for me. What interests me is Downey, and Long Beach—how big Long Beach is. Strange sorts of demographics, and how things used to be. The black people who used to live around the Coliseum don't anymore, and the Japanese kids who I went to University High with have moved into other neighborhoods.

That's more what interests me, and somehow I get the songs thereby, not by what makes this place so weird and different. To me it's like somebody growing up in Las Vegas. If you deal with gambling every day, you're not going to be there long, because they'll take all your money away. You have to just live there and ignore it.

I live five hundred yards and four million dollars from where I grew up. Out here where we are, it's kind of unbelievable, but it isn't unbelievable to me. I remember when it was all lemon groves out here.

My dad wanted me to be a film composer, like I said. And I had some talent for music, which is hereditary in part. Without a doubt it runs in families. So that's what I did, thank God. I don't know what else I would have done.

I'm always conscious that I'm very lucky, and I'm always conscious that when I'm working with an orchestra, I'm getting to work with people who have put in years and years sitting alone and working hard to get great at their instruments.

The Hollywood String Quartet, four musicians from the Fox orchestra, made maybe the best record ever of the Beethoven Late Quartets,
which are considered by musicians to be the peak of musical expression.
That performance came out of Hollywood, and that might be the best
thing to ever come out of Hollywood.

Part VI

Mythology

luis VALDEZ

Award-winning playwright Luis Valdez has written or directed for TV, theater, film, and flatbed trucks. Born in Delano, California, in 1940, he is the second of ten children and worked in the fields with his family as a boy. He had a televised puppet show as a teenager and was writing such plays as *The Shrunken Head of Pancho Villa* by the time he was in college. In 1965 he founded El Teatro Campesino, a theater company that would dramatize the farmworkers' plight, the ongoing grape strike in Delano, and the work of farmworkers' leader César Chávez. His highly acclaimed 1978 play *Zoot Suit*, which was first produced at Los Angeles's Mark Taper Forum, was the first play by a Chicano to be presented on Broadway. Later plays include *I Don't Have to Show You No Stinking Badges!* and *Bandido!* He wrote and directed the 1987 film *La Bamba* and is currently writing a film about Chávez. On the founding faculty of the Center for Teledramatic Arts and Technology at California State University, Monterey Bay, he lives with his family in San Juan Bautista.

⌣

There are two things that you can do when you're in the San Joaquin Valley. You can look down at the ground and become involved in agriculture or you can look up at the stars and become a dreamer.

It's no coincidence that George Lucas grew up in Modesto and started making movies about outer space, because what you have in the San Joaquin Valley is a lot of sky. There's just so much space out there that it takes you into interior space in self-defense.

Both my parents were born in Arizona and settled in the San Joaquin Valley with their families in the late twenties. Refugees from the Mexican Revolution found ready employment in the Southwest in agriculture, mining, or the railroad.

In 1929 movie producers came to the San Joaquin Valley to film the Oklahoma land rush in *Cimmaron*. They needed good mule drivers, and my dad, who could drive mule team wagons, became an extra for the wide shots.

There were hundreds, maybe a thousand extras in the picture, but my dad recalled it throughout his life with a great deal of delight. For one, *Cimmaron* won an Academy Award. Two, he was well fed. It was the beginnings of the Depression, and he was impressed with the amounts of food the caterers brought.

California's major industry is still agriculture. We're losing agricultural land to urban and housing development, but there are still a lot of people stooping over the same fields that I worked in when I was a kid.

Those fields stretched up and down the San Joaquin Valley. There were oranges, potatoes, cotton, grapes, tomatoes, pears, peaches, onions, garlic, carrots, and lettuce, and we'd stay as long as it took to pick the crop, which could be two, three, four weeks.

There were ten of us, five boys and five girls, and I knew the pleasures of a tight family group. But I could already see we were working very, very hard to make very little money. Even as a child, you knew you were at rock bottom, and there weren't other kinds of work below you. So you had nowhere to go but up.

We went to a number of schools, each for a very brief period of time, but I was generally aware of the importance of school. In those days the school districts didn't care if migrant kids went to school. No one went out and got you. You had to make an effort. There was a bus that came by, and we got on it. That was basically it.

In 1946 there were paper shortages, and I remember that one day my lunch bag was missing. I discovered my teacher had used the bag to make a monkey mask for the school's Christmas play. I didn't know what a play was then, but she explained it to me, and I later auditioned to play one of the monkeys. I was measured for a costume, and I had shoes with little curly toes. It was just magical.

Before the play went on, we had to leave. It was the end of the cotton season. I never got to be in the play, but a number of elements came together for me with absolute clarity. I had fallen in love with papier-mâché, the theater, and masks, and I began to play at theater with my friends.

We put together plays in empty houses and barns, and a few years later I started organizing productions. My friends really weren't as interested as I was, and they'd get tired of repeating. So I went to puppets. I found it much easier to start making my own little actors out of papier-mâché.

My puppets were crude at first, but they got better as time went on. I took a cardboard box, cut a hole in it to make a proscenium stage, and put in a lightbulb so I could do it after dark. I painted my puppets. I even began to use fruit, carrots, and potatoes. I was always out in the fields during the potato season looking for puppet faces on the ground.

It was all child's play, but it began to take on an aspect of performance and production. I began to develop a sense of story and timing. I performed with the puppets in my grandfather's garage.

In the early fifties, when I was in high school, I acquired a used Jerry Mahoney dummy and became a ventriloquist. I repainted him and changed his name to Allie Nelson. I gave him a little moustache and a goatee. He was a cool cat—cool enough to hang around with me.

I remember in a couple of labor camps sitting around the campfire and entertaining the workers with my dummy. Then I created a balsa-wood Mexican character called Marcelino Pipin, and all this attracted enough local attention that in 1956, when Channel 11 in San Jose opened up, I was invited to be on the inaugural broadcast.

The station had one Spanish-language half hour on Sundays—to satisfy FCC regulations, I guess—and I was on that opening shot. The producers got enough positive response to invite me back, and every Sunday for about eighteen weeks, I was live on television for five minutes with my dummies. I was living in Salsipuedes, which means "Get out if you can," still working in the fields, and I was on television.

I did some theater in high school, but I knew enough about the realities of life to know it couldn't sustain me. It was my passion, but it was not a job. I certainly didn't want to be a farmworker, that's for damn sure, and I didn't really want to do menial labor. But I didn't consider theater a serious career choice.

I took the hard-core math-engineering course and graduated from high school in 1958, when the microchip had just been invented. I got a scholarship to go to San Jose State, where I majored in math and physics my first year.

My brother stayed with it and became an engineer, but I didn't. I took a quick left turn the second year. We all wore our slide rules like swords in those days, and I remember I was listening to these two students talk about how much money they were going to make. Maybe it was just the tone in their voice or something, but it really upset me.

I found myself thinking other things are more important, and I made a beeline for the drama department. I switched my major and I began to write plays.

By the time I finished college, a number of things had happened in the world and in my life. The Cuban missile crisis politicized me. I thought the world was going to end. I dropped out that year because I decided, What the hell, what's the sense of studying, if the world's going to blow?

⌐⌐

The early sixties were the turning point for me. We started holding discussion groups on campus about the war in Indochina. The Cuban revolution had already happened, and then the Kennedy assassination. All of that catalyzed my political thinking. Especially after Kennedy's death, it seemed to me that the world and the country were going to hell, and I had to do something.

I had two choices. My roommate went to Mississippi in 1964 to register black voters, and I went to Cuba on the SCTC, the Student Committee for Travel to Cuba. It was the first time American students had gone to Cuba, and the Cuban revolution was five years old.

We all changed there. In Cuba I went from being Mexican American to being Chicano. The women went from being radicals to being feminists. And the blacks went from being Negroes to being black militants. It was a little crucible. Mississippi did that too, but to a different group of people.

Meanwhile, I had studied theater as literature when I was in college. I was influenced by Bertolt Brecht, and I found out about the Mexican popular theater of the 1920s. I studied labor history and learned about the Wobblies and the New Jersey Textile Mill workers and about the Federal Theater Project. All that stuff really and truly moved me.

I became a Lorca expert. Lorca had gone into the Spanish countryside in the 1930s, with students from the University of Madrid, and formed his own company, called La Barraca. He had taken this truck and toured all over Spain doing his own work as well as others'. I knew less about it then than I know about it now, but the thing is that it became again another influence.

The final missing piece was actual outdoor performances. I had seen the San Francisco Mime Troupe in San Jose, and when I moved to San Francisco in 1964, I began to work out in the parks with them.

I talked to people about my idea for a workers' theater. My shtick was that I was going to organize a theater company and go out into the labor camps, and I started seeing some of the leaflets that César Chávez was putting out.

My family knew the Chávez family in Delano. César and my cousin Billy were *pachucos* together in the forties. I was about six, and I began to notice these young men were wearing strange homemade suits with overgrown, baggy pants and fingertip coats. In fact, when I sat down to write *Zoot Suit,* thirty years later, my "El Pachuco" character came out of my impressions, really, of my cousin and César. I saw them from my little six-, seven-year-old perspective, and they seemed mythic to me.

But I didn't remember César Chávez as a *pachuco* then. I just recognized his name as someone who was working with farmworkers. Then, before you knew it, of course, there was a strike, and all these lines converged for me.

It was moving so quickly that I had to make a choice: stay in San Francisco or go to Delano and join César. I spoke to César about my idea for a workers' theater that would tour the labor camps. Because of the strike I saw an immediate, urgent need. I told César that I would be willing to come for nothing and organize a workers' theater.

He told me there were no actors in Delano. He said, There's no theater. There's no money. There's nothing. There's a strike, that's all. If you're willing to come and do what everybody else does, we can use you.

Our first job was to write strike songs, and we performed first on the picket line, then at Friday-night strike meetings. César was very much in favor of our singing songs to end the meetings on a high note, and, of course, the strikers themselves were with it immediately. They loved all the clapping and the shouting. It had the feeling of a religious revival.

We started putting on skits—*actos*—in the meetings. People would bring their kids, and César dangled us like a little carrot. The meeting kept going on and on, and then finally we'd come on for fifteen minutes.

We inevitably showed the growers losing and the strikers winning, and of course everybody cheered. So in that sense it was very heartening to have the Teatro. Particularly our first winter, when things were really bleak for the union, whatever good feeling we created was important to the survival of the strike and the union.

In the 1966 march on Sacramento, we decided to use as much pageantry as possible and have the Teatro perform on a flatbed truck. And performing on that march, for twenty-five days and nights in a row, gave the Teatro Campesino a continuity that we'd never had before. By the time we got to Sacramento, we were a polished group.

Other people saw us, and we ended up being invited to San Francisco and Los Angeles. It was 1966, after all: The sixties were starting to ferment, and we seemed to be just the ticket. People said, "Farmworkers' theater. Good idea."

In 1967 I was still in Delano, and I got a call from Pete Seeger inviting us to come to the Newport Folk Festival. We made our first cross-country tour, with Newport as the anchor, and ended up performing in Washington, D.C., sponsored by both Robert Kennedy and Ted Kennedy, in the Senate courtyard.

In 1971 I was invited here to San Juan Bautista, and I fell in love with the place. San Juan Bautista sits on the San Andreas fault, and we're very close to Hollister, the earthquake capital of the world. We get rumblings here all the time, but it's just part of the way of life.

Over the years I've become convinced that the influence of the San Andreas fault is more positive than we suspect. We tend to think only of the disastrous effects, but you have to look at what an earthquake is. An earthquake is the splitting of the earth's crust, and it releases tremendous amounts of telluric energy because it comes from the heart of the planet.

The upside is that these tremendous releases have creative energy. It's no coincidence that Los Angeles, Silicon Valley, and San Francisco lie in

the path of these fissures in the earth. I think the earthquakes rain peri-
odically a certain amount of energy on the state of California, which
drives us crazy. It explodes out of the ground through an earthquake,
and then it just dissipates in the atmosphere, comes down, and hits us.

It flattens a few people, if they happen to be in the wrong building or
on a bridge or an overpass. But the rest of us, believe it or not, have had
our batteries charged.

culture **CLASH**

Culture Clash was launched in 1984 in San Francisco at Galería de la Raza's Comedy Fiesta celebrating Cinco de Mayo. Richard Montoya was born in San Diego, son of the poet José Montoya. Ricardo Salinas, born in El Salvador, was raised in San Francisco, studied broadcasting communications, and performed there with Teatro Latino. Herbert Siguenza, born in San Francisco, trained in the visual arts before performing there with Teatro Gusto. Their comic riffs, rap, and social commentary are reminiscent of agit-prop theater, commedia dell'arte, and California's own El Teatro Campesino. All born around 1960, they are comics, oral historians, and political satirists, reflecting not just the Marx Brothers and Cantinflas but the interview-based documentary theater of Anna Deavere Smith. Their full-length plays include *The Mission, Radio Mambo: Culture Clash Invades Miami, The Birds,* and *Culture Clash in Bordertown.* They've performed at Los Angeles's Mark Taper Forum, New York's Lincoln Center, Washington's Kennedy Center, and San Diego Repertory Theatre and are regular performers at Latino and comedy festivals around the country. Their work has appeared on PBS's *Great Performances,* and in 1994 Fox TV ran thirty episodes of a Culture Clash show. They all live in Los Angeles.

Richard Montoya: My parents were both organizers for the United Farm Workers union. I remember seeing El Teatro Campesino perform in the fields and camps, and I don't think I've ever seen a group of performers that visceral and exciting.

César Chávez would be in the front row, with a lot of little kids huddled around him. As children we tried to get in the front row, and sometimes the stage out in the fields would be lit by cars that would shine their lights on the stage. There was an urgency, a life-and-death kind of feeling, with those early productions that we try to inject in every one of our shows.

Ricardo Salinas: When Culture Clash got started we were doing political theater, very much what the San Francisco Mime Troupe and El Teatro Campesino were doing. Mind you, this was during the Reagan era, so we had a lot of ammo there. A lot of universities and cultural centers were doing political theater, and we were performing at parks, rallies, or cultural centers.

Herbert Siguenza: René Yañez, the director and curator of Galería de la Raza, had this idea about forming a comedy show for Cinco de Mayo in 1984. He was going to call it Comedy Fiesta, and phoned people he knew who might do comedy.

Marga Gómez and Monica Palacíos were already stand-up comics, so he invited them. He invited Richard, who was funny and great at improv; José Antonio Burciaga, a humorist and poet from Stanford; and he invited me, out of the blue, to emcee this show. I was just an actor then, and I go, "Yeah, sure, I'll emcee. But I'm not going to be funny." Then I started getting into it. So I impersonated different people that night, like Paul Rodriguez, the comedian, who was popular then. Michael Jackson. Julio Iglesias.

We put on this show in a little gallery. There were fifty people jam-packed in there, and magic happened. It was just a bunch of us with one mike and some sound cues. It was so simple and so effective.

Salinas: It was very San Franciscan because it was almost like a wink to the audience, in terms of its political astuteness.

I think we were one of the first groups who were doing politically incorrect material. We eventually tweaked our material and got more sophisticated, yet sometimes we throw in that politically incorrect stuff just to rattle the boat.

Siguenza: It was two sold-out nights. Then some people at El Teatro Campesino were there and wanted us to do the same show in San Juan Bautista. So Culture Clash got on the fast track right away. We were excited because El Teatro Campesino to us was the most successful Chicano theater in the country. Luis Valdez was our hero.

I knew Ric was a Latino rapper, and I said, "Wouldn't it be cool in the middle of the show to just throw in a Latino rapper and jazz it up?" "Lat rap" was just new then, and sure enough, Ric hit the stage and people went wild. He break-danced too, so it had an exuberant hip-hop feel to it.

We needed a name. Comedy Fiesta was the name of the first night, but we did not have a name as a group. So René came up with this idea of calling it Culture Clash, and we all liked it because it has different meanings. It has the clash between mainstream society. The clash between ourselves. The intercultural clashing between Latinos.

Salinas: The shows that Culture Clash had prior to 1988 were almost vaudevillian. We would each go up to the mike and take what we called our star turn. I did bilingual rap and stand-up comedy. Herbert did impersonations. Richard would talk about growing up with all white classmates in the suburbs not speaking Spanish, which was a great culture clash.

José Antonio Burciaga talked about growing up in El Paso. He was very much a Chicano Will Rogers—he basically came out dressed like a cowboy, a *vaquero,* and just talked. He died two years ago from cancer, but he was with us for so many shows.

Siguenza: José Antonio toured with us for a couple of years, but he was about fifteen years older than us, had a family, and the touring was just not good for him. The two women went off because they were already a duo, and they were more seasoned than us anyway. They had their own following.

So the three of us regrouped as Culture Clash in 1988.

Salinas: We quit our day jobs that year.

Siguenza: That's when we wrote our first play, *The Mission.*

Salinas: We really got serious. We decided to do a play so we'd get reviewed. The other shows that were cabaret style never got reviewed, so we locked ourselves in my apartment and said we weren't coming out until we had a play.

We tied together all the sketches that we had written before and put them in this thin plot. At the time they were trying to canonize Father Junípero Serra, the priest who established the twenty-one missions along the Camino Real. But we totally took the opposite side. We really love retelling history the way we think it should have been told.

The Mission was about three struggling actors who would do anything to gain national attention. They eventually kidnapped Julio Iglesias, who turns out to be the illegitimate great-great-great-great-great-grandson of Junípero Serra.

Writing *The Mission* was really important for us because back then we couldn't get parts in theaters. They wouldn't hire Latinos. It was really us rebelling against the system in this play.

Siguenza: And producing our own work.

Salinas: We wrote it. We did the sets. We did everything. Then, in 1990, we brought *The Mission* to the Los Angeles Theatre Center.

We wanted to make fun of the Industry and Hollywood, but sure enough they loved it and came in droves. And eventually it got picked up by Fox TV for a half-hour sitcom. But they converted it into something else. That adventure in Hollywood went really sour.

Siguenza: The positive note was that we found a huge Latino audience that loved our humor and would come back over and over again. We were having a hard time getting audiences in San Francisco, so in 1991 we decided to move here.

Salinas: The three of us are these Latino guys who were weaned on TV of the sixties. Abbott and Costello, the Marx Brothers, Buster Keaton, Danny Kaye, Red Skelton, Jackie Gleason, Lucille Ball, Desi Arnaz— all are huge influences on our work. So are Jerry Lewis and Dean

Martin. Cantinflas. Groups from San Francisco like Pickle Family Circus. Cirque du Soleil.

Bob Newhart, Lenny Bruce, Richard Pryor. We were right in that era, but we were grabbing from the past and this new future. And then, being in San Francisco, we saw Robin Williams, Steve Martin, Lily Tomlin, Whoopi Goldberg. We are influenced by all these people.

A lot of times you'll read our scripts and man, they're not a good read. You have to watch them, because it involves slapstick, timing, and fusion of different comedic styles.

Siguenza: We are a California group. We go to New York, and they have another style of comedy.

The tempo is different. Ours comes from another base. It comes from a literary base. It comes from a farmworker base. It's political. It's more laid-back. When they see *Radio Mambo,* people think we're Cuban. But we intentionally made that play have the speed and tempo of Miami. *Bordertown* has another tempo, because San Diego's another tempo.

Salinas: Yes, we're from El Salvador and our group is influenced by Central America also. But it's merged with the Chicano aesthetic, and there is a definite Chicano aesthetic that's very Californian.

Siguenza: California has not lost its sense of being the last frontier. It is to me the beginning of something new, and I think that our parents and all the people that come to California are looking for something. They're looking for a better life, better home, and better education, and most likely they'll find it here because California is very abundant. It has a lot of resources.

The California economy is in great shape now. People are buying homes. They're feeling good again. But politicians during the Pete Wilson era were saying that immigrants were bringing the state down. You would never hear anything positive. *Bordertown* was a reaction to that. We wrote it during the Wilson era, and it still has that anger.

Salinas: All my life I've been an alien, being from El Salvador. I've seen on my forms "Alien." It really makes you feel like a second-class citizen. Even though I became an American citizen, and I vote and work for causes, you still feel like a second-class citizen. In *Bordertown* we really wanted to include this whole notion of aliens.

Being in San Diego and doing the play *Bordertown,* we found that as much as people want to say that it's really cool to be a Californian and laid-back, people really don't talk to each other still. They really are not communicating with their neighbors.

I think Californians are people who believe that they are in the land of milk and honey. Although the milk might be a little sour and the honey might not be as sweet.

I think it's still a state that does have cultural amnesia, though. People here forget what made California a great state. How it started as a Mexican place, as a Spanish place, as a place where the Chinese came and built the railroad.

Montoya: So many of the interviews that we gathered along the way for *Bordertown,* so many of the people that populate that new work, were sons and daughters of farmworking parents. At the turn of the century here, that just strikes me as such a quintessentially American saga.

I go to coffeehouses and see monologues about a Latino actor's struggle to be recognized in the Industry. I understand that struggle. We've taken that up as well. But let us not forget that there are generations of people that put us here. Culture Clash is just not going to let that go too easily.

I look out at our audience and it's not just Chicano, not just Anglo. When I see a real mix in a Culture Clash audience as I saw last night, then I know we're doing something right and making people think. That's really all we can hope for.

We're not going to change the world, you know. El Teatro Campesino did not change the world. But they did provide a hell of a lot of inspiration for this kid.

jon **JERDE**

The architect Jon Jerde is perhaps best known for the "festive federalism" of Los Angeles's 1984 Olympics and for Universal City's CityWalk entertainment area, but his Jerde Partnership International has created large-scale urban "experiences" from Minnesota's Mall of America to projects in Rotterdam and Shanghai. His award-winning Horton Plaza retail development in San Diego led to a commission for the huge, $1.4 billion Canal City Hakata complex in Japan, and over conversation in early 1999, he observed that the only continent he wasn't working on then was Antarctica. Born in Alton, Illinois, in 1940, he spent his childhood being shuttled back and forth between his peripatetic oilman father and his mother's place near Long Beach, California. His oceanfront office in Venice is replete with green walls, red bookcases, an American Indian carpet, and a Robert Graham sculpture. For several years Los Angeles's Urban Design Advisory Coalition of artists, architectural historians, and preservationists met Saturday mornings in his office, trying to come up with a way to "decode" the city and figure out its future. The big theme of Los Angeles, he says, is that there is no theme.

⌒

I was born in Alton, Illinois, where we lasted three days and left, which was the story of my life. My father was a superintendent for Fluor, a big construction company, and he went to various sites where

they were building oil refineries. We'd move from place to place starting up projects and moving on to the next one. Wherever there was oil
in America, we went.

We traveled in a gypsy caravan of forty or so people, moving every
three or four months among trailers, motels, or houses broken up and
shared. Because I was never anywhere for any length of time, I had no
allegiances. I had no hometown. I was open minded about everything.
As far as I was concerned, it was all great and yet to be explored.

When you moved as a kid into these little Texas Panhandle towns, you
were an outsider. You really had to use your wits to get into local society
just to keep from getting battered. So you'd transform yourself to fit, and
I learned to adapt myself to whatever place I was in. Home base was
Grandma's hotel in Los Angeles. The Florence Hotel mainly catered to
businesspeople coming in from various parts of the world, checking in
with headquarters, getting a new assignment, and leaving. My dad had
come in from somewhere, and that's how my mother met him.

My uncle Gordon Adams, my mother's brother, was an artist, and my
grandmother had a room for him at the Florence Hotel, too. He was the
only adult who took a real interest in me, and he taught me how to
draw and paint. We went to Clifton's Cafeteria, where the whole facade
was waterfalls and rock clusters, and inside was a redwood forest with
terraces. I remember thinking it took a genius to figure out something
like that.

Whenever my parents had a fight, my mother and I would jump on
whatever train was around, go back to LA, and move in with Grandma
and Uncle Gordon. Some time would elapse, my mother and father
would get back together, and off we'd go again.

As I got older, Mother would send me to live with my father. He
didn't know what to do with me, and he got me jobs in the construction
industry. We lived on the construction sites, and that was where I
played in the daytime. I would spend huge amounts of time in oil
refineries, these incredible spherical things with catwalks and bridges

and lights at night. When my father was working late and everybody else had left, I had the run of the place and would spend all this time climbing around these fantasy cities.

When I was seven or eight, my grandmother helped my mother get her own place in Belmont Shore, a very charming community near Long Beach. I went all through high school there, although I would leave and come back, leave and come back.

I was very lonely. Long Beach had the Pike, an old amusement zone, and every Saturday morning, I'd walk the bluffs to the Pike. It was a very busy, crowded thing, a tremendous source of entertainment for me, and a feeling of well-being. I'd always buy fried shrimps and fries for a quarter, then spend the day wandering around and looking at all the people.

My mother couldn't drive, so I used the garage as my studio. I would take a wagon and go up and down the alleys and get all this great stuff out of trash cans, like old radios and pieces of metal. I would create a bar or a post office, and these were big-scale, ceiling-to-floor, complete tableaux of scenes I would invent.

Like everything else in Southern California, Belmont was just developing, so there were lots of vacant lots. I would go out and dig a hole in the ground and then sculpt the walls of the hole and make cities with roads, bridges, and building facades out of sticks and stuff. They were very elaborately done.

I'll never forget when I was working on Horton Plaza, we had a twenty-five-foot model, and the facade had this big curving part. I'm sitting there, in the model, working on it, and thinking, This sure feels familiar, and I realize I'm back in one of those Belmont holes working on the wall. It's astounding how things you do as a little kid naively you end up doing later on professionally.

I think that all those years of free invention led me to architecture. I always wanted to be an architect, although my father told me,

"Whatever you do, don't be an architect. You have to have long hair and wear a cape and be strange. You must be in math or science. That's hard, reliable stuff. This art stuff is crazy."

I went to UCLA, the only place I could afford, and studied engineering to be obedient to my father. But I hated it. I started adding art courses, taking a patchwork architectural education. I taught myself drafting, and I had this summer job working for builders who hired me to be the draftsman.

One day, when I was getting building permits for my bosses, this old guy asked to look at the roll of drawings I had with me. I showed him, and he asked where I went to school. When I said UCLA, he said, "There's no architecture school there." I said, "I can't afford to go to USC," and he said, "Come and see me Monday." It was Arthur Gallion, dean of the school of architecture at USC.

My second year at USC, our projects were always "Mr. and Mrs. A and B live in a house with children D, E, and F," and we had to design a house for them. I went to my teacher, Don Hensman, and said I wanted instead to design a school of architecture and its curriculum. My classmate John Rhone, whose basement I lived in, and I took his van to a site in Malibu, surfed in the afternoon, and wrote a curriculum. We mounted our project on corrugated cardboard, and presented it while John played guitar and I did a soliloquy about the soul of the school. It was so cornball it was unbelievable, but we got A's. And I'll never forget how important it was for this guy to let us have the freedom.

At the end of my fourth year, I had a traveling fellowship of $2,500 and a year off. I got married and went to Europe. We saw every museum and cathedral, but what I liked was the anonymous stuff. I'd go up behind the cathedral and look at the vernacular buildings.

That's when I discovered the Italian hill towns of Tuscany. These towns are built on top of hills for reasons of defense. Because they're all stone, builders can't change them, so they really have to build on what's there. If there's a great boulder in the road, the town just moves around it. There's also agreed-upon vernacular style of architecture and a set of colors. If one guy builds a house and another guy shows up fifty years later to build a house, it will complement the first house. Everybody knows what to do. There's an Italian term that means "the way." It's not stated. It's not written. People just know about "the way." That blew me away.

You have to remember it's utterly anonymous. There's no genius connected to it. It's strictly the work of a collective society over a long period of time. Architecture is taught as genius: Great men rise up and point the way. Howard Roark. I was trained as a modern architect, and everything I saw made me feel everything I learned was wrong. Dead wrong.

I began to form this feeling that has to do with collective accomplishment. One thing happens, then another. Taken as if the whole town were architecture, considering the visceral effect it had, it was experiential. It changed your experience. I began to sense that designing experience was by far the higher art form than designing things.

I worked for an architecture firm that specialized in suburban shopping malls for thirteen years, doing things on my own as well. But it really bothered me that everything is the same all across America. All the things I learned in Europe were contrary to this.

I had to get away, and I went to Seattle for a while in 1977. One morning I was sitting outside my little log cabin in the San Juan Islands, looking at a pond, when all of a sudden I was engulfed by a ball of blazing white light. Luminescent, pulsing white light. This is true. I was communicated with. Not talked to. I was being led to see something, and the lesson was: All is one.

This changed my life. Most people will say, "Another dope-smoking California wacko," but everything I've done since then was a function of that event. I've made an art out of garbage. I work with the humble stuff. I don't use the highfalutin stuff at all. I try to make the ordinary extraordinary.

The history of architecture is the history of objects, but that's not what we do. What we do is design what happens in the space between objects. We call it experiential design, and what it means is that we create the theater within which a vast variety of experiences can occur that would normally never occur in standard settings.

The first place I got to apply all that was Horton Plaza shopping center in San Diego. Just a few months later, out of the blue, Ernie Hahn, one of the great giant developers, calls. He says, "You know all that junk you used to talk about? Its time has come. Come out of retirement and save me and San Diego."

He gave me three weeks before he would bring in the mayor, lenders, tenants, and insurance people. We began to design the project in cardboard. No time for drawings. We built a twenty-five-square-foot model for the presentation. I put the staff in black and had them on the rafters with these high-power flashlights. I'd say, "Here's the hotel," and *phoom,* there was light on it. Afterward everyone just said thank you and left. We sat there, wondering what happened. Then, three days later, I get a phone call from the head of the redevelopment agency. He asked, "Can you really do it?" And I said yes.

About the same time I got a call to direct the design of the 1984 Olympics. I was told to use the stock system of Olympic colors, graphics, and other iconic images. That seemed incorrect to me because this is California, and even more specifically, this is LA. The world is going to be demanding a show. We've got to do something spectacular. We had no money and no time, but I knew how to do it using string and cardboard and paper.

We transformed the stock images and colors to the language of LA. John Aleksich had the idea of renting scaffolding, dipping it in the Olympic colors, and making towers, gates, and other structures. I got hold of Deborah Sussman, a graphic designer who had showed me her work on Horton Plaza. She had this color scheme of magenta and turquoise, and when I said there is an official set of Olympic colors, she said, "These *are* the official Olympic colors—just the LA version."

We called it "festive federalism," and color is a big part of our vernacular. It's not really possible in most of America because of the quality of light, but it is in California. For instance, Horton Plaza is mainly cheap stucco buildings, but there are seventy-two different colors in it, and that's what I did with the Olympics facilities. I'm forced to build things cheap by virtue of the projects we do. These are common projects for common people. One way to get a tremendous amount of impact inexpensively is color, and in California you can do that.

Horton Plaza opened right after the Olympics, and later came CityWalk at Universal. All of this wild stuff couldn't have happened anywhere else in the world but California, and particularly LA. That's because with every click you go east in America, you become more and more ossified by tradition and powerful preexisting power structures. You can't just go in and rewrite the book.

In Boston you do buildings like Boston. In New York you do buildings like New York. But LA is a teenager. It's a punk city. You can do anything you want around here. So there's creative freedom, not only for artists and architects but for everybody. This is the one last place where the cannons are still loose. You can begin to look at tomorrow here.

robert **GRAHAM**

Since his first completed public monument, the twenty-thousand-pound 1984 Olympic Gateway, sculptor Robert Graham has immortalized the celebrated of our time. His sculptures honor Joe Louis in Detroit; Franklin Delano Roosevelt in Washington, D.C.; Duke Ellington in New York; and Charlie Parker in Kansas City, Missouri. Commissioned to create the "Great Bronze Doors" for the Roman Catholic Archdiocese of Los Angeles's new Cathedral of Our Lady of the Angels, he also created the National Medal of Art for the National Endowment for the Arts in 1985. Born Roberto Peña Graham in Mexico City in 1938, he became an American citizen in 1950. He was trained at San Jose State College and the San Francisco Art Institute and began his career as a painter. His first exhibition, tableaux of small figures, often in erotic poses, was at Palo Alto's Lanyon Gallery in 1964. But he soon turned to larger work, and particularly bronze female nudes he created using the lost-wax process, and often employing former gang members at his foundry workshop. Graham also designed the beachfront Doumani House in 1982 and, in 1994, a house for his wife, the actress and director Anjelica Huston, and himself. Graham lives and works in Venice, California.

⌐

I was very fortunate to have a family that supported everything I did. I was an only child, and I was very pampered. I always made drawings and little things out of plasteline, the sort of clay I'm still using, and everything I did was celebrated in some way. So I always assumed I was an artist. I could probably have been a thief or a lawyer—or actually a thief *and* a lawyer—and they would have been quite proud of me.

My mother always took me on weekends to outings around Mexico City. We'd go to nearby towns to see the cathedrals and murals and we'd go often to Teotihuácan, where the three pyramids now stand outside Mexico City. Murals were everywhere, especially those by the contemporary muralists Siqueiros, Orozco, and Rivera. We would walk by the Palacio de Bellas Artes on our walk. That was my neighborhood.

Going back to the Palacio de Bellas Artes for an exhibition of my work there in 1997 was like going full circle for me. It was inaugurated around the time I was born, and it was very emotional for me to go back to a place that was about the same age I was.

I was exposed to a lot of stuff as a child, but I never considered it art. That was somehow defining for me because none of it was, "Let's go to the art gallery." You just went to places and saw things. What we call art was very much a part of people's lives. This is the way you go through the ancient towns in Italy, too—you see things that weren't necessarily called art, although they were made by artists.

I say that in retrospect. I wasn't aware of it then. But with the monuments that I've been doing, I'm making works myself where the authorship is not important. I think back to my first experiences with art and how artworks had a different purpose. People grew up around them in a different way.

When I was about thirteen, we followed my uncle from Mexico to San Jose, California. I couldn't speak English, and the way I could communicate and not feel like an absolute dummy was to draw. I would draw on the blackboard, and I became kind of the class clown-artist.

I probably learned English quickly, but at that age a year can be a long time. It was maybe two years until I started thinking in English. After the air force I went back to San Jose and studied art first at San Jose State, then at the San Francisco Art Institute. I was still at San Jose State when I had my first show, at the Lanyon Gallery in Palo Alto, where Nicholas Wilder, the pioneering Los Angeles dealer, was then its director.

I started out in college drawing and painting, then began to make three-dimensional small objects and figures. I did some work at home and some at Woolworth's, where I was working part-time as a sign painter. I continued making small objects after moving to Los Angeles with Joey, my first wife, and our son, Steven.

My tableaux came out of an idea I had about California culture. It wasn't so much that I was part of it. I was just commenting on it. I only did a few because I couldn't figure out what to do with the human figure. I wanted there to be a narrative but I didn't want it to be illustrative, which was always the problem of working in the figurative mode during those years.

When I went to the San Francisco Art Institute, my teachers were Richard Diebenkorn and Frank Lobdell. They were both doing very abstract work, and I could already see how differently artists were treated in the United States. Compared to the Mexican muralists, they didn't really have jobs. They were jobless and had to invent their own patronage. That situation is very artificial and destructive to creative ideas. You really are doing something that's controlled by very few people—museums, galleries, and collectors—and not something that gives you a real sense of being in tune with the rest of your life.

I began to work at different studios in Venice in the late sixties. I already knew several of the Venice artists—Bob Irwin, Kenny Price, Billy Al

Bengston—and I thought it was great to be in a larger studio. I was always in a portable suitcase studio; I could go anywhere to do those small pieces.

I liked Venice. I liked the cross-section that reminded me of Mexico City, Tokyo, London. It has a real urban feel to it. Yet it's not a stultifying city. If I go to Beverly Hills, I feel like I'm going to this ghetto. I actually suffer. I see all those plants and flowers and driveways and gates and no people on the streets.

I started working larger, with larger studios. When, in 1971, I decided to work in bronze, I looked everywhere for foundries, and none of them came up to the standards I needed. They were too coarse, too crude. I found a couple of people, especially Skip McClelland, and he and I started a foundry at my studio on Windward Avenue.

It was a very good thing to be in Venice because so many industrial outservices were here. I could also find models for my sculptures easily here. Some were waitresses I saw in Venice restaurants or other women I would have someone approach on the street.

I was interested in the human figure always, even when I was a child. I feel in retrospect that one has a certain kind of something, a predilection, that scars you for that for the rest of your life. I know that some artists I'm very close to and respect don't have the same feelings for the figure. Throughout time there have always been people who are interested in the background to the figure and others interested in the figure itself.

I started doing what I consider now to be my civic work when the landscape architect Larry Halprin asked me to participate in the Roosevelt Memorial thirty years ago. I was still making the small figures, but he came to me and asked if I thought I could participate. I didn't think I could, but I said yes. I had no idea how I was going to do it, but I made a lot of studies, and by the time we finally built it decades later, I had a repertory company of thirty years of faces and bodies to work with.

When I was a child, the idea of going to pyramids and seeing ancient work was a very normal thing. That was my cultural heritage. When you go out of it and come back, you have a sense of anger at the Spanish colonials for having come in and destroyed an unparalleled culture. The palaces and churches we see of the colonial era are somehow a hybrid that wouldn't have happened without the destruction of the original. They actually killed something to make something new.

I feel now that being an artist is just remaking stuff. There's nothing that hasn't been made before. It's probably the rhythm of culture to go up and down, on a curve that goes from the archaic to the classic to the mannered to the decadent and then starts again. So in California the lack of any real history or fixed idea of culture is invigorating in the sense that you're remaking stuff that Californians don't know existed. If they'd lived in London, they wouldn't be so surprised. In a way, it allows you to make things again without people jumping on you.

The pyramids of Teotihuácan were made for a very specific purpose. They exist now as remnants of something that you can't understand because it's not your culture. But you know it wasn't built on a whim or with no one watching.

Every grand structure that was built throughout time has a very specific purpose and a very specific program. When California tries to make its monuments, it doesn't have the common ground that existed when those things were made. Even New York or Chicago has a historic culture of three or four generations, but California doesn't have that kind of cultural identity. So we're making it up, and we don't really have a common ground to build on.

I built our house here for Anjelica because I was commuting to Beverly Hills where she lived and I hated it. Somehow I talked her into coming to Venice, and that was a very audacious thing for her to do. I asked her what kinds of things she wanted in the house, and I promised her the same kind of comforts here that she had before. That was my task. Since I'd been living with her stuff for a couple years, I knew what she wanted and designed the house around that.

I know what a house feels like because I've lived in houses. I've felt space like that. I've seen it. Or I've been somehow scarred by it. There's no way for me to make anything that's not about my experiences.

You can have a concept that doesn't really get crystallized or realized until you make it, but to try something that you have no understanding of, which sometimes happens in terms of our ideas of modernism and avant-gardism, is bogus. What I've made are *my* reflections on Charlie Parker or Franklin Delano Roosevelt. My childhood immersion in the Catholic faith allows me to work on the doors for the new cathedral. You don't have any business doing something you don't know anything about.

My task now in the cathedral is to capitalize on my understanding and experience within that world, and that idea again goes back to the construction of the temples in Mexico and to the Olympic Gateway I designed in 1984. That Gateway was my first confirmation that I could exist as an uncompromised artist on a public commission and have my take on something that was way bigger than any one artist.

Authorship wasn't important. I'm known for having made the Gateway, but only a very small number of people know that. I can still stand in front of it when people come look and take photographs. They couldn't care less who made it.

maxine hong **KINGSTON**

Maxine Hong Kingston's *The Woman Warrior: Memoirs of a Girlhood Among Ghosts* won the National Book Critics Circle Award for nonfiction in 1976 and went on to become the book by a living writer that is most often taught in U.S. colleges and universities. Both *Woman Warrior* and *China Men,* published in 1980, chronicle the real and mythical journeys of Kingston's family from China to California. Kingston, who was born in Stockton, California, in 1940, first spoke only Say Yup, the dialect of her parents' Chinese village. She went on to attend the University of California at Berkeley, where she held eleven scholarships, and where she has been a professor of English since 1991. *Woman Warrior* and *China Men* were adapted for the stage, and she has written other books, poems, short stories, and articles. Winner of a National Humanities Medal, she lives in Oakland with her husband, actor Earll Kingston.

~~

My sense of reality is Central Valley, Stockton, California. I was fortunate having been born and raised in Stockton at the time I was because I got a good sense of city and country life. I saw the trucks come through and pick up the farm labor in the morning. At night, when they came back, the workers would bring not just money but dinner they gleaned from the fields. My parents were part of that, so I had a very deep sense of seasons, nature, and farmwork.

I think being connected with the earth and the land is really important for a writer. When I was growing up my uncles and great-uncles were still alive, and they farmed the land. They had a stage-coach they turned into a vegetable truck. I knew their horses. We raised turkeys, ducks, chickens, turtles. It was a city lot but could be like a farm.

We lived right across the street from the sloughs—the wetlands—before the rivers were paved, and across from the Santa Fe Depot. There were always people living in the sloughs and jumping trains, and it's still like that. There are lots of interesting stories that came out of Stockton, and I think it's because they are real people who lived lives there. A sense of the Wild West is still there.

I've never seen such a population of hobos—now you call them homeless, these people who live under the trestles and railroads. I was always aware of them, and I think it is good for a writer to know these things. I see my brother raising his children in the suburbs and he has to *tell* them about the poor and people who don't have cars. He has to inform them.

Both my parents were in America illegally, and in writing about them, I had to find a form to accurately portray the way people would talk about their own immigration. The amount of illegal immigration that's in California may affect the kind of fiction that we write. We have to protect people. We have to maybe write fiction instead of nonfiction. We have to move the facts through an imaginary process in order to tell a story. We have to imagine the facts.

My parents had a laundry in New York, and when that folded, they came to Stockton. They chose it because there were a lot of people in Stockton who had come from their village in China. People who were their neighbors in China became their neighbors in Stockton. They knew each other when they were kids. I met a man, an immigrant from

China, who was about my age and said my mother, who was a doctor in China, gave him his first immunity shot.

During the war my father ran a gambling house. Then, when that closed down, you could always get work in the fields. It was something that could be a last resort because it was such hard work, but it was always there, and so were the canneries. Those were very colorful, interesting things to do during hard times—gambling or agricultural work or artwork. I always think of those as things you can do when you are in extremis.

Growing up in Stockton, which is a very racially integrated city, gave me a view into many areas of life and many different kinds of people. We were all living in the same area, so I knew people from various backgrounds. It's wonderful for a writer to be able to move in different worlds and various sensibilities.

I also had a good chance to hear the language of all different kinds of people. I heard not only their foreign languages but also the way they spoke American English. I could hear English with a Mexican accent, a Filipino accent, a Chinese accent, Japanese, black, all these various ways of speaking. I think that was very good for my ear as a writer.

It was my brothers, sisters, and I who brought English into the home. I think that growing up with another language again trains the ear so I can hear English and American speakers better. And it gives you a fascination for languages. One certainly doesn't take language for granted. And I think it gives me a fierce need for communication.

In California and in Hawaii, which I also know well, the various cultural groups have celebrations which are semipublic, so you see people of various groups celebrating Chinese New Year's or Cinco de Mayo.

I felt really good when I was in Riverside, and the children at a grammar school were celebrating Chinese New Year's. They had made a dragon, and they were all underneath this dragon doing a little dragon dance. You could just see their legs, and they were all different colors. They kept talking about "our dragon" and "our New Year's." It just made me feel that those children had become Chinese and were cele-brating a Chinese holiday.

People are so afraid of losing their culture and getting assimilated, but I don't see that happening in California. I see more of a sharing of all the specific cultures. Probably the reason is the numbers of various people. There's a lot of each ethnic group, so that people can support one another in keeping a culture and language alive.

In Stockton we always had Chinese language school and a Chinese cultural center. It's a very stable community. They don't have this American wandering, where everybody leaves and disappears. There are Chinese organizations and clubs, family associations, and benevo-lent societies that must be one hundred years old. Filipino organizations there might be one hundred years old too. I think this kind of stability is very important for keeping these cultures going within the larger American society.

Another thought goes through my mind: The general American cul-ture is so blah and, in some ways, so uninteresting, that everyone finds it fun to participate in an ethnic festival. I think that's part of what keeps it all going. These are colorful, interesting customs. They make things more lively for a culture that has been taken over by television and McDonald's.

My three brothers, two sisters, and I all worked at our parents' New Port Laundry on El Dorado Street. I think that was so cool—the New Port Laundry on El Dorado Street. It was right at the edge of the port in Stockton.

When I walked out of the laundry, I would see a meat- and fish-processing plant and next to that, the river coming in, with the railings, piers, and ships. Then, to the right, as you went up El Dorado Street, was the Stockton Hotel, which was very fancy at that time. Along the street were a cigar store, clothing store, grocery, bar, and pawnshop. Gypsies had a little storefront where they told fortunes.

Now I live in Oakland, eighty or eighty-five miles away from Stockton. We went to Hawaii, then came back because my parents were getting old, and I wanted to be here. I went to Berkeley to college and I liked it a lot. Oakland is almost Berkeley, but the feel of it is more like Stockton. It's a very multicultural place, with a lot of working-class and poor people. My husband, I think, is fourth-generation Oakland.

Our house burned down in the Oakland fire in 1991. I was working on a book based on the Chinese idea that there were three lost books of peace. I was conjecturing what might be in them, and I was going to write a book of peace for our time. That book, the fourth book of peace, burned in the fire. So I'm working on the next book. It's called the fifth book of peace. I started it as soon as I could get going again.

It was interesting that my book burned in a fire. Afterward, writing again, I thought a lot about the waves of creation and destruction. In some ways creation seems to come from nothing. You have to make something out of nothing. On the other hand, it's also making something out of whatever is here. Whoever comes across your path. Whatever circumstances you find yourself in. That's the raw material for making the next book.

I guess California is my reality. Even when I was living in Hawaii, I was writing about California. It could just be because I was born and raised here, and maybe I don't have enough imagination to see other ways of being real. But I feel if I can just write the feelings and thoughts that come when I'm in California, and when I contemplate California, then I will have created something. I will be making works of art.

California is like a mother lode that keeps paying off. There's always more. It's bottomless. It's endless. It goes on forever. The mine keeps opening up.

david henry **HWANG**

Born in Los Angeles in 1957, Tony Award–winning playwright David Henry Hwang is perhaps best known for his 1988 play *M. Butterfly*. From his 1980 play, *FOB*, which was first staged in his Stanford University dorm, to his contemplated restaging of Rodgers and Hammerstein's *Flower Drum Song*, Hwang has explored and articulated the hopes, dreams, frustrations, and losses of Asian Americans. While most of his plays have debuted in New York—and largely at the Joseph Papp Public Theater—he honed his craft with Sam Shepard at Los Angeles's now-disbanded Padua Hills Playwrights' Festival. Today a writer of opera librettos and screenplays as well as plays, he both profited from and contributed to San Francisco's nurturing of Asian American theater in the eighties. He lives with his family in New York.

The only writing experience I had, before college, was when I was ten years old and is the genesis of my play *Golden Child*. My grandmother fell ill, and we thought that she was going to pass away. She still lived in the Philippines—in Cebu, the second-largest city, after Manila—and she was the only one of that generation who remembered all of the family's history. It seemed to me at that point that if she died and this history was lost also, it would be doubly a tragedy. So I asked my parents if I could spend a summer with her in the Philippines.

They agreed, and I went over and did what I guess would now be called oral history. I got it on cassettes and compiled a ninety-page non-fiction novel which got Xeroxed and distributed to my family. It was a history of my family basically, with stuff made up to fill in the gaps.

My mother is from a Chinese merchant family in the Philippines. She came to the States in the early fifties to study piano at the University of Southern California. That's where she met my father.

My father grew up in China and Taiwan, but he was always very Western oriented. He would see Western movies and somehow got it into his head relatively early on that he wanted to come here and be an American. He left to go to Linfield College, a small liberal arts college in Oregon, and after a few years there made his way to Los Angeles. He was studying international relations in the graduate department at USC when he met my mother at a foreign students' dance.

The LA of my growing up was very much like a small town to me. The city of San Gabriel was fairly multiracial and pretty solidly middle class. My friends' parents were barbers and insurance salesmen. The thing about LA that's sort of unique is that if you grow up in the suburbs, you don't actually realize that you're living in a city until you learn to drive.

My senior year in high school, I transferred to what is now known as Harvard Westlake School, and that was an important year because it opened up a lot of horizons for me. I debated competitively, and Harvard recruited debaters as opposed to football players. All of a sudden I was commuting to the San Fernando Valley and meeting kids whose parents were in the entertainment industry. I started reading books like *War and Peace* and *Les Misérables* and began to see some plays.

The next year, when I started Stanford, I saw more plays and began to feel something very much like in *A Chorus Line*—"I can do that." So I tried to write some plays in my spare time. I took a drama class from

John L'Heureux, who's a novelist and was the head of Stanford's Creative Writing Department, and showed him some plays I'd written. He said that they were really bad, which they were, and that my problem was that I had the desire to write plays but I didn't actually know anything about the theater. He became my adviser, and over the next few years I saw and read as many plays as I could, which essentially became my education.

We're talking about the late seventies in the Bay Area, which was a very big time for new plays. Sam Shepard in particular was debuting a lot of his work at the Magic Theatre. Then, the summer before my senior year, I was back home and I saw an ad in the *Los Angeles Times* "Calendar" section that said "Study playwriting with Sam Shepard." It was the first year of the Padua Hills Playwrights' Festival, and only two people applied to be students so we both got in.

I had a real breakthrough at Padua because Shepard and that whole theater-genesis school of writing is very influenced by the unconscious. Previously I thought the way that you wrote a play was you sort of structured a bunch of scenes and then executed them, which is more or less how you write a movie. This really taught me to delve into areas of myself that I didn't understand.

I found that as I was doing these exercises, various concerns and issues began to appear on the page that I had not necessarily thought I was interested in—issues of ethnicity, culture clash, East-West immigration, assimilation, those sorts of things. In a way I started to become an Asian American writer by virtue of these exercises which caused me to look past my own conscious mind.

I went back to Stanford and read Maxine Hong Kingston's *The Woman Warrior,* which was a big breakthrough for me also, because of the juxtaposition of her hyperrealistic view of growing up in Stockton against this kind of mythological backdrop. I started to feel that I could find my own voice in that area. Very soon after, one of the exercises that I'd begun writing at Padua evolved into my first play, *FOB,* which stands for "fresh off the boat" and which I wrote to be done in the dorm at Stanford that spring.

FOB was accepted at the O'Neill Playwrights Conference and was directed there by Robert Allan Ackerman, then a resident director for Joseph Papp at the Public Theater. Joe fortuitously was looking for Asian American plays to do, and Bob Ackerman brought him this play. It was produced at the Public in June of 1980 and did well. Joe subsequently produced my next four plays, and I had a career.

Mako, who was artistic director of Los Angeles's East West Players for a number of years, directed *FOB* in New York. I did an internship at East West the summer before I went to Padua, and I have a long history with them. My parents were friends with Beulah Quo, one of East West's founders, and I think when East West decided to do Menotti's opera *The Medium* around 1967, my mother just seemed the natural choice for a pianist. I was about ten and I hung out around rehearsals.

My father, an accountant who became East West's bookkeeper, always had a kind of tangential interest in show business. It's not something that he was ever able to pursue, being an immigrant and needing to make a living, but when I was around twelve, he started taking singing lessons. By the time I was in college, he performed in *Amahl and the Night Visitors,* which East West did as a Christmas show. I think that that part of him made it possible for him to accept the idea that I was going to be a playwright.

At first when I started writing plays, it was obviously not something that my parents were particularly keen on. I remember my dad looked at *FOB,* saw some swearwords, and said, "We send you to this good university and all you write is this junk." But when we did *FOB* at the dorm, my father told my mother, "Well, you know, we should go see it, and if it's good we'll encourage him, and if it's bad we'll tell him to stop." They came up to Stanford and were actually very moved by the production. From that point on, they were very supportive of my writing, which is an unusual and progressive thing for Asian immigrant parents to accept.

I started doing a lot of work at the Asian American Theater Company in San Francisco. It was located on California Street, in an area which was rapidly becoming a second Chinatown. It was in an old storefront that had been converted into a ninety-nine-seat theater, and there was just about enough room for the stage and the audience.

East West was even then becoming somewhat more institutionalized, but AATC was just a bunch of kids. We were all in our twenties and thirties. People would hear about it and come in, so you were constantly meeting young Asian Americans who may very well have ended up walking in off the street and being cast in a show. Or working on the lights. It was very egalitarian, democratic, and wide open, so I directed a number of plays there. It was communally artistic in the best sense of the phrase.

The roots of the Asian American experience basically center in California, and most of my early work was set there. For a long time, I didn't know if I could write a play that wasn't set in California. San Francisco was the first major port of entry for Chinese immigrants during the gold rush years and the railroad years, and it continued to be the locus of Chinese Americans. The first major Chinatown was in San Francisco.

I was very conflicted about New York. I actually came out to test the waters once during a spring break, and I found the place completely baffling and intimidating. I came back during the eighties because I had this relationship with the Public, and, despite the fact that yes, the regional theaters are where the important work gets done in this country, there is still something about the imprimatur of a New York production that makes it easier to get other productions.

I've lived both places on and off since the eighties, and moved to New

York permanently in 1994, just before my son was born. The California influence per se has probably weakened as I've grown older, but I feel like it is always going to be part of me because that's who I am and where I grew up.

The thing about California that I really love is that it's the incubator for ideas and culture in this country. So many things spring from there—new ideas, trends, conflicts, problems. The sorts of problems that Californians deal with now, in terms of immigration and multiculturalism and all that, are really the forebear of what's going to happen for the rest of the country.

California becomes this fascinating crucible in which the future of America can be seen. That's why it's an exciting place to be, and that's also why, in a more parochial sense, I think the notions of both Asian America and therefore Asian American theater began in California. I was fortunate to have been there while that was happening, and it infused my artistic and political sensibilities in a meaningful way.

If I'd been at a different place at a different time, who knows? But the point is, the idea of trying to create an Asian American culture made sense to me at a point when I was also struggling to find my own voice as a writer. And those two things came together in a way that enabled me to produce a body of work. Now, is it possible I could have been infused by some other idea? I don't know. But those are the particular circumstances. It was also incredibly exhilarating to have been part of a very young community of artists who were also engaged in the same explorations.

If we believe that I've had some kind of impact on the American theater, the sensibility is essentially an Asian American sensibility that comes from California and that I am disseminating to a broader cultural establishment. America is really about this constant infusion of energy and ideas that comes oftentimes from people whose histories in this country are relatively new, and who are taking pieces of old worlds and from them forging something new and different.

betye **SAAR**

The artist Betye Saar calls herself a "junkie"—one who collects junk—and it is a passion she has passed on to her daughters, the artists Alison and Lezley Saar. Calling themselves the Saarettes, the singing art group, Saar and her daughters have carried on the assemblage tradition of Simon Rodia, the creator of Los Angeles's fabled Watts Towers. Born in Los Angeles in 1926, Saar is a graduate of UCLA, where her parents first met. Her works range in size from small fabric collages to full-room-size installations, and she has had solo exhibitions at such museums as the Los Angeles County Museum of Art, the Studio Museum in Harlem, the Whitney Museum of American Art, and the Fresno Art Museum. Drawing on ancestral, biographical, mystical, and historical images, she incorporates in her art everything from twigs and shells to handkerchiefs, old photographs, and washboards. She lives and works in Laurel Canyon.

⌒

The reason that I am where I am today, living here in Laurel Canyon with this nice studio and this nice family, is that my grandmother had to work at a sewing machine. Her mother had to be a midwife. Her great-great-grandmother was a slave. And somewhere back through slavery, somebody had to come over and survive being chained in the belly of a slave ship.

My father passed when I was six, and until my mother remarried, when I was about twelve, we lived with my mother's great-aunt and great-uncle. They worked as a cook and maid in wealthy people's homes, and they had a particular kind of taste and elegance.

I grew up in Pasadena, but during the summer, my brother, sister, and I would spend part of our summer vacation with my grandmother in Watts. It was rural, with lots of vacant lots around, and at one point Simon Rodia's property came very close to the railroad track where we would walk to go do our shopping.

Simon Rodia was building the Watts Towers then, and I was very curious about them. Then, when my grandmother's husband passed, I spent one semester with her, and I would always walk the long way back and forth to school so I could look at the Towers.

I have a very active imagination, and when I first saw them, they seemed like fairy-tale castles to me. It was the first exposure I had to a self-taught artist and to a rough kind of assemblage. He used everything from broken plates and bottles to tiles, corncobs, and imprints of tools.

Those Towers just really made an impression on me and, later, on my daughters, and it has influenced my art. I was not even aware of it, but that's probably where I thought of my motto, which is "You can make art out of anything."

I liked to collect things. I was always finding shells at the beach, and when we visited my grandmother, we would dig in the dirt or look for things alongside the railroad track. We were hunters and seekers.

Because of the Depression, my family was project oriented anyway, and we all made things with whatever materials we had or found. My grandmother and my mother were sewers and quilters. My mother made my sister's and my clothes, and we all made gifts for each other.

When Mother wasn't working, she would always spend time with us drawing and taking classes, and I did the same things with my own children. On rainy days we'd cut up magazines and make collages. They always had crayons and paint, and they always wanted to make something.

In 1968 I saw Joseph Cornell's work in Pasadena. His boxes were exhibited like little jewels on pedestals or in showcases, with an intense little pinspot light on each of them. It was like looking into a separate little special world. The Watts Towers were a big fairy tale because they were larger than life, and these boxes told a whole story in a tiny little box.

My imagination was fired up. Joseph Cornell's work was so elegant, beautiful, and mysterious. I had been doing drawings and prints, and they were very detailed, and it just sort of worked very easily into putting them in boxes and windows and so forth.

I began to collect things from swap meets and yard sales. I'm still using what I got at one yard sale many years ago, where this man had been a photographer, and he and his wife never threw away anything. There was a photo album of their life together, some clothing, bric-a-brac, ornaments. There was a Pegasus, which was probably from the Flying A gas stations, which I remember buying for a quarter or something, and which turns up in an early piece I made from the base of a sewing machine.

Most of my materials come from California. First of all there's the availability of materials through yard sales, thrift stores, and flea markets. Then there's being surrounded by nature and organic materials; I get a lot of things from just tree branches. My piece *Spirit Catcher* is made from twigs, straw, shells, beads, and things like bones.

Alison and Lezley also collect junk for their art. So does my youngest daughter, Tracye, who gives it to Alison, Lezley, or me. We buy for each other, too, and if something's expensive, we buy it back from the person who bought it. It's a family affair.

When Alison was living in New York, we would send things in the mail. I was beachcombing in Haiti and found these shards of plates and things that I collected and sent to her because she was doing *her* Watts Towers bit, carving a piece and covering it with shards of glass and ceramics. I remember another time being in Australia and finding some copper pieces for her.

The scale of my work has always been small. Even if I do an installation, it's just a lot of small things put together to fill up a room. Basically I want to be able to handle it and store it. Alison has always liked to work large. Maybe that's from the Watts Towers, and maybe it's just from wanting to be different from Mom. Lezley started out small, but now she works quite large, too.

Alison got a Guggenheim before I did. It's like there's this art relay race. I'm running, but out of the corner of my eye I see her catching up, so I hand her the baton. Her work was also purchased by the Metropolitan before mine. Lezley now has a dealer in New York and will be having her second show in New York. When we talk about ourselves, we call ourselves the Saarettes, the singing art group.

Because I always had a young one around, I've always worked at home. I was a stay-at-home mom. When I was doing printmaking, my kitchen was my studio. I never really thought that I needed another place to go to be an artist, but several years ago I built this studio where we're sitting now. Having a separate studio gave me the opportunity to leave everything out and be able to look at it. And it's still home.

I've always been interested in nature, and I've always been fortunate to live in a house where there was a garden. We could be outside and see the sky. I haven't moved very much, and this is maybe the fourth house I've lived in since I've been married.

Our house was built in the twenties, and in 1956 there was a terrible fire in Laurel Canyon. My house was one of the few remaining houses, but the landscape was scorched. We made an adventure, my daughters and I, of excavating in the ruins. Even now, when El Niño strikes, dirt is pulled away, and we find melted pots and bent glass and things like that.

Laurel Canyon used to be in the country. Down on Hollywood Boulevard and Crescent Heights were bean fields, and the other way was the Valley, which was farmland and very rural. This house still has that feeling of being in the country. Unless they're doing some building or some gardener is cutting down a tree, it's very quiet and peaceful. I like solitude. I like to make art in silence.

I guess I'm also rather protective about my environment. Classes always want to come in, but unless it's a really special friend, I don't like other people's vibes coming into my space. My grandkids can come over. And I have places for them to make art and be part of the garden.

Even now I'm interested in yard art and environments and so forth. If you look out my window you see my little grotto that I'm building over there. The garden is important to me, like the garden was important to my mother. I have several little patios, and I like to sit there.

I also get inspiration from natural history museums. Years ago, when I was in Chicago, I went to the Field Museum, which was the first time I had ever seen such a large collection of Oceanic art, Egyptian art, and African art. I made lots and lots of sketches.

I began to make these altarlike structures, boxes that were like fetishes, trying to find out who I was and what my unknown African ancestry was. The autobiographical part of my ancestry I knew from photographs. And the other part of that legacy, between slavery and the autobiographical things, was the sixties with the whole civil rights movement and Martin Luther King's murder.

In the early seventies, I was invited to participate in a show in Oakland at an African American community art facility. I had been collecting these derogatory images of Aunt Jemima, Uncle Tom, Black Sambo, and so forth, and I decided to do this piece called *The Liberation of Aunt Jemima,* converting her from a servant and slave to a warrior.

I had found something at a flea market where in one hand Aunt Jemima had a pencil that became the handle of a broom, the other hand was on her hip, and her apron was a notepad. I recycled that to make her a warrior: The broom handle became a rifle, she had a hand grenade, and I think there was a raised fist, which was the black independence symbol at that time. And that was *The Liberation of Aunt Jemima.*

The Liberation of Aunt Jemima became a series about recycling derogatory images of African Americans into a positive aspect. I considered Aunt Jemima a heroine. Her activity was her way of surviving by being a maid, a caregiver, a nurturer.

Now here we are at the end of the nineties, the end of the millennium, and racism has been showing its ugly head again. So I did an exhibition in New York in 1998 called *Workers and Warriors, the Return of Aunt Jemima.* The message didn't get across before, so she needed to be angrier and tougher.

The gallery director passed out my statement, called "Unfinished Business, the Return of Aunt Jemima," about why I returned to these images. It concluded: "She symbolizes the painful, ancestral memories of the Middle Passage, of slavery, of Jim Crow, of segregation, and of continuing racism. Aunt Jemima is back with a vengeance, and her message: 'America, clean up your act!' "

I wanted to honor all of those people that I don't even know but I still have strong feelings about, because that's why I am where I am now. That's why my children are where they are now.

ruth **WEISBERG**

The artist Ruth Weisberg has long used her canvases as a visual journal, and the subject of that journal is as much the Jewish people as it is Weisberg herself. Since her first major work, a book about a Polish *shtetl* that she wrote and illustrated in 1971, her connections to art, feminism, spirituality, and history have become almost concentric circles in whose center she is firmly rooted. Born in Chicago in 1942, she studied in Italy and Paris as well as at the University of Michigan, and her artwork reflects her interest in classical as well as Jewish themes. Working primarily in painting, drawing, and printmaking, she has participated in more than two hundred solo and group exhibitions and written dozens of articles, reviews, and essays. She has been teaching since 1970 at the University of Southern California, where she has been Dean of Fine Arts since 1995. She is a former president of the College Art Association, which in 1999 gave her its Distinguished Teaching of Art Award. She lives in Santa Monica, California.

⌒

I began taking classes at the Chicago Art Institute when I was six, and after three classes I had made up my mind to be an artist. I still remember telling my parents and how they didn't laugh. Their reaction was: "Oh, wonderful!"

Instead of going right home after my art classes, I would go into the

galleries. I think it was '52 when there was a huge Picasso show and
then in '53 a huge Matisse show. I saw those shows for their entire run,
eight or nine times, and knew the galleries and the Art Institute by
heart. In fact, when I went to Italy I used to put myself to sleep by walking the galleries. That was my way of counting sheep—I would just go
from room to room in my mind.

I was often transported in the museum. It was just a place of such
delight for me. I can close my eyes right this minute and see the Georgia
O'Keeffe, like a close-up bone looking through to the blue sky. The Art
Institute, thank God, had women artists, so I was able to imagine that I
could be an artist, which I think a lot of women of my generation had
trouble with.

My mother was a fantastic role model and still is, for that matter. She
was on the first Commission on the Status of Women in Illinois, and
she's still full of intellectual curiosity. My father was an architect and
really attuned to the visual. Taking a walk with him was always a constant visual adventure, where he sensitized me to what I was seeing.

Of course it's of tremendous advantage to know so early what you
want to do, especially if you're going to build mastery in something like
drawing. I know it's in some quarters not popular that you think about
mastery, but I have never believed that and certainly have not acted on
anything but a belief in mastery vis-à-vis my teaching at USC.

Another really important early influence was my summers in the
Indiana sand dunes, where our family went every summer. We lived
without the benefit of most twentieth-century technology, and played
all sorts of wonderful games. We were free to roam through this incredibly beautiful landscape and felt we really owned it. My friends and I
named all the places.

I've used them in my work, those images. It was a lost and innocent
place, really idyllic, and sparked ideas that are at the heart of my work,

ideas about wanting to hold on to things at the same time you recognize that is impossible. I suffer perhaps from the opposite of nihilism. Life to me is just full of meaning; it's loaded with significance.

I spent my sophomore and junior years of college in Italy. I initially went because it had been inculcated in me by my father that the Renaissance was the most important moment in our history. I didn't take art history via slides—we went and looked. It was an extraordinary education and clearly a deep influence on my work in terms of narrative—the importance of the figure and how the figure exists in space.

When I went back to the University of Michigan in 1962, it was a terrible era for women. People at the university sat me down, as they did every woman student in my class who wanted to go on for graduate work, to tell us that we were never going to get to teach. I think it's important for people to understand that our activism really came out of experiences of exclusion. Sometimes you hear things about the sixties, and we're demonized in ways that don't make sense if you lived through it.

By the late sixties, I had my M.A., had married psychologist Kelyn Roberts, and was teaching at Eastern Michigan University. In 1969 Kelyn had an offer to teach at UCLA, and I was ready to leave Eastern Michigan because I felt that the women faculty were not being treated equitably.

When we got to Los Angeles, the first person who really took me under his wing was Lee Chesney, who at that time was the Associate Dean of Fine Arts at USC. I think part of my attachment to USC, where I've been teaching now since 1970, is that by being there I found a base, a community, and to some extent an identity.

I really feel that I didn't find my voice as an artist until just before I came to LA. Starting with *The Shtetl, a Journey and a Memorial,* which I began in Michigan and finished here, my work began to deal more with memory and the past.

One of the things that Judaism emphasizes is the value of remembering. As a post-Holocaust person, I really understand that human culture is a repository for our accumulated meanings, and if you destroy a people, you're also destroying a culture. Even in my work that does not have Jewish themes—some of it does and much of it doesn't—I draw from multiple identities. We are linked to the past, and we carry values, meanings, ideas, and images forward. There is for me something glorious in this lineage.

I grew up with a strong Jewish tradition, but we didn't go to synagogue and there wasn't attention to the religious observance aspects. I've become observant as I've gotten older, and Los Angeles has a very strong Jewish feminist movement. That meant I could combine two strong interests of mine.

I think Los Angeles, more than most places, acts as a vessel for the histories of people who come here. I am very attracted to the water's edge, as I was in childhood. My studio is three blocks from the ocean, in Venice. Sunlight on swimmers through the surface of water is an image I have woven through my work from the seventies onward.

I try to mix knowing things intellectually and knowing things intuitively and physically. I feel that both ways of learning feed my work as an artist. In the seventies, for example, when I wanted to do an image of birth or rebirth, I spent the day in my friends Elyse and Stanley Grinstein's swimming pool. I was pregnant at the time with my daughter, Alicia, and I wanted to have the sensation that a fetus would have in the amniotic fluid. I think one of my strongest early works comes out of that experience of being in the Grinstein pool and taking that fetal position over and over.

Los Angeles in many ways is an ideal place to be an artist. It offers both community and anonymity. It's also an important place to be, which matters. You can do wonderful work in Ames, Iowa, and you never become part of the common discourse. Not enough people see your work for you to become a reference in the other work of your time or for your work to have a broader national or international audience.

I feel very at home in the paradigm of the new Los Angeles, partly because I helped create it. I feel like a player. There are tremendous intersecting networks of people who may look casual but who are working hard. Sometimes people assume being a university dean must be so administrative, just pushing papers around, but we are affecting the future through the lives of a lot of young people.

I should talk about art schools in California, which are rather different here than in other parts of the country. Artists like Ken Price, Wayne Thiebaud, Chris Burden, and the late Richard Diebenkorn all taught for significant periods. A lot of the cross-fertilization, dialogue, theorizing, and other activity that might take place in a SoHo or Chelsea takes place in art schools and university art departments in California, north and south.

Many people have remarked that Southern California is the best place to come for graduate study. One reason is to study in a place where you ultimately want to settle, and I think a lot of people feel that the future is in Los Angeles. So why go to art school somewhere else?

We value in Los Angeles visual culture. We are the producers of visual imagery in the world, and whether our graduates are going to have traditional studio careers, invent new techniques of computer animation, or do imagery that relates to games, toys, or movies, they're going to have this huge impact. I was lecturing my undergraduates just yesterday on how they needed to think deeply about their responsibility in all this.

It isn't palm trees, Los Angeles. It's at the heart of the creation of images. So-called fine artists are using animation techniques from the film and computer industries, and people who work for Disney are taking serious figure-drawing classes, sometimes taught by USC graduates. So it's very much a time to throw out old definitions and old

boundaries and to really look at the production of culture and the dif-
fusion of images globally.

You know, it's LA in the world, not LA, the West Coast of the
United States. That's why all these young people are coming here. The
role and meaning of being an artist in the twenty-first century is going
to be distinctively different, and LA is going to be the primary place to
explore that.

Part VII

Land's End

matt GROENING

Matt Groening grew up watching a lot of television in Portland, Oregon, where he was born in 1954. He is the creator of *The Simpsons,* referred to by the *New York Times* as "the best show on television," and one that essentially brought animation back to prime-time television. Introduced in 1987 as animated shorts on *The Tracey Ullman Show,* his smart, funny, and colorful Springfield, USA, family became a regular weekly show on Fox TV in 1990. His new animated series, *Futurama,* set in New York in the year 3000, followed in 1999. Groening thinks of himself, however, not as an animator but as a print cartoonist. Several collections of his cartoons have been published, and *Life in Hell,* which began in the *Los Angeles Reader* in 1980, is syndicated in more than 150 alternative, college, and other newspapers. He lives in Los Angeles.

I grew up in the west hills of Portland in a house that was in the middle of the woods. It was a good half-mile walk from my house to the nearest bus stop, down windy roads through the forest. It was very deep green and absolutely gorgeous.

My father, Homer, among other things made movies that had to do with water: surfing, skiing, underwater movies, fishing, and so on. He shot a lot of his movies in California while I was growing up, and I could never understand why we lived in Oregon. We should be where the sun and the surf were. But he thought it was more beautiful in Oregon, and I have to agree.

The first time I went to California was when I was five. It was a trip to Disneyland, which was Mecca for little kids. Every one of my friends and I were completely obsessed by the idea of Disneyland, basically from watching Walt Disney TV shows. Usually we drove from Portland to Disneyland, but my father was also an airplane pilot, so we flew down a couple times in small Cessnas.

I've been writing since I was a kid. I was always interested in creative self-expression, although that's obviously not the term I used. My friends and I used to make up poems, limericks, stories, and comic books, and we made little movies. I thought the difference between me and my friends was that *they* were playing, and I knew that this was what I was going to be doing for the rest of my life. I didn't think I was going to make a living at it, but I knew that I'd always be doing some form of child's play.

One of the things I find most refreshing about California, having moved here finally when I got out of college, was that where I grew up in the Pacific Northwest, if you asked someone what he or she did, they would define themselves by what they were actually doing at the moment. In California people define themselves by what they wish they were doing. So a waitress in Portland is a waitress. A waitress here is an actress. I thought that the optimism of people in California was often misguided and foolish, but it sure beat the bitter resignation of some of the people I left behind in Oregon.

I arrived in August of 1977, and as I was driving into town, my car broke down in the fast lane of the Hollywood Freeway. I finally got it started, and it broke down again on Sunset Boulevard. I had no money, and that was very disconcerting. The incredible range of wealth from high to low is probably as extreme here as anywhere. So there's nothing like having my little lime green Datsun stalling on Sunset Boulevard near Beverly Hills, with big fancy sports cars zooming around me and honking. In fact, whenever I go by that corner where my car stalled, it all comes back to me.

I was listening that night to a disc jockey who had just been fired, and it was his last show. He was drunk on the air, and he was berating the radio station. The next DJ up was Tom Waits, who was on as a guest DJ, and I thought, Man, if this is the way radio is, this is going to be great. That was probably the best radio I heard in twenty years.

One inspiration for my moving to Los Angeles was Frank Zappa. I grew up listening to his music, and I thought if LA was good enough for him, I should check it out. But I could never bring myself to live in a canyon like he did, because I'm afraid of fire. I edited an article once about the ecology of Los Angeles and how these brushfires are natural and normal in this region, so I've never lived in a canyon. I like living near the water because, when I moved here, I had no air-conditioning. When I'd drive out to the beach, I'd go, "My God, it's twenty degrees cooler here."

The very first job I had in Los Angeles was as a movie extra. I played a member of a lynch mob in a TV movie that was set in the 1930s. They gave me an old wool suit that was about three sizes too small, and this was in August, when it was really hot. They bused us to San Pedro, and the shooting went on and on and on. At about midnight there was no end in sight so I snuck in the back where our regular street clothes were kept. I grabbed my own clothes, and I hitchhiked back to Los Angeles.

I wanted to be a writer, and I had no idea how to go about doing that. So I looked up help-wanted ads for writers in the LA Times, and I found one for a "writer/chauffeur." I answered the ad, and got the job, which was to take and chauffeur an eighty-eight-year-old retired movie director around Los Angeles during the day and listen to his stories, and then in the evening try to turn them into his memoirs. While I was out driving him around, there was another guy at his house who was typing up the stuff from the day before.

It was quite an odd job. We would drive up into the canyon and he'd go, "There's Cary Grant's mansion. I'll never forget the parties there."

And he'd tell me some story about Greta Garbo and Jimmy Stewart and whoever. We'd drive by the same mansion the next day and he'd go, "Ah, look, Laurel and Hardy's house." So not only did Cary Grant's house turn into Laurel and Hardy's house, but he somehow had it in his mind that Laurel and Hardy lived together. I did that for a couple of months. He fired me because he didn't like the quality of my writing.

Then I started working at a little photocopy place. I hated Los Angeles so much that I started doing a little Xeroxed comic book called *Life in Hell,* which was inspired by my misadventures here. I just gave them away to friends.

I got a job working at a record store, Licorice Pizza, up on Sunset Boulevard, right across from the Whiskey A Go Go. There was a little corner of the store where they sold punk singles and little 'zines, and that's where I sold *Life in Hell.* It was just basically Binky the rabbit ranting about how awful Los Angeles was and about the smog and the trendiness and the stupidity. I am completely a black-and-white line drawing type of guy. I think I would like colors if I could do them fast, but one of the reasons why my drawing style is so simple is that I'm in a hurry to get to the next idea.

I worked for the *LA Weekly* for one issue. Then I worked for the *LA Reader,* and delivered newspapers. I showed the editor my comics and he hired me to deliver the paper. There were the publisher, the editor, and me. I delivered the paper from Glendale to Malibu—I got deliveries up to sixty thousand, from twenty-eight thousand—and the only reason we delivered to Malibu is I wanted to end up there so I could go swimming in the ocean.

I started doing the cartoon as a comic strip in 1980, and in 1984, my girlfriend at the time, Deborah Caplan, put up the money to publish my cartoons as a book, *Love Is Hell.* We sold twenty thousand copies or something like that. Pantheon picked up the book, and *Work Is Hell,* which Deborah had also published. But I wasn't making that much money. I was still scraping by.

Polly Platt, a movie producer who worked with James L. Brooks, liked my cartoons and bought some of my original art and showed it to Jim. When Gracie Films, Jim's production company, started *The Tracey Ullman Show,* they brought me on board in 1987 to do little animated shorts. Originally I was going to do the *Life in Hell* characters, but I found out shortly before the meeting, at which I was supposed to present my ideas, that whatever I did Fox would plan to own, so I thought, Well, I've got a good gig with my own characters, so I'd better make up some new ones. I made up *The Simpsons* in fifteen minutes. I named them all after my own family, and I just drew them really fast. They were pretty ugly to begin with, but they've been refined over the years.

When I first pitched *The Simpsons* to Barry Diller, when he was running Fox, he said, "So where is this Springfield located?" And I said, "Well, I think it's vaguely some mythical town in the Midwest." And he said, "Hmmm, I thought it was the San Fernando Valley." I said, "Yeah, it could be," and that's when I realized it *could* be the San Fernando Valley. The Springfield state of mind is definitely San Fernando Valley. In both Springfield and the San Fernando Valley, it seems like there's this lack of awareness that there's anyplace else to be.

I'm fascinated by novels of California decadence. I read Nathanael West's novel *The Day of the Locust* when I was a high school student, and it was a huge influence on me. I'd also tried to write my own novel, then called *Mean Kids,* which was about my struggles in high school, and it starred Bart Simpson and Homer Simpson, who was inspired by Homer Simpson from *Day of the Locust.* I once said that Bart is an anagram for "brat," but actually I just thought it was a funny word for Homer to say. It's comical because it sounds like barking.

I look at Los Angeles and say, If you're doing something that's unique to this city or you work in some element of the entertainment industry, then I can understand living here. But if you're a dentist or fix cars or something—boy, somewhere else in the country would be much better. It's too dirty here. Too smoggy.

There's also a level of menace here. When I lived in Venice years ago, I'd gone out for dinner on New Year's Eve to a really fancy restaurant, and when I came out of the restaurant at about midnight, the valet parking people were wearing metal salad bowls on their heads because there was so much gunfire. They wouldn't even get my car. They gave me the keys, pointed down the block, and said, "You don't have to pay. We're not going out there." It's better now, but you know what? It's not even so much that you're actually in danger. It's just the possibility of it.

Part of my work is just observations about life and then part of it is taking my memory of what television meant as a little kid, and how boring it was, and how glued to the TV set I remained because there was so little of interest that you really wanted to hang on for the stuff that was any good. So, yeah, I watched way too much TV. In fact sometimes I think that one of the reasons why I went into television is to justify all those wasted hours watching TV. I can say it was research.

I was a big fan of *Leave It to Beaver* and *Ozzie and Harriet*—a lot of those family sitcoms. I would say that *The Simpsons* is more inspired by *Ozzie and Harriet* than just about anything else. A little bit by *Dennis the Menace,* but only because I was so disappointed. When I heard that [the cartoon strip] *Dennis the Menace* was going to be on the air, I was thrilled that there was going to be a sitcom about a kid who was a menace. But after he comes out animated as a little cyclone, it turns out to be this very namby-pamby Jay North, who didn't really do anything bad at all. So I thought, When I grow up, I'm going to do my own TV show, and there's going to be a kid who really *is* a menace.

I've always thought that *The Simpsons* was a celebration of America.

And what made it work for me was that we acknowledge the contradictions, the absurdities, the authoritarianism that are rampant in our culture, and I think that people really resonate with that attitude. A lot of people think, Boy, if I could have my own TV show, I would do it like this or that. I got to do it.

bill IRWIN

Born in Santa Monica, California, in 1950, Bill Irwin was raised first in Oklahoma, then back in California. He studied at UCLA and at the California Institute of the Arts in suburban Los Angeles, and in San Francisco performed on street corners as well as with the Pickle Family Circus and the Oberlin Dance Collective. Whether working with his frequent partner, David Shiner, or alone onstage, he incorporates the spirit of such great film clowns as Buster Keaton, Charlie Chaplin, and Harold Lloyd, who also came to California. Onstage, his well-honed physical comedy has resulted in such theatrical successes as *The Regard of Flight, Largely New York,* and *Fool Moon.* The first active performing artist to receive a five-year MacArthur "genius" fellowship, the actor and clown lives in New York, where he works in theater, film, and television.

I can't remember not thinking and strategizing like a clown. When I was seven or eight, I would baby-sit my sister, and I knew I could keep her from crying if I kept falling down on the bed. A bed, of course, was much easier to fall down on than a stage floor. But the early kernel of a clown idea was there—you're trying to get up on the bed, you confront the endless Sisyphean dilemma of not making it, and each time you think you're going to make it, you miss and smash down on your face. She'd stay with it as long as I would.

When I was a student at CalArts, I would perform in San Francisco on weekends. I was enamored of a girl in San Francisco, and I found myself commuting. I'd go to school all week, then hitchhike to the Burbank airport, count out quarters for the sixteen-dollar one-way flight, and make enough money performing in the street to eat and to fly back and forth. That was my college job for a while, and I can remember the exhilaration of feeling I was making a living at what I wanted to do.

Herb Blau, who ran the theater school at CalArts, went to Oberlin College in Ohio, and I left the brilliant sunshine to go work with him there. In Ohio we did this very intense, elitist, avant-garde work, and for something to do other than that, I'd go to the library and read about famous clowns. I was looking backward to really popular forms. I had a desire for information and craft, so when our company disbanded, I seized the opportunity to go to the Ringling Bros. and Barnum & Bailey Clown College in Florida for ten weeks—ten intense weeks.

Immediately upon finishing I went back to San Francisco. I learned to eat fire because it was a kind of impressive thing around which you could build a comic monologue. My ex-wife, Kimi Okada, and I did a brick-breaking act where she would break a brick on my stomach with a hammer or vice versa. It's an old carny trick—the brick absorbs the blow as long as you hit in the right place, and your stomach muscles are tight. That and the fire-eating were flashy skills which were audience catching and which kept me out of the dreaded stand-up comedy milieu, where I probably would have been too scared to go anyway. I was essentially doing stand-up comedy, just built around spectacle.

I was casting about for something to do, and I saw this ad in the paper. I can remember every word: "Wanted: jugglers, tumblers, equi-librists for formation of new circus." I called Larry Pisoni, who had placed the ad, and I could hear his heart sinking when he talked to me because he'd talked to nothing but clowns. But we got together, and I auditioned. I was practicing the morning before at a friend's apartment, and I broke a plastic plate, a precious prop, and I didn't think it boded well. But I did become a founding member of the Pickle Family Circus.

The Pickle Family was an outdoor show. We played under the sky, which worked 85 percent of the time. There was a big drought in 1977, and we had a great summer. Then in '78, it did all the raining it hadn't done the year before, which made us realize we had been living on illusion and borrowed time. But my memory is always of cloudless sky.

I also worked with the Oberlin Dance Collective. It was a group of Eastern collegiate types who transplanted themselves to San Francisco for lots of different reasons, sound and unsound, and I was blessedly lucky to be able to work within the scene that they helped to create for themselves. Not unlike the Pickle Family, they were forever pioneering their own spaces. I painted more floors and redid more walls in those years than I ever had or have since. It didn't create a huge high-profile performance opportunity, and in many ways I wasn't ready for that. We were performance artists and could do whatever we brought in that night. That was the primary place I got to experiment with taking popular entertainment forms and working with them in contemporary theater pieces.

That's something that California either nurtures or tolerates. For me one of the things that happened in California before I made the move here to New York was a mixing, almost like a kid's chemistry set. Just put things in a beaker and mix—a circus aesthetic with an avant-garde aesthetic. The solo performer as poet or artist. Jerzy Grotowski's notion of stripping theater back to its essentials: a performer, a bare space. I took lots of different kinds of work, and I like to think I was both celebrating their power and satirizing their pomposity.

When you're finally ready to create a piece of performance, the audience is the other end of the guitar string. That's one of the parts of the physical comedy craft that's particular unto it. If you go back far enough, tragic acting, radio announcing, and physical clowning are essentially the same. They're all basic acts of performance, but turn out to be quite different in craft. The relationship to the audience is very different for a clown and for an actor, and woe unto us if we forget which craft we should be calling on.

The clown is listening to and including the audience in a different way than the actor is, I think. *Waiting for Godot,* for example, is a play that calls upon a clown's craft, but I don't think it is one in which you include the audience. If I'm onstage with David Shiner in *Fool Moon* and somebody in the third row sneezes, and it's loud and everyone hears it, if it's a place where I can do so, I'm almost irresponsible if I don't acknowledge the sneeze. I don't have to look at David or him at me. He'll pretend to wipe off his sleeve, and I'll offer a handkerchief. That's part of the story being told. But when you're doing *Godot,* even at its most comic, and even though the playwright plays with that idea by having the characters look at the audience, if you stop in the middle and acknowledge the sneeze, it may be a big laugh, but I don't think it's a proper telling of the story for that play. (I know because I've tried it.)

My sister and brother and I watched a lot of animated stuff on television, for better and for worse. I can only speculate as to what sense of movement reality I was drinking up from all those creatures whose legs could stretch forward as they walked. You wonder how much easier it would have been to be a physical comic before people saw animated creatures who can do anything. I remember Marcel Marceau being described to me as a human cartoon, and it was a profound compliment. Visually and narratively, the silent film comedians and all the Disney animation that came into our lives have changed people's perceptions and expectations of physical comedy.

Some days I think, How lucky of me to have been there, at CalArts, learning these things. Other days I think it bolstered my smorgasbord dilettantism. I'm sure it was both. I'm very glad for tai chi training and hope to go back to it as a middle-aged performer. To do tai chi outdoors for an hour, then work on text by Brecht, was a great gift. But it also is part of a California tendency that sometimes leaves artists wondering whether they've really followed any one thing as far as they ought to.

Chaplin, born in the slums of England, toured the world as a comic and ended up in California, where he did his great work. Keaton, same thing. Born near Omaha, he toured the world, encountered film in New York, but did his greatest work on the West Coast. I had to leave California because so far, anyway, my main work has been in the theater, which is an indoor place and is built on bodies being willing to mass together and come in out of the outdoors. Ironically, I've toured to California and been paid nicely to perform in California, but only because the show emanated from New York.

My son is eight now, and I watch him with a mixture of wonder and jealousy. He moves with an abandon I sort of remember but don't have anymore. I was looking at a picture of him running on the beach near where his grandparents live, in Northern California, and I was struck with the feeling of what a beautiful physical creature he is and how beautifully situated this moment is on the beach in California. I will always think of myself as a Californian.

john RECHY

El Paso–born and raised, writer John Rechy spoke only Spanish until he started school. His first book was *City of Night*, a semi-autobiographical story of a gay hustler that began as a letter to a friend, stayed on bestseller lists for more than six months, sold more than a million copies, and has been in print since its 1963 publication. There have been twelve books now, three plays, nearly two dozen short stories, and as many articles, essays, and book reviews. Once called "the country's most important author on homosexual life in America" by the *New York Times*, the so-called sexual outlaw in 1997 received the PEN Center USA West Lifetime Achievement Award. He has been an adjunct professor in creative writing at the University of Southern California since 1983.

⌐⌐

I was born into memories of loss. My grandfather, who had come from Scotland to Mexico, was Porfirio Díaz's personal physician, and my father was a child prodigy who played piano at Díaz's palace. His family fled to El Paso, Texas, during the Mexican Revolution, and, with the Depression, my father's high social and artistic status declined.

I started writing when I was seven or eight, and I did comic strips first. But they were very literary comic strips. Every one was called "Long Ago." The ladies always had long, full skirts, and the gentlemen always had plumy hats. I saw a lot of movies, including *Marie*

Antoinette, with Norma Shearer and Tyrone Power, and my very first novel was about Marie Antoinette. There I was, a Mexican kid living in pretty bad poverty, writing a sympathetic novel about Marie Antoinette.

Probably I was just trying to get out into my imagination and escape my life. I was the youngest of five children, and our lives were so very, very poor. My father's decline—psychological, financial, and creative—had been devastating, and my mother, who had been a great beauty, had some money and all of it was gone. All that remained were the *attitudes* of money. My mother was teaching us how to signal the servants that we wouldn't have seconds when we didn't have firsts.

When I got out of the army, I set out for New York. I spent more than a year there, living mostly on Times Square. I was writing short stories, but by then I was so involved in another kind of performance, the street performance, that even in my own mind I had to separate it. So I never showed anyone the writing.

I first came out here to visit my beloved sister, Olga. I was in my early twenties, and I don't know that I knew anything about California. I landed in downtown Los Angeles with that feeling of fear and exhilaration that I remember so well. I just walked a few blocks, and I was in Pershing Square.

I was overwhelmed by the sensuality, the eroticism, and the possible display of flesh, which I would soon join. When I was in that scene of abundant sensuality, there was no idea of writing about it; the times didn't nurture that. I wasn't in the closet about my sexual life, but I was in the closet about the writing. *City of Night* finally brought together the writing and the activity that I had so kept apart.

My body changed in Los Angeles. I came here with a New York body—I was slender, very cute, very streety. Then here were the spill of the sun, the emphasis on bodies, the possibility of wearing no shirt. I was the first one to walk Hollywood Boulevard without a shirt and with a leather jacket open. I paved the way for the scoop shirts that are international now—I used to get ordinary shirts, put them in hot water, pull them down so that they had a low cut, then put them in cold water so they shrank.

I love the rampant, unabashed narcissism and exhibitionism in Los Angeles, the concern with physicality, bodies, flesh, glamour—even the homeless have tans. I think that's one of the reasons that people put down Los Angeles and ridicule it. It's a kind of envy of beauty. I swear it is.

But along with the emphasis on physicality, there's a deep, equally exhibitionistic soulfulness, a sort of promiscuous spirituality. We have every religion, every cult, every sect here. All those factors create a unique artistic climate that is further influenced by the very vastness of the city. Los Angeles doesn't have one singular identity, but many distinctive ones—a sort of grand schizophrenia of diverse personalities. Our artists can't be categorized into one "school."

I hate Los Angeles being called "la-la land." It's not a stupid city; it's a very profound city. I think of it very much in terms of a grand Grecian city, where all occurrences are possible. You're aware of fate swirling about you every time you get on the freeway. You're in a current that is like nothing else. Every car, potentially lethal, is dashing about, and then at night, when traffic gets slowed and you look at the opposite lane, you see this whole row of ruby red lights, halted. It's quite dazzling. The freeway arcs, those swirls, those entanglements, those architectural creations are really statuary, and it's amazing that they're so terribly dangerous.

There's here in Los Angeles a fascination with disasters. We dance before the void both in challenge and acknowledgment. I think that's a very profound attitude that runs as an undercurrent among artists, and certainly myself. A kind of acknowledgment that this is the last frontier. This is where the sun sets. As the sun moves to the west, all the energies of the country, bright and dark, gather here before that last stop. But it's a defiance of the setting sun, too. We idolize the sun, but accept its inevitability. It *will* set.

It's that edginess. The floods may come, the earthquakes may shake us, the fires . . . There's terror, sure. But there's also an exuberance in survival. People go ahead and build their homes right on the edge. We write about it even while we're terrified of the actuality. We have so many catastrophes, and they're almost gleefully announced. You turn on the news and here comes this very cheerful person, telling us that the city was just about wiped out or another upbeat declaration of doom. I think that permeates the city.

If you look at it, Southern California is shaped somewhat like a coffin, with its headquarters in glamorous Forest Lawn, where I hope to be buried. I love Forest Lawn. I love the whole splash of it. It's the acknowledgment of death and endings but also the challenge to live right with it. I think that one can extrapolate that as a current in Los Angeles.

The other headquarters is Hollywood. There's not an artist who hasn't been influenced profoundly by movies. I certainly have. My book *Bodies and Souls,* which is about Los Angeles, replicates scenes from my favorite movies. I don't know that there would be one person, one writer, one painter, who would not be forever inspired by the end of part one of the movie *Gone With the Wind,* that ode to fakery and drama when Scarlett swears never to be hungry again. I pay homage to that scene—and to the movies—all the time.

Forest Lawn and Hollywood actually resemble each other. They're polarities—two powerful currents. One is the acknowledgment of death, and the other is the defiance of it. Each is as extravagant as the other in its way.

The vocabulary of stardom, if it does not originate with Hollywood, thrives with Hollywood. By extension it invites one to be what I feel one should always be—the star of one's own life. I think there are more people in Los Angeles who play their lives like stars than there are anywhere else. I commend that, because how terrible to be a supporting player in one's own life. Some people live as if they're walk-ons, but you must never fade in. We could take lessons from the thirties and forties and fifties. Stars looked like stars. They dressed in a certain way, moved in a certain way, and talked in a certain way.

Los Angeles is also the headquarters of bodybuilding. Bodybuilding really is an assault on the body, which is why it's called progressive resistance. Get your mind going with metaphors: progressive resistance—what is life but that? Bodybuilding is doing unnatural motions, motions that the body doesn't ordinarily do, see? In some kind of miraculous way the body, if you increase the resistance, knows that it is under assault, and to meet that challenge becomes stronger and grows muscles. You do increasingly more repetitions, lift heavier weights, break down in order to create. Break down, create, break down, create, always keeping the creation ahead of the breakdown. Otherwise, of course, the body will decline.

It's not unlike the structure that one brings to a novel, which you also want to be admired. Bodybuilding is very exhilarating, and I hope I'll continue that forever. When I'm hurt—for example, I have a bad shoulder—I have to lay off every now and then. I'm very unhappy, actually depressed, because then I think, The body is now in decline. The writing is the same. This will be my twelfth book, but can I do another one?

A large number of my books—among them *Bodies and Souls, The Miraculous Day of Amalia Gómez, Numbers*—are set in Los Angeles. I constantly move more toward metaphor, and this is a city that is rife with metaphoric elements. Just the name Los Angeles—"the angels." I refer to it as "the city of lost angels" very, very often. *The Coming of the Night* is set one day in Los Angeles during a Santa Ana, and I use the Santa Ana winds as a metaphor for a violence that is invading the city.

Everything is grand in Los Angeles. The winds are like no other. They can push heat into even cold weather, and they make the sky glow in a very eerie orange way. Gay cruising becomes quite exaggerated during that particular time, and I think there's truth to the legend of the sexual devil winds. They stir the blood, and so sexuality runs rampant, but so, alas, does violence. The moment you step into them, you're enveloped by this unique sense of everything astir. They are part of the array of what makes Los Angeles so spectacular and so much the city of daily apocalypse.

joan **LA BARBARA**

Vocalist and composer Joan La Barbara bends, extends, and ex-
plores the voice the way other musicians experiment with their
instruments. Called "one of the great vocal virtuosos of our
time" by the *San Francisco Examiner,* she has worked with such
contemporary musical masters as John Cage, Philip Glass, Steve
Reich, and her husband, Morton Subotnick, as well as in collab-
orations with the artist Judy Chicago, the choreographer Bella
Lewitzky, and the fashion designer Holly Harp. On the faculty of
California Institute of the Arts from 1981 to 1986, she com-
poses and performs her own work here and abroad. She was
born in 1947 in Philadelphia, and currently lives with her family
in Santa Fe, New Mexico, and New York.

I started piano lessons when I was four, and one of my early teachers
was the composer Louise Christine Rebe. At an early age I came into
contact with a woman who was not only teaching piano but also happened to be a published composer.

Although I studied piano for a number of years and was an accom-
panist for my high school orchestra, at a certain point I started to get
very nervous about playing. My hands would get kind of cold and
clammy, and I was afraid they'd slip off the keys. But singing was very
easy for me. I loved singing and being onstage. So when I was around
fifteen, I switched my focus to the voice and began to take private

STATE OF THE ARTS

306

STATE OF THE ARTS

lessons. I was also in a folk-music group with three friends from high school.

At Syracuse University I studied traditional Western classical voice. My junior year there, one of the composition teachers had a Moog synthesizer I was fooling around with, and I became curious about what I could do with electronic machinery. I was also going then to Tanglewood in the summers, and began to get much more exposure to contemporary music. I saw instrumentalists experimenting with their instruments, and I began to be curious about what the voice could do.

Anxious to get my career going, I transferred to NYU for my senior year. I was still studying traditional classical music, but I took private lessons with Marion Szekely Freschl, a teacher from Juilliard. As a student in Hungary, she had been friends with Bartók, and she encouraged me to work with composers, saying it's so hard for them to write for the voice because they don't understand the instrument. Although two of my earlier teachers had also done so—Helen Boatwright at Syracuse had done first performances of Hindemith, and Phyllis Curtin at Tanglewood had done Ligeti premieres—Freschl was the first to really push me in the direction of working with composers.

I started working with some jazz musicians. I began to imitate things like the sounds of other instruments and to put myself in positions where hopefully a surprising vocal sound would come out. I began to think about composing.

Around the same time I did a number of commercials, mostly for composer Michael Sahl, including one for a Japanese perfume where I was hired to imitate the sound of the Japanese voice. They weren't quite sure what they wanted, so they also had me imitating the sound of a harp imitating the sound of a Japanese koto. We finally came up with something that sounded a little like a Japanese Astrud Gilberto.

I also started working with Steve Reich when he was developing his piece *Drumming*. I wound up imitating the sound of a marimba. We did the premiere at Town Hall in New York and, not long after, in the galleries of the Los Angeles County Museum of Art. I found California a very open, inviting, and enthusiastic place as far as contemporary music was concerned. I wanted to come back and investigate it a little bit more.

I relate California to electronic music and experimentation. In 1974 I did my first solo concerts in New York of my compositions, and in '76 I brought those concerts to California. One of the pieces was *Vocal Extensions,* which was essentially a live improvisation using electronics almost as a secondary performer, and the recording of my performance at the University Art Museum in Berkeley became my first LP.

I was working with John Cage around that time. He was asked to do concerts at California Institute of the Arts, and he agreed if he could bring me. I performed the "Solo for Voice 45" from his *Song Books,* with twenty pianos playing his *Winter Music* in the main gallery at CalArts. I felt very positively about CalArts, and a few years later was back to teach a workshop on extended vocal techniques and experimental voice.

Being at CalArts was very much what I had suspected it would be. It was a very open kind of situation. I did a piece with some of the members of the class, which was called *As Lightning Comes, in Flashes,* in 1981. Some of the performers were in the trees, others on the grassy courtyard. There were costume pieces that the dancers gradually removed and left behind as a kind of reminder of what the performance was. One of the intriguing things about performance is that it happens in real time and disappears, and all you have is the memory or the tape of it. This was a way to leave a physical remnant behind.

A lot of the inspiration that I took from California had to do with the rolling hills, the openness of the landscape, the air, the freedom, the vegetation, even. The outdoor pieces were works that I would not have done if I hadn't been in California. And it wasn't just the inspiration of the landscape and the area, but also having the opportunity to work with people who were willing to try things out and do that kind of experimental work.

One sees that with the gamelan groups that have sprung up around the West Coast. When one thinks of California, one thinks of Harry Partch and John Cage—the experimentalists, the inventors, the rugged individualists.

When you think of New York and the East Coast, everything is so serious. There's such a vested interest in East Coast professors having their students win prizes. On the West Coast there's not such a support system. You almost have to do it yourself: Make your own career and declare who you are and what you're into and construct the scene. You see a lot more people starting up concert series and otherwise not being afraid to try things out and generate a world for themselves.

I still think of myself as from New York. But I know that a lot of the work I did would not have been done if I had stayed in New York. First of all the access to electronics and studio equipment was much greater in California. I'm giving you mixed answers, but that's who I am. One part of me will always be in New York, and another part has strong ties to California.

I do think the air there has a positive effect on the voice. I lived in Santa Monica, where the air comes right off the ocean so there's moisture in it. The moisture makes the voice a much more fluid, flexible, relaxed instrument. In Santa Fe it's so dry that one is constantly drinking water to try to relubricate the throat.

Recently I've started to do some vocal work on commercial films, and that is certainly part of the Southern California scene. I did the voice for the alien newborn in *Alien Resurrection,* where I was called upon to create an unearthly sound that was quasi human but otherworldly. Earlier I had created an angel voice for the film *Date with an Angel,* and last year my voice was used on the sound score of *I Still Know What You Did Last Summer* to heighten the tension and scariness of that film.

I love doing film work. I love being on a soundstage and talking to

the director and sound designer about what sound they want and what
reaction they want from the audience hearing the sound. I'm putting
into play my experience in improvising, composing, singing, and even
acting. It's very different from sitting in my studio and generating all
the ideas out of my head.

bill **VIOLA**

Bill Viola was born in 1951 in Queens, New York, learned to make videos at Syracuse University, and in 1981 brought his still-new art form to California. Drawing images and narrative largely from his own experiences and thoughts about spirituality, life, and death, he records the human heart and scream, the bird in flight or the animal in decay, water that begins in the eye or fills huge pools. He has been an artist-in-residence at WNET-TV in New York; Sony Corporation's Atsugi Laboratories in Atsugi, Japan; and the San Diego Zoo; and speaks of being influenced by Persian poets, Taoism, Sufism, Zen Buddhism, and mysticism. The first video artist to have major exhibitions at the Los Angeles County Museum of Art as well as New York's Museum of Modern Art, he is a regular participant in the Whitney Museum of American Art's Biennial and has been called by that institution "the leading video artist on the international scene." He lives with his family on a quiet residential street in Long Beach, within an hour's drive of Los Angeles and a mile from the Long Beach Museum of Art.

O n my first trip to California in the seventies, I went to Death Valley. We drove down into the valley floor to camp, and I remember watching the dawn rise. Lying on my back looking up, I'd never seen light like that in my life.

It was revelation after revelation on things I had been thinking and reading about. How we perceive space. How the body deals with scale, perception, and sound. It changed my life, and the experience is still buried down there in everything I do.

The desert is so empty. I'd never seen emptiness, growing up in New York, and it was liberating my senses. There I was, this kid from New York, going, What is this? Where are we? What planet is this? It was the most magical thing I'd ever seen.

I grew up in Flushing, Queens, in a neighborhood that looked like something out of the movie *West Side Story*. Tall cyclone fences. Brick buildings with fire escapes. Concrete schoolyards. No trees.

There was a real mix of people—Jews, blacks, Cubans, Poles, Italians—with lots of kids around. Most of us couldn't afford to go on vacation so we all just hung around the schoolyard playing stickball and waiting for the ice-cream truck to come by every afternoon at four. I remember the soles of my sneakers getting soft, actually, on some of the hot days.

My mother likes to tell how I drew a boat when I was three, and I've been an artist for as long as I can remember. I was always the class artist in grade school, getting perks even when I was eight years old. The principal would ask me to draw a winter scene or something, and I would always be excused from class. Like today I'm excused from a real job.

I grew up with TV, and the advantage of when I grew up was, of course, that the TV I saw is not the TV of today. They didn't have enough content to put on the air, so they were running Humphrey Bogart movies, *King Kong,* and all these great old black-and-white movies. Crazy young jazz nuts were doing these wild things with animation. That's what I saw on TV.

My first video experience, which is an important line in my bio, was as captain of the TV Squad at P.S. 20 in Queens, when I was around nine. In those days public TV was truly educational TV. University professors and teachers taught Spanish, French, physics, or basic math on

TV, and some of those programs were incorporated into the curriculum for grade-school kids.

They needed people to wheel this huge TV into the classrooms and plug it in, and I volunteered for what they called the TV Squad. They kept all the equipment in the TV Squad room, and we used to hang around there. We'd tune the TV to different off-channels so you'd get all these distorted faces and stuff. It was a little game we played.

When I was twelve or thirteen, my dad had an eight-millimeter movie camera, and I made a few films fooling around with it. He worked at Pan Am as a flight attendant, and they also had all this audiovisual equipment he could check out. He would bring home this big, open-reel audiotape recorder, and I'd make my own radio programs.

All this personal-recording media really has to be distinguished from television and radio, which were one-way transmission coming into your home. It's totally different to have a camcorder or a VCR or an audio recorder, because you actually record your own stuff. That was happening for the first time with my generation.

I wanted to go to Rhode Island School of Design or one of those famous specialized art schools, but my father thought I should go to an art school in the context of a larger university environment. I went to Syracuse University, and it ended up being the greatest thing that happened to me, that decision, because that's where I got into video. I would never have gotten into video had I gone to one of the smaller art schools, because they didn't catch on to video until after I had graduated.

It wasn't artists who were doing this stuff at that time. It was a mix of people from all different backgrounds. Video came out of the communication and journalism school, the TV and radio departments, and the student union at Syracuse.

I spent a year teaching after I graduated so I could continue to work in the media center. I could never afford to buy any of that equipment myself, and I was able to continue my work on my own schedule. I also had a job at the local art museum in Syracuse as a video and technical installer working with Nam June Paik and other artists.

I moved to Florence after college. I was getting known as a good technical guy who could help artists realize their projects in video. I had a job as a video technician at Art / Tapes / 22, one of the early video art studios in Europe.

After Florence I went right back to New York again. If you rewind back to the seventies, you didn't really have an option as an artist to go anywhere but New York. Even the European artists were moving to New York. It was the happening place.

Then, in the early eighties, I remember talking to a young artist there who said he was moving to LA, and my jaw dropped. My generation didn't move to LA. You moved from LA to New York. You moved from Cleveland to New York. You moved *from* anywhere, but you were going *to* New York. That's when I thought, Whoa, something's different. Something changed.

There was a cultural movement in the 1980s in California that is extremely significant in art and cultural history in America. Museums and galleries were opening. The 1984 Olympic Arts Festival brought important performing groups from Europe, and LA felt like a unified city.

These West Coast artists—Bruce Nauman, Jim Turrell, Robert Irwin, John Baldessari—were tremendously influential for me and others. West Coast art now had come out of the closet and was acknowledged. California became a place you came to. It pales in comparison to people uprooting families and coming over here at the turn of the century, but our move to California was also a form of immigration.

I'd actually been interested in California since I was a kid. My parents had gotten me a Venus Paradise colored pencil set, and there was a whole series of color-by-number California landscapes. The giant redwood trees were amazing, and these do-it-yourself drawings weren't like taking photos. You spend time when you're coloring them in by numbers, so you can think about them.

My first solo show was at the DeSaisset Art Gallery in Santa Clara, California, in 1973, and I'd been in Los Angeles in the mid-seventies performing experimental music with David Tudor's music group. I'd come out from New York for a little West Coast tour every year and a half or so, going to video art centers at UC, San Diego; the Long Beach Museum of Art; CalArts; maybe San Francisco and Seattle.

When I left New York in 1980 with a fellowship to go to Japan for a year, my wife and collaborator, Kira, and I packed up knowing we weren't going to be coming back. I didn't come with a job, but I had a couple of shows here and we both figured, Let's try living on the West Coast.

We opted for Long Beach because I'd known it from my experience with the Long Beach Museum. The video scene was active here, and the museum was having regular screening programs. Artists were coming to make and show pieces. They had a great collection and they still do, one of the best west of the Mississippi.

Long Beach was also not LA. It's a lot like LA, but it just doesn't have an edge to it. You come down here and you sort of chill out. You calm down. It ended up being a good place to raise kids, too, but I didn't think of it in those terms then.

It was a quiet town, and after Tokyo and New York, I didn't want to live in a big city anymore. I didn't want to get a loft in downtown Los Angeles and pretend I'm in New York. I don't want to just see concrete, thank you. I want a garden.

In fact, one of the first things we did after we rented a little bunga-
low here was make this huge vegetable garden in the back and start
growing giant Goodyear blimp–size zucchinis. There I was with my little hoe, and I thought, If my friends in New York could see me now.

After Japan it was essential that I break with that frenetic pace. We
had a room behind the garage that I filled with all my books, and I sat
there just reading and studying.

Aldous Huxley called LA a city for writers—you could be totally isolated—and I think that suited the recluse part of me, which has always
been there. I need solitude to work, and I could just disappear for long
periods of time here.

Nearly all the installations I did came out of that little room behind
the garage. In a twelve-by-fifteen-foot room I was making thirty-by-
forty-foot video installations. I was working them out on graph paper
and sending off notes on how big to make the space and where to build
walls. I didn't see them for the first time until I actually went to the
museum to install them, because I never had a studio or anyplace to set
them up.

We're now in my little private domain, and it has the quietness that I
need. In New York I felt even if I had the doors and windows shut, I
was surrounded by millions of people. You just walked out on the
street, and there was something always going on. In New York it's an
aggressive act to not engage, to not involve with people, to not go out
and see the latest thing. In LA it's an aggressive act to go out and connect with people. It's completely the opposite. You have to make an
effort and get on a freeway to drive somewhere.

I do, of course, have that contrast between being in a quiet environment like this, then getting on a plane for a European capital somewhere where I'm right in the middle of the art scene, having dinner
with amazing people, and seeing great works in great museums. I prob-

ably wouldn't have ended up staying here if I didn't have that range of experiences.

I also thought I could be a little bit out of the way but still connected. I wasn't interested in Hollywood, but all of a sudden I'm here, and I realize there are all these resources. Videotape houses have people on beepers, and if you run out of tape at two in the morning, you just make a phone call, and within an hour some guy's at your door with extra tape. That's pretty neat. I rented a zebra once for a project. I don't think I could do that in New York.

If I want green grass, sunny skies, and people in T-shirts, I can shoot that any time of year. If I want snow, I just drive up to the San Bernardino Mountains in wintertime. That's why Hollywood's here.

The presence of nature here is very real. Earthquakes, for instance, are very mystical. So much of our stability in life is rooted in the earth, and the very foundation of physical existence, which is not supposed to move, moves here. You feel like you're still in this creative process as far as the earth goes, and then you add to that the brushfires and the floods.

Other than the occasional hurricane in New York, it's mostly man-made disasters—power outages and stuff. But floods washing away a trailer park? In the middle of a major city, a wall of fire just rolling down the hills and wiping out a whole neighborhood? That's pretty astounding.

You read that the grasses and shrubs that grow on the hillsides surrounding LA need fire in order to germinate and survive. All of a sudden you realize they were here way before we were, and they'll be here long after we're gone.

john **BALDESSARI**

Once called "the dean of West Coast conceptualism," artist and teacher John Baldessari uses photographs and words the way other artists use paints. Perhaps best known for his combined images from films, newspapers, and other sources, he has focused on conceptual art since burning all his paintings in 1969 at a San Diego crematorium. Born in National City, near San Diego, in 1931, he has been based in California most of his life and has been on the art faculty of the University of California, San Diego, the California Institute of the Arts, and UCLA. He is six feet seven inches tall, with a white beard and a contagious laugh. Continually on the road, he is as well known abroad as at home and in 1996 won Austria's Oskar Kokoschka Prize. He lives and works in Santa Monica, California.

M y parents were both immigrants. My father was from the Southern Tyrol and an Austrian citizen but spoke Italian and German. My mother was from Denmark, and my sister and I could never quite figure out how they met in the States.

Reading was important to me. There was a local library, and I spent most of my days there, checking out the maximum number of books. My mother would get novels sent to her from Denmark, and I can remember slicing open the pages for her. She played piano, and there was a lot of music in the house. Because of her I took piano and drawing lessons.

My father was basically the provider. He had a salvage business tearing down houses and, with those materials, building other houses. He wasted nothing and recycled everything. He had bins for steel, iron, brass, copper. I had to take nails out of lumber and straighten the nails and take apart faucets to clean and paint them, so I have this feeling for things like that.

Somehow I got a book on chemistry for photography, and I started mixing up my own developers. I had to have something to develop, of course, so I started taking pictures. My father fixed up a darkroom for me, and I was developing photographs at three o'clock in the morning. Probably I got interested in photography that way, and I remember going to the library and looking at camera and photographic journals.

I always felt different. I always had a sense that somehow I wasn't really American in some way. My father died at ninety still speaking broken English. But I became very aware of communication. I was trying to make myself clear to my father, talking in as clear sentences as possible and saying things in an understandable way.

As I began to teach, I could see the same need. But I already had been primed for it. And as I continued with teaching and art, I began to see how they both shared the same problem of communication. I saw how you could obfuscate, be crystal clear, or do anything in-between. You could play your audience like a musical instrument.

After I graduated from San Diego State, I felt I couldn't just go out in the world and call myself an artist, because I didn't know what an artist was. I began teaching high school and junior high school until at a certain point, I wanted to have more time to paint.

I got a call to teach at a California Youth Authority camp in the mountains behind San Diego. It was an honor camp, no walls. One of the kids there asked me to open up the arts-and-crafts room at night so they could work. I made a deal with them: If they would cool it in class and pay attention, I would open up the classrooms at night. It worked like a charm.

I had an epiphany when I saw that these kids cared more about art than I did at the time. My idea of art then was just some sort of masturbatory activity that didn't help anybody out in the world at all. I had this sort of social conscience, I suppose, and I thought here are these kids who really value art for some reason. So I figured my gifts are in art and I'll just work in art, and maybe somewhere along the line I'll figure it all out. I can't say that I have, but at least it did kickstart me.

I found a summer workshop being taught by Rico Lebrun, who was pretty well known, and I went up to UCLA for the summer to study with him. He would come by and stare at what I was doing, and when a visitor would come in, they would both stare. He devoted about half of his last lecture to talking about my work and afterward he took me aside and said, "You really ought to be an artist."

Nobody had ever said that to me before. I wondered, How do you do that? He suggested I move to Los Angeles and study at the Jepson Art Institute—which later became the Otis Art Institute—which I did. I tried painting for a while there, but somehow things just didn't click in for me, and I moved back down to San Diego. My father owned some old buildings, including a Laundromat that had some room in back and that he couldn't seem to rent out.

That room became my first studio. It was at the corner of Main and First Streets, an all-American address. No windows. I set up shop and just started painting. I was teaching part-time to support myself, and I found a few other artists, the avant-garde, such as it was, and we all sort of hung out together.

In the late sixties, it became clear to me that somehow I was on some wrong track defining art as painting and painting as art, and that what I was doing wasn't painting. I wanted to do something symbolic and in 1969 I had this idea—God, now it all comes back—that some pigments come out of the earth and are made into paint on your canvas. I would just continue that circle by burning them and sending the paintings back into the earth again. Even now it sounds very strange, but it made sense to me. I found a crematorium that would do it after hours.

My total output was nine and a half boxes of ashes. I still have them. I put some of the ashes in an urn that was shaped like a book, and it became part of the first conceptual art show, which was at the Jewish Museum in New York around that time.

I was doing text and photo paintings and paintings solely with text. The text paintings were things culled from my reading. I had ignored photography for a long time, thinking it was a high school infatuation, but now I had this idea that I would do visual note taking, just like I was taking notes of books. I would go out with my camera and take photographs of things that might be information for my paintings. Then I got another epiphany. I asked myself, Why do I have to translate all of this information into painting? Why can't it be art in itself?

Now it's not such an interesting idea but that was a little bit heretical, I suppose, at the time. You have to remember that I was still in National City, and I had given up all hope of ever getting out into the world. I took shots randomly out of my car window, which I combined with notation of the street address done by a sign painter. The photographs could have been done by somebody else, but I did them because I didn't have any money then to hire anybody.

I remember at the time taking these canvases with text and photos around to Los Angeles galleries and just getting blank stares. The only sympathy I got, although he was also a little bit baffled, was from dealer Nicholas Wilder who introduced me to the New York dealer Richard Bellamy. Bellamy also said he didn't quite know what I was about, but he introduced me to other artists in New York, and I found I didn't feel so crazy.

Really, I didn't feel so crazy anyway because I didn't care. I was just going to teach high school and do what I did and have a family. I was having fun, and since I didn't have to please anybody, I thought, Well, why not do this stuff? I'm going to enjoy doing it. I think that's a great lesson—not to care.

I was exploring all kinds of ways to appropriate images from other sources: shooting things randomly off the TV or with an automatic timer. Having a camera outside my studio. Anything where my own selection process wouldn't come into play. I began to shoot things out of magazines and books, imagery that wasn't meant to be art. I was probably trying to figure out why some things are art and other things are not.

I began using movie stills. I would go into processing houses and rummage through their Dumpsters for any print rejects. Then I found this bookstore out in Burbank that sold movie stills that came from movies you'd never even heard about. They had them in these big cardboard boxes for ten cents each. So I began spending hours going through these things and pulling out images I thought somehow might be interesting. It was only as a by-product that they were from movies. That wasn't the intention.

I usually seem to be incapable of using a single image. I always seem to have what I call "colliding images." The best metaphor I can think of is how a writer puts words together. A writer could use single words, but it's more fun to put two words together or even three or four. They're both units of a language, and I'm building structures with images as a writer would build structures with words, to create some new meaning.

Living in California as opposed to New York or Europe affords a certain kind of freedom, because we don't have the weight of history in Los Angeles. If I'm sitting in a café in Vienna, say, people are going to tell me that Mozart used to sit where I'm sitting. If I'm in New York, there are galleries, museums, and publications around constantly to remind you that art is very real. It's a major industry there.

I think it was an advantage living here in that I got away from this pressure of history. I think it was a disadvantage in that you miss all the networking and talk, especially the talk. In New York, artists are thrust together because that's the nature of New York—space is at a premium. It might take you half an hour to get from one end of a street to the other, you just run into so many artist friends. Out here you walk outside your studio, and you never see anything. You're certainly not going to see an artist.

Do I think Los Angeles has any influence on my work? I always answer that by saying that a shark is the last one to criticize salt water. If you're immersed in something, you can't see it.

I'm twenty minutes from LAX, and I can be in New York in six hours. Probably half of my year is spent traveling. I've been in Europe once a month in the last four or five months. In the last two months I've been in New York three times, and so on. You have to be someplace.

For art there are three points in the world where one could be: LA, New York, or Europe. As long as you're at one of those points, you're part of that configuration, because everybody else in art traverses that same triangle. For about five years I did have an apartment in New York, which I called my vacation home, but now with the Internet and fax and e-mail, it really doesn't matter.

It dawned on me that I had to live someplace that I thought was ugly, and Los Angeles was my choice, probably because it replicated National City. If things are too beautiful, why would you want to create anything beautiful? If things are too idyllic in my environment, I go somehow crazy. I could not live in Beverly Hills or Bel Air.

If you're driving around constantly, as one has to in Los Angeles, you become aware of the overwhelming blandness and sameness. It has to reinforce something visually, and I think for me it's a fascination with monotony and boredom.

I think there's something psychologically going on, too, that I live near the ocean. I have to be at the edge of something, and I notice where I had my apartment in New York was the same distance from the Hudson as it is from my house here to the Pacific. It's like staying at the edge of a crowd. Like convicts keeping their back to the wall, so nobody can sneak up behind them.

My studio is a mess. I trip over things, and it's full of books, records, and magazines. I know where everything is, but I'm a pack rat. I think I've replicated my father's salvage store. He couldn't throw anything away because he saw value in everything. I see visual value in everything.

Part VIII

Minimalists

joan DIDION

The writer Joan Didion was born in 1934 in the same Sacramento Valley her ancestors first came upon by wagon train in the 1840s. Generally considered California's chronicler of record, she has described Sacramento as "a place in which a boom mentality and a sense of Chekhovian loss meet in uneasy suspension," and California as where "we run out of continent." She moved to New York soon after graduating from the University of California, Berkeley, but a few years later so missed her Sacramento birthplace that she immersed herself in it to write her first novel, *Run River*. In 1964, the year after its publication, Didion headed back to California with her new husband, the writer John Gregory Dunne. Author of nearly a dozen books, including such novels as *Play It as It Lays* and such distinguished essay collections as *Slouching Toward Bethlehem,* Didion has also written several screenplays with Dunne, including adaptations of both her novels and his. Didion and Dunne moved back to New York in 1988, where they live on the Upper East Side.

⌒

My mother's family came to California in the 1840s, and my father's family in 1852. They came looking for richer land. There wasn't anything glamorous or dramatic. They weren't propelled by some mission. I think it was something to do.

Some of them kept journals. I remember somebody in my father's family describing grass growing so high you could tie it over the saddle.

I wanted to be a writer, and my mother encouraged me. My father didn't discourage me. We just didn't have that discussion. I taught myself to type by typing out other people's fiction. I did a lot of Hemingway. You found out how the sentences work. I got very fast as a two-finger typist by typing out Hemingway's short story "The Hills Like White Elephants" and the whole beginning of *A Farewell to Arms.*

I went to Berkeley in the spring of 1953. It was quiet and smaller than it is now. As far as the culture went, it was kind of beat. People listened to jazz and expected to smoke a lot of cigarettes, drink a little too much, and be unhappy.

I was sort of in a depressed mood at Berkeley, although I think everyone was. I couldn't quite feature how I was going to get to the next step or what the next step should be.

I was the editor of the literary magazine and took what few writing classes there were. Then I got put off writing fiction because it was so clear that everybody had already done it. It wasn't likely you were going to be as good as Henry James.

I wrote stories, and somebody on the faculty had mentioned me to a publisher who happened to be coming through. The publisher wrote me a letter asking me to send him some stories, and I never answered. I was so fearful that they would be rejected, that they wouldn't be good enough, I simply ignored the letter.

I thought I wanted to be a writer or an actress. It was undefined. I was a guest editor for a month at *Mademoiselle* magazine when I was a junior at Berkeley, and that was the first time I ever went to New York. It was the first time I was ever on an airplane, for that matter. After that month I wanted to go back in a really strong way.

The following year I won a contest at *Vogue,* and they gave me a job in New York. I was homesick and started writing my novel *Run River.* By the time John and I got married in 1964, I had published *Run River* and was on extended leave from *Vogue* because I was supposed to be writing a second novel. In fact I was not. I was really frozen. It's harder to write a second novel than people think because you haven't got a clue how to do it.

John was working then at *Time* magazine and had some disagreements with his editors over its Vietnam coverage. It seemed a good time to take a six-month leave of absence and go someplace.

Our first thought was we'd go to the Caribbean, but that was ridiculous. Neither of us really wanted to go to the Caribbean, and I'm not sure either one of us had ever been there. Also this was an unpaid leave of absence, and we couldn't make a living. I had a little sinecure of three hundred dollars or four hundred dollars a month for movie reviews for *Vogue*. That was our entire income, so we had to go someplace where we could make some money.

Once we decided to move to California, Los Angeles seemed the obvious place because (a) we had this demented idea we could make a living writing television, and (b) I got depressed in San Francisco.

I don't know why we thought we could write television, but we actually made appointments with people who ran a lot of television shows in New York. After we moved to California, we sold a story for one thousand dollars, which saved our lives. Then we just started writing magazine pieces.

I changed the idea for the novel I'd been not writing to another idea, which I was not writing, which turned out to be *Play It as It Lays.* But when I finally got around to writing that, I practically wrote it all in one session.

Los Angeles was a great place to live. We went out for six months and stayed twenty-four years. For the first three or four years, we stayed six months at a time. John just kept extending his leave of absence. And finally *Time* told him that they weren't going to extend it anymore. We lost *Time*'s medical plan then, but we decided to stay.

You ask if it's true we made seven thousand dollars that first year, and if we made that much, I would be surprised. We had many low-income years. I think the year we adopted our daughter, Quintana, we made practically nothing. I don't know how they ever gave her to us. My father loaned us some money to pay the hospital. We didn't have a regular income until 1967, when the *Saturday Evening Post* asked us to do "Points West," a column John and I alternated writing.

We rented a house sight unseen. I put an ad in the paper, and I got an answer from this couple who had a huge piece of property in Portuguese Bend. The family built two gatehouses but lost money in the Crash and never built the big house on the point. We had wild peacocks and a pergola with wisteria.

We paid very little rent, but part of the deal was that the exteriors could be used for movies. I remember a Chrysler getting washed out to sea because they were shooting a Chrysler commercial in the surf and wouldn't believe me when I said the tide was coming in.

It was a beautiful house. We lived there until we adopted Quintana. We needed help to take care of her so I could work, and the owners didn't want a lot of extra people there.

We stayed all those years in Los Angeles because we loved it. John always realized how much he loved it. I didn't realize how much I loved it until we left.

We moved here to New York in April 1988, and I went back to Los Angeles that June on a Jesse Jackson campaign plane. The plane landed at LAX about sunset, and we drove in a bus to a rally in South Central, and I had tears streaming down my face because it was the most beautiful thing I had ever seen. And we're talking about LAX to South Central. It was the openness. Just the feel of it.

I didn't start driving the freeways until then. When we lived in Los Angeles, I never drove, not unless John had a broken leg or something. John always drove. I might have driven on a freeway about twenty times the entire time I lived there because I learned how to get almost anywhere on surface streets. The whole beginning of *Play It as It Lays* is something that somebody who is intensely terrified would spin a fantasy about.

So then the question of why we decided to leave Los Angeles comes up. It wasn't because we didn't like it. It was because we wanted to jump our lives a little bit. Quintana was in college. We were each between projects. We were feeling stale about work, and a move seemed like something to do. It was sort of like moving west.

We had a small apartment in New York, so we started spending more time there. It wasn't really big enough, and it became irritating to be supporting this large house in Brentwood. It became clear that if we wanted a bigger apartment, we would have to sell the house in Brentwood.

I'd always wanted to live in a hotel in Los Angeles anyway. I was always drawing up these charts showing how it would be cheaper. Now I'm so at home in a hotel there that when I come back, it takes me a week or two not to dial nine to get out.

My family didn't perceive California as an easy place to live, and it's not a particularly easy place to live. A place like Sacramento that floods every year isn't particularly easy. Los Angeles isn't easy. It's easy to get your clothes to the dry cleaners, and it's got big supermarkets. But think about the fires. You don't need winter clothes, but at the same time your house can go. That was another thing I missed when we got here—fire season. The drama of it. You're always looking for something to take you out of your daily routine, and that did it.

I think people who grew up in California have more tolerance for apocalyptic notions. However, mixed up with this tolerance for apocalyptic notions in which the world is going to end dramatically is this belief that the world can't help but get better and better. It's really hard for me to believe that everything doesn't improve, because thinking like that was just so much a part of being in California.

You thought if you bought a house, of course it was going to increase in value. If you bought a piece of property, of course you could sell it for a subdivision. And that was just at the crassest level. But you really believed that the town was going to grow for good. The dam was going to help the river. All these kinds of fixed wrong ideas. But there they are, fixed.

Growing up in California influenced everything about me. I can't imagine not having grown up in California. Look around this apartment. It's full of flat horizons. I have to look at flat horizons.

jules **ENGEL**

The artist and filmmaker Jules Engel was born in Budapest on
March 9, 1918, a Pisces who observes that "fish have a lot of
problems because they're always swimming against the current."
A California resident since the thirties, the hard-edge abstract
painter has also been called "the dean of American experimental animators." He has made about forty short films, including
thirty abstract animated films and ten live-action films, and his
film *Coaraze* received France's Jean Vigo Award. His decades of
paintings, prints, drawings, and constructions have been exhibited
at galleries and museums in New York, Los Angeles, and elsewhere. Engel created the Chinese mushroom dance in Disney's
Fantasia, and as a cofounder of the United Productions of America studio was instrumental in developing such UPA cartoon
characters as Gerald McBoing Boing and Mister Magoo. Director
of the experimental film program at the California Institute of
the Arts since its founding in 1969, he lives in Los Angeles.

In Budapest, when I was a child, we'd put on our best clothes and go
to the museum on Sundays. I enjoyed it, but I don't think I ever
decided to become an artist. I just kept doing art. I'm a firm believer
that some of us come ready-made.

When my family came to America in 1930, my teacher at Evanston
Township High School in Illinois would have the class go out and draw

the scenery. But she told me, "You just stay back and you do whatever you're doing," which was drawing squares, triangles, and circles. Now I don't know what made her do that. I wish to hell I could talk to her now.

Where did the ideas come from? I have no answer for that. I didn't know about abstract art at all. I simply felt that whatever I put on the paper—these shapes and forms—would be of consequence. This is why I come back to the word "ready-made."

I remember once I came around a corner and saw an automobile that had a square front and lines this way and that way. I'm talking about responding to something without trying to make anything of it. I did not know about abstraction. I just saw this car's grid, and it hit me so hard.

I'd try to go into an art class where you have a model. I would sit there, and in about thirty minutes I'd say, Now what am I doing here? I never had any desire or need to draw people or go out and draw nature. Absolutely none.

Something else happened when I was in high school. This young kid said to me, "Jules, I'm going to go see the Ballets Russes de Monte Carlo, and I would like to invite you." I had no idea why he invited me—I didn't know him—and thought maybe a teacher put him up to it. But anyway, he took me to the Ballets Russes de Monte Carlo. Well, I tell you, when that curtain went up and those men walked in with their purple tights, it was an awesome experience. I saw for the first time movement. I saw for the first time a background, a painting. I heard music. And it knocked the hell out of me.

That experience changed my whole thinking about movement. A while later I ran in a big track meet, and when I finished the race, I went back to my locker, took off my track shoes, sweat suit, and everything else, put it all in a suitcase, and left it in the locker. I was finished. I was done with that.

The ballet clarified for me the importance of movement. It gave me an idea that I wasn't aware of before. It took some time before that idea came to reality on paper, but it was germinating in my mind. And now I sought out the world of dance that I hadn't known about before.

When I finished high school, I got on the bus and came to California. I was very much interested in the sports world, and Southern California had a large presence in athletics. Where could you see bodies in motion more eloquently realized than in Southern California?

A lot of people don't understand athletics. They don't understand the magic of seeing a human being do something so special, so beautiful. The movement of athletes still fascinates me and gives me a thrill. When I saw Flo-Jo at the Olympics run a 2:20, it was magic. It's movement, and it's pure joy. They are dancers, but maybe with spiked shoes on their feet.

The first film I worked on was *Fantasia.* I had some friends at Disney, and they knew how crazy I was about the ballet. They were working on *Fantasia,* and they recommended me to Disney because they had had a problem storyboarding the Chinese Dance mushrooms sequence. They could draw, but some of these guys had never seen the dance world. They had never been exposed to it.

At that time I was beginning to get involved with abstraction, and I was making small eight-by-ten paintings. My first exhibit was in 1945, and I remember I was still in uniform at that show. It was after Disney and before UPA.

UPA was United Productions of America, although we never used that title. UPA actually grew out of Hal Roach Studios in Culver City, where armed forces training films were made during the war. We had a freedom there we never had at Disney or anyplace else, so we were trying out all kinds of ways of running and inventing film.

At UPA we created well-designed characters, and the movement came out of the design. Magoo would still be fairly close to live-action movement, but with Gerald McBoing Boing the movement came out of the graphic. We also brought a different kind of color into the animation world, using the colors of Picasso, Braque, Matisse. I was responsible for the color at UPA, and when we were working on the credits, I didn't want "Background by Jules Engel," I wanted "Color by Jules Engel," or whoever else was working.

Then, after fourteen years at UPA, several of us opened our own studio. We opened it with something which was very popular, *The Chipmunks,* because that gave us the bread-and-butter income the studio needed. We sold twenty-six half-hour shows to Hollywood, so we had something going for us immediately. *The Chipmunks* sold over three million records and gave us that chance to open our studio.

The animation industry fell apart after our fourth year in business. You couldn't sell anything that was animated. It was just dead. But there were other big jobs here that kept me involved with animation, and by that time the painting world was moving for me.

I almost moved to New York, but the California Institute of the Arts came on the scene. I was an abstract painter; I did abstract films; I would teach experimental animation.

As an artist I'm primarily a hard-edge, geometrical-architectural kind of painter, although I will go away from it every once in a while. And when it comes to making films, I was interested in carrying that kind of art into the animation world. The art in motion was important. Not the music. Other animation artists work to music. I never worked to music in my films.

For me it was the drawing itself. The shapes and the way they function on paper are for me the most important thing. It must function without music. If the structure and all the activity in a film are working, and you bring in sound, it would enhance but never equal or top what people see visually. The music would function with the image, but the image is first for me.

You ask if the painting influences the filmmaking and the other way around. It works both ways. I do think of a film as a canvas, and my films are pure graphic choreography.

Sometimes I might see an image like a newspaper photo of a dance group in a certain position that turns me on. Another time I came home, and there were signs all over my apartment house saying WET PAINT, WET PAINT. Well, I liked that title, and it propelled me to do something with this idea of wet paint. So that film came about.

Another film, *Train Landscape,* came out of the landscape I saw on my way to New York. I sat in the train by the window, and I knew I was going to do something with that. *Shapes and Gestures* was pure dance; I saw a dance event and used some of those ideas for movement. But then movement comes at you from anyplace and every place.

Painting comes more from other sources. I can invent a total composition. Sometimes seeing something is enough to initiate the texture or character of the rhythm in the painting. But painting is a very difficult world. You're dealing with Michelangelo, Leonardo, Pollock, Motherwell, de Kooning, Mondrian, Cézanne. You really have giants on your back when you come to the world of painting.

In the world of painting if you put two lines on a piece of paper, one horizontal, one vertical—that's Mondrian. So you have to be very careful. So much has been accomplished that in order not to look like this or that, you have a very difficult time.

I don't find giants in the film world like in music and painting. When we did Gerald McBoing Boing, that was new, that was fresh, that was something very special. Jackson Pollock did it, but it's very, very difficult to come up with a painting that has that enormous presence.

Sometimes people ask me how I start a painting. Generally my best preparation is to take a play that I'm familiar with and read the first or second act. It gives me a feeling for structure, and a sense of relaxing, but at the same time it brings me into the mood of trying to start a painting composition.

I read Chekhov's *Uncle Vanya,* or *Three Sisters,* maybe Neil Simon. I think it has something to do with the way I structure sometimes even my paintings. A well-written play will have a wonderful sense of almost architectural structure. I never read novels, but I always read plays.

Recently I saw the musical *Chicago,* which is all movement. I tell my animation students they must read, they must see plays, and I highly recommend they see musicals, because an animator deals with movement, and a musical is all movement. You'd be surprised how few ever read or see a play, but I tell them gently.

When I deal with young talent, I think back to going to the Ballets Russes and realize they too are at a point of discovery. I remember this young student of mine. I said her drawing reminded me of Giacometti and she, who was eighteen, asked, "Who?" She'd never heard of Giacometti. So the next day I got two books and gave them to her. I said, "These books are yours. Maybe you will see things you didn't know existed before."

george **WINSTON**

The musician George Winston performs more than one hundred shows a year around the United States and overseas, and during the past decade has performed in thirty-four California cities, from Humboldt to Ukiah. While often inspired by his Montana childhood, Winston's impressionistic solo piano music has long been associated with California, his home state since the seventies. The Grammy-winning performer also plays the guitar and harmonica, and in 1983 established Dancing Cat Records to record the otherwise unrecorded masters of Hawaiian slack-key guitar. Born in 1949 in Hart, Michigan, Winston first came upon the music of his mentors, Fats Waller and Professor Longhair (Roy Byrd), in California public libraries and says he still goes to libraries whenever he can. "You never know what you're going to find," he says. "They're like museums."

⌒⌒

I had a few piano lessons when I was seven or eight, and I wasn't interested at all. But I was a fan of instrumental music, particularly organists. And when I was eighteen, I was so crazy about organ music and R & B and jazz and rock, I felt I had to do something besides listen. So I got a compact organ and started to play in bands, stuff like that.

A few years later I was living in Redwood City, north of Palo Alto, and went to the Redwood City Public Library. I'd been studying Jimmy Smith, the great jazz organist, and saw an album, *Jimmy Smith Plays*

Fats Waller. So I got it, and liked it. Then later, on another trip to the library, I saw a Fats Waller record, and said, Let's check this guy out. After thirty seconds of listening to that great stride pianist, and his great piano solos, I was on another planet.

That wiped the organ and the band stuff off the map forever. It wasn't even a decision. It was just—I'm going to play solo piano now. I decided to hitchhike to a campus, find a practice room, and start playing piano. I'm very thankful for the Stanford University practice rooms. That's where I went and started climbing the mountain; I'm still only halfway up it.

I met the pianist Vince Guaraldi in 1971 when he was playing at In Your Ear, a club in Palo Alto near Stanford. I played the intermission for him, and I asked if he minded if I played his tunes. He said, "No, go ahead," and was very encouraging. I was just starting to play piano, and I'm sure I didn't do them that well, but he was very nice about it.

I later recorded an album of his tunes, including one called "Treat Street," which is where Fantasy Records was in San Francisco's Mission District. It reflects the music you hear coming out of the windows there to this day. His music to me is very San Francisco—the fog, the kids playing—and reflective of the whimsicalness and multicultural way of San Francisco. San Francisco has nothing to do with the rest of California. It's the equivalent of New York, which has nothing to do with New York State. It's almost like a country to itself. In fact, if you're coming from anywhere but the north, you have to pay to get into San Francisco—you pay to go to the carnival.

When I heard and later met John Fahey, whose record label Takoma did solo piano, I agreed to do a record and moved to Los Angeles in '72. LA has so many different people from different cultures, you can hear a lot of different music there—jazz, rock, pop, Latin influence. You knew it was a good music town. But there wasn't much chance to play. It was the disco era. Nobody wanted to hear solo piano playing. There wasn't much chance to do anything but practice and study Fats Waller.

I also got my second wind of piano in Los Angeles. At the public library I saw a record by Professor Longhair, founder of the New Orleans rhythm-and-blues school. Stride piano came out of ragtime and wasn't the music I grew up with. I grew up with Booker T and the MGs, Ray Charles, and the Ventures, so when I heard Professor Longhair, I thought that was so perfect.

I had actually quit playing. I love stride piano, but I didn't know where I was with it. I had the folk piano style I'd made up for the melodic things. But there was 98 percent missing. I heard Professor Longhair, and I said, "That's it." Later, in Northern California, I heard James Booker, who was another great New Orleans pianist influenced by Professor Longhair, and later Henry Butler. I heard all these pianists in California.

Every place has a feel. Do I translate it into music? I don't know. I let things make me play differently, subconsciously. California is definitely an inspiration, and I do particularly enjoy Central California. I like the plains, the flatland, and I've played all over there—Bakersfield, Fresno. I get inspiration from everywhere—California, Japan, you name it— but the big chunk is Montana, where I grew up.

In 1980 I did the *Autumn* record, which was strange—I made the songs up in LA, but they're about Montana. Usually I don't make up all the songs on a record. I've never done that since. I'm not really a com- poser. I make up a tune once or twice a year, just because it kind of hap- pens, but I made up all those *Autumn* tunes in Los Angeles. Seven out of seven. I think LA made me miss Montana. They're so opposite. LA had summer down pat—nothing but sunshine and no seasons, hardly— and I think that actually contributed to me doing season records.

I used to go places where there was a dead tree and I'd just look at it and pretend I was in the fall. I didn't have any money so I couldn't get out of LA. I couldn't go anywhere. I didn't see snow, and I didn't see fall foliage. All I could do was remember it.

But then, California is where I needed to be. The record companies are there. My record company, Dancing Cat, is in California. I was going to be touring, and I could live anywhere I wanted, and I'd been in the big city, Los Angeles, and did what I needed to do. It was time to be in a smaller place. I grew up in Billings and Miles City, Montana, which hasn't changed since 1954. Everyplace else has. Miles City is still ten thousand people. Santa Cruz, where I live, is near two airports, and it's nice to be in a smaller place like where I grew up.

The style I'm best known for is simple, melodic, folk, and rural. Rural folk. There is urban folk—Bob Dylan, Joan Baez—and rural folk, which is what I do. Other people may call it new age, but I don't play "meditation music." I just play. I don't have any intent, none of this highbrow stuff that I'm enlightened or anything.

When I started out, my main passion was jazz, but I was always so much more a rhythm-and-blues than a jazz player. I wanted to play everything, and it was interesting to narrow it down. The longer you play, the more you become who you are. When people just are themselves like Frank Zappa or Randy Newman, that's an inspiration, even if it's completely different. I want to do my thing like they do theirs.

I'm just very grateful for all the inspirations I've had. I'm not an innovator. I'd be nothing without all these people. I wouldn't know what I was or what I'm to do. I did make up the folk piano, the thing I'm best known for, but it was a reaction. It was to do something besides the r&b and stride. I didn't intend to make up that style. I wanted to do something melodic and simple as a complement. You know how you listen to a fast song and want to slow it down? That was it. Let me do something slow. Everything comes from my mentors, even things I made up. Without my mentors, I'd be wandering around lost.

otto **NATZLER**

Born in Vienna in 1908, Otto Natzler fled Hitler in 1938. With his late wife and artistic partner, Gertrud, he moved to Los Angeles, where the couple created more than twenty-five thousand individual ceramic pieces before Gertrud's death from cancer in 1971. Already recognized in Vienna by the time they left, the Natzlers won their first U.S. honor at the National Ceramic Exhibition in Syracuse in 1939. Their work was included in a 1940 group show at the Metropolitan Museum of Art, and retrospectives have been held over the years at such museums as San Francisco's M. H. de Young Memorial Museum, the Los Angeles County Museum of Art, and in New York at both the American Craft Museum and the Jewish Museum. The early kiln and potter's wheel they brought with them from Vienna are today in the collections of the Smithsonian Institution. Following his wife's death, Natzler began to work in clay himself, and he stopped only after a bad fall in the mid-nineties. A U.S. citizen since 1944, he lives with his second wife, the photographer Gail Reynolds Natzler, in the Hollywood Hills.

⌣

If I hadn't met my late wife, Gertrud, I probably would never have touched clay in my life. We met at the country house of her parents in Vienna in 1933, and on the train back to Vienna together, Gertrud told me all about clay and how wonderful it was.

My school training was in textile design, manufacturing, and weaving, and for several years, I had been unhappy with a job that I didn't care for. My only recreation was listening to music or making music myself. I played the violin, and I loved to play chamber music. Concerts and the opera in Vienna were my home away from home.

The word for clay in German is *ton,* which also means "sound" but I didn't connect the two at the time. In fact, what I'd seen before in ceramics didn't really interest me, and only after Gertrud told me about clay and what pleasure she got out of it, and after I had fallen in love with her already at first sight, did I discover that ceramics are made of clay.

March 11, 1938, was the day of our destiny. We received a very official envelope from, I believe, the Ministry of Commerce. We had five small pieces exhibited in a juried show at the Austrian Pavilion of the Paris World's Fair, and the letter informed us that we had been awarded the Silver Medal. It was great encouragement and our first recognition. I still have the letter.

That same evening, around ten, I went to walk her home. We heard a lot of shouting and singing and when we got to the Maria Hilferstrasse, there was a horde of people on the sidewalks and on the street. There was no traffic except the German army driving in with armored vehicles, and on the sides, people waving swastika flags.

I knew we had to get out. There were demonstrations all over Vienna, and every building had at least one huge swastika flag hanging. You would have believed that everybody in Vienna was a Nazi, which wasn't the case, but people had to protect themselves.

The eleventh was a Friday, and everything was closed on Saturday and Sunday. We went then to the American Consulate in Vienna and were told we had to get an affidavit of support from somebody living in the United States. I had a cousin who emigrated to Los Angeles four years earlier, and he was kind and brave enough to send us the affidavit.

We needed passports to get visas, and the Nazis didn't make it easy.

The passports we had were invalid, and we had to go through a bureau-cracy that you cannot imagine. You had to bring documents for every-thing. That you paid your income tax. That you paid your customs duties for imported goods, even if you'd never imported anything. That you'd paid your dog tax, even if you had never had a dog. I had to get a document that I was 100 percent Jewish, and Gertrud had to get all the same documents. And wherever you went, at every office, there were lines and lines of people, and you had to stand in line for hours.

It took forever, but we finally got the passports and visas. Getting passage was fairly easy because very few people went to California. Even fewer would choose the circuitous route we took through the Panama Canal and up the coast, a trip which took five and a half weeks from Trieste to Los Angeles, with various stops.

We brought Gertrud's kiln and potter's wheel, but we couldn't take them with us on the ship. We arrived on the twenty-eighth of October, 1938, in Los Angeles, and they arrived on a German ship around the middle of December.

We used different materials here than we had in Vienna. At first Gertrud didn't find commercial clays satisfactory. They were too rough and sometimes not moldable enough for throwing. I don't know how many different clay samples we tested, first by themselves and then in various mixtures, until we finally decided on two different clays.

Both of the clays came from the Alberhill region of California, near Corona. One clay was called Alberhill Red, and the other was called Hill Blue. The red fired red and the Hill Blue fired to a buff color. I mixed the two together and added various ingredients to improve the quality.

It took more than a year until we finally settled on a clay composition because we wanted something that fired red, had the working qualities that Gertrud wanted, and wouldn't warp too much in drying or firing. We stayed with it until, years later, both the Alberhill and Hill Blue mines ran out of clay.

After several years we moved to this house in 1946. It was surrounded by chaparral and weeds. You could see three mountain ranges, and there was a row of young eucalyptus trees planted along the driveway. There was hardly any traffic on the street, and when a car went by, we usually looked: Who might that be?

Of course our work reflects California as it had Vienna because you live in a landscape. I know, for example, that the desert landscape influenced our thinking of texture very much.

Some of the glazes, such as the rough lava glaze I made in the forties, rather unconsciously came out of what we saw. You accept various impressions, and translate them into your work, and it is a process that you are not even aware of while you are doing it. Some of the things that I made after Gertrud's death were inspired by rock formations that I saw at Mono Lake.

I get up usually around six-thirty, earlier in summer. I take the dog for a walk, for an hour or so, longer at weekends. Then I come home and do an hour and a half of yoga. Unfortunately I don't work anymore, something I miss very much, since I broke two of my fingers in a fall several years ago. I used to work until the light started to fade.

If I take a simple bowl from the late sixties and compare it to what we did in the forties, there's a tremendous difference, though very few people will see it. Whenever I create one of the more complicated glazes I do it up to a certain point, but the rest is up to God, and the vagaries of the kiln. There's always a big unknown and always to the very end a great excitement when you open the kiln after a reduction fire.

It is very much unlike painting. When paint dries, it changes a little bit. But the blue will always be a blue, and the red will always be a red. I put a glaze which looks red or gray on something, then fire it, and it turns green or blue or yellow, even white.

I never had any formal training in glaze chemistry or anything, and when I started out, I used my high school chemistry textbook. In the beginning I ruined half of Gertrud's work because we had all these mishaps. I didn't know anything, and she didn't know anything. There was no place to read up on it.

We live in earthquake country. I recall the last earthquake when Gertrud was still alive, and we were both awakened by the rattling in the closet where we had a lot of ceramics. Then the lights went out, and we heard things fall down and shatter.

We had various things on top of our window boxes, standing unsecured, and they crashed down and broke. Gertrud said, "Here goes our life's work," but after daylight, we saw we had altogether four pieces completely broken, and just six or seven that were damaged. It sounded terrible, especially with those things that fell down from a height, but everything else survived.

The creation of form, especially on the wheel, is very spontaneous. It seems like a miracle, but it comes just out of two hands. And one brain, of course. It was such an aesthetic wonder to see Gertrud create a vessel. Her hands moved like the hands of a dancer.

The whole creative process is something which cannot be explained. You breathe in air, and it makes you do something. You see a landscape, and it inspires you. So does music. I always like to listen to music when I work, and I recall that one day I was listening to *Parsifal* on the radio, and I started and finished a whole piece during the five hours of *Parsifal*.

When Gertrud died, I felt completely lost. I thought that this was the end, because we were 100 percent collaborating in our work from when we started practically until the very end. She was responsible for the form, and I took over after the form was finished.

During the first couple of years, I tried to complete the unfinished work that was left. Just for recreation, I made some mobiles.

Then I had met Gail, whom I married in 1973. She used part of the workshop for her sculpture, and she decided that the wheel, which was not used, was in her way, and she created a table over it. But before she could use the table, I had put some clay on it and started to play with it.

I hadn't touched clay at all except in handling the pieces that Gertrud had made, and I found it quite interesting to feel clay again. I made slabs of clay, and all of a sudden I found myself building some sculptural pieces and vessels. Poor Gail, who had made the table for herself to use and found herself deprived of it because she didn't want to interrupt my creative impulse.

Of course, this process is very different from throwing clay, and since I'm a different person, my forms had no relationship to what we did before. Gertrud's work was very ethereal. My work was heavy and more massive, but it gave me satisfaction to work in such contrasts. There were new glazes which I still wanted to invent, and here was something I could use to apply them to. And since I was the only creator of this work, I felt a little more reckless in firing it. I felt very badly when I experimented with Gertrud's work and ruined something that she had made.

I always feel that when you go to a museum exhibition of ceramics, you get only half of the pleasure that you can get when you are in a home, where you can pick a vessel up, handle it, hold it against the light, turn it. You'll see that sometimes even the color and texture change.

Ceramics are more than three-dimensional. There is an inside to a vessel which cannot be seen if you look at it just from one point. Even the form can sometimes not be comprehended when you see it through glass, stationary in a museum.

You have to be in close contact with ceramics. It is not enough to just look at them from a distance. Vessel ceramics is really the chamber music of art. Chamber music doesn't sound right in a huge hall. You can hear the notes, but you don't hear the texture.

robert IRWIN

The artist Robert Irwin blends such California interests as hot rods and surfing with the intellectual rigors of philosophy and science. Teacher or mentor to many other prominent visual artists, he calls himself a "question junkie" and has journeyed from abstract expressionist paintings to sprayed aluminum disks, room installations of light and space, and, in 1997, the creation of the Central Garden at Los Angeles's Getty Center. Born in Long Beach in 1928, Irwin lived primarily in Los Angeles until 1988, when he moved to San Diego, saying its slower pace reminded him of Los Angeles in the fifties. He visits regularly, however, to check on his plants and trees at the Getty, which is where this conversation took place.

⌐⌐

I was born in Long Beach, California, on the side of Signal Hill. Seaside Hospital. Made in California. When I was six, we moved up to Los Angeles, so I'm probably about as California as you can get. In fact, once, when I got off one of those long flights from Europe at two in the morning, I was ready to sleep for two days but too jazzed. So I bought a Coca-Cola, got in my car, put the top back, put on my big-band tapes, drove onto the freeway, and got these incredible waves of well-being. It may not be very sophisticated, but I knew who I was.

Artists in California have a sense of humor, a little levity about what we do. Artists in New York do not. There's this whole idea that art grows out of angst and that was the only way that weighty things have been brought on. I think the biggest thing that bothered New Yorkers, and still bothers New Yorkers about me, is that I had a happy childhood. Growing up in California was a footloose and fancy-free sort of thing. You're an incredible optimist, even to the point of being Pollyannaish, and that's a big difference.

When I went to Europe the first couple of times, I'd be in a place like Paris, which is so beautiful, so rich, and so refined that you almost want to cry. I entertained the idea of living there, but I realized that a place that beautiful is very difficult. You're tied to the past, not in the negative sense but really in a positive sense. You're surrounded by all this richness and beauty, and it's very difficult to be heretic under those circumstances.

The beauty of growing up in California at this moment in time is that you have very little dead weight. All the things that New Yorkers would say to me was wrong with California—the lack of culture, place, sense of the city and all that—is exactly why I was here. It was very possible to entertain the future here.

The risk you run in being not in the center is naïveté. You could easily reinvent the cotton gin, which of course would be a day late and a dollar short. So there was some risk of not going to New York. But what I realized later is that when I first went there, I expected a kind of dialogue. I was looking forward to that. I really needed it. But instead of conversation, I got confrontation. Everybody had positions, and everybody was extremely sophisticated and able to defend those positions and make arguments for them. In the beginning I was constantly getting my ass kicked.

I was beginning to consider and to entertain something that they had no interest in at all, so it was in a way the last place for me to be. For me to have a studio next to de Kooning, or have a dialogue with those people, was interesting. But it was not nourishing in the sense that I needed it, and I realized that for good or for bad, I was probably going to have to live out here, which I have continuously.

I got my first car when I was fourteen years old, and it was a '34, five-window Ford coupe. I was not allowed to drive it until I was sixteen, so all I could do the first year and a half was work on it, which was half the fun. It started out blue, and it ended up white, icebox white, and it was my first passion. The car I actually wanted was a '32 B roadster but my parents didn't have any money then, so I was limited to what my own funds were. I still want that '32 B coupe, to this day. If I could find it, I'd buy it.

Your first car is sort of like your home away from home. You work on it for fun, but also to give it a kind of identity. I remember one time having a dialogue with a New York critic, who was trying to tell me how superficial all that was. I was trying to explain to him that building hot rods was a genuine folk art, and he was saying no, folk art is Indian blankets and what have you. I disagreed. Folk art is when you take something utilitarian, something you use every day, like a cup or a blanket, and at some point you mark it. It becomes an extension of you. When that's been around for a hundred years and you start making them to sell on the side of the highway, it's not folk art anymore. It has to be tied to function. Building a hot rod at that time was, in a sense, a kind of California folk art.

Every summer I would go off and be a lifeguard at Lake Arrowhead or Catalina, and it was a very pleasurable thing to do. I had absolutely no time to be an artist. That was the downside, and it took me until my mid-thirties before I started to do anything of any consequence. I had a lot of facility, and no one confronted me with my lack of weight until I finally became aware, looking at my own work, that it wasn't going to make it.

I had a show at the Felix Landau Gallery, and I had one of those great moments that happen in your life, in which I had finally the opportunity to look at my own work. I mean clearly. You want to like your own work, so you color it and bring to it all your ambitions and feelings about it, and sometimes you don't get a very clear view. But I saw it, and it was terrible, which was shocking five minutes before the gallery doors opened. All my friends came in and patted me on the back and said how terrific it was, which is why they're my friends, I guess. But I had to teach myself some very fundamental lessons, so I spent ten or twelve years in the studio, twelve hours a day, seven days a week, and became an artist.

The second sort of major moment of my life came when they finally had a show out here of abstract expressionist painting. I cut my teeth as an abstract expressionist, but I'd never seen an abstract expressionist painting. Standing fifty yards away, I saw my first two abstract expressionist paintings. One was a James Brooks, about twelve feet by twenty feet. Very strong contrasts. Big powerful painting. Next to it was one of those little Philip Gustons. Grays. Pinks. Scrumbly, sort of. A very, very low-key-looking painting in terms of style and technique.

Yet the Philip Guston blows the James Brooks right off the wall. And I said to myself, Whoa, how's that possible? By everything measurable, the Brooks has to be the stronger painting. But it's not, and the lesson was very simple. In the James Brooks two and two makes four. In the Philip Guston two and two never made less than five. I wanted that power in *my* painting.

So I spent the next ten years taking my whole world apart, and questioning everything in it, in that everything in a painting either works for you or it works against you by its simply being there. My paintings were filled with stuff that didn't need to be there, so I started going through, step by step, throwing out things, and came to a kind of new mantra. There's a famous line, "less is more," and I came to the position that less is more only when less is the sum total of more.

Then one day I looked up ten years later, and I went from these very rich, impastoed, thick, gestural paintings to two orange lines on an orange ground. Everybody said, "What the hell are you doing?" and other than being able to backtrack what I've just said, I couldn't have told you. All I know is that those two lines did more than the five hundred lines in the paintings that I had been doing ten years before.

It was never a negative and never an antithesis. It was always just a very careful looking at my own work, deciding what was interesting, and trying to maximize that, and looking at what was not interesting and trying to get rid of it. And what I saw in all these fifty lines that weren't doing anything was my own superficiality. The problem with the painting was me. So I had to put myself on a major learning curve. I could have never been an artist if I hadn't spent that ten years buried in the studio.

The disks were my first attempt to try and paint a painting that didn't begin and end at the edge. Since the square canvas had four critical corners on it, which were very demanding, I opted for the idea of a circular format. Later on people attributed it to being spiritual, like mandalas or chanting or what have you. I understood that, but it just shows you how little that was a real issue for me because I wasn't even aware of that.

When I took the disks to New York, after having spent twelve years in the studio with them, and put them on a wall, and saw that the wall had little holes in it, and the baseboard was black or something, I carefully painted all that out, because it was a visual distraction. I was trying to create this thing that just floated, and they immediately attributed that to excessive potty training, as if I was incredibly anal. Their criticism was very strong. They really hated them and just completely discarded them as a part of the historical structure. That blew another myth: this idea that you can move your work from one place to another and it's understood.

The criticism never really addressed the issues that I was involved in, and it never made any real issues. So going to New York reaffirmed for me this whole thing of why I stayed in California in the first place, because I was obviously not a part of that dialogue. I was not doing what they were interested in doing. And that sort of confirmed my California-ness.

If I could do something that lasted forever, and was brilliant, or if I could do something and it only lasted for an hour, but it was infinitely brilliant, which do I do? From a classical point of view you do the former, and in terms of my point of view you would do the latter. It becomes this whole issue about permanence and about the death of things. It starts to challenge the idea of transcendence, which is a very beautiful idea, but basically in our lives there's nothing that's really transcendent. We have children to carry on our lives. We try and leave our mark in the sand in some way, but probably in any causal sense, that's a kind of futile activity.

We put structures in the world to live in and through. In other words, all information is contextually bound and all understanding is understanding within a frame of reference. Without it, information just floats around—we can't make any sense out of it. So we have these structures that we set in motion as a way of organizing, collecting, and understanding the information that we're getting or gathering for our efforts.

This garden here at the Getty Center was a great opportunity to try and find an extended frame of reference, and it is very much a part of what one can assume to accomplish in California. I tried to make every decision based on all the cues of being in this space and place—how you come to it, what your expectations are, the physicality of the space, the phenomenon of the sun, and so forth. And if I do that really well, somebody walking through this garden doesn't have to know about me and they don't have to know about art, because they have all the same cues that I had. In other words they can critique it, because it has a frame that it is operating in. And they do it in the direct sense—experientially rather than intellectually—and they do it in real time rather than abstract time.

Californians approach the world differently. Other people in New York and places like that assume everything there is to know is either known or eminently available. Growing up on the West Coast, you start out with the assumption that everything there is to know is to be found out. What you've done is put the question in front of the answer. It's not about answers, it's about questions, and the key is establishing quality questions so that the answers in a sense become inevitable.

When I started doing installations, that was not something anybody was interested in or wanted to do. Now, my God, there are nine thousand installation artists in the world. I got involved in light and space twenty or thirty years ago, and it has now become a thing. I guess there's something to be said for standing still long enough for history to catch up with you.

clint **EASTWOOD**

Mayor of Carmel, California, from 1986 to 1988, the actor and director Clint Eastwood was born in 1930 in San Francisco. A onetime surfer, lifeguard, and swimming instructor, he dug swimming pools at one point to make a living. A jazz aficionado since his teens, he played piano in an Oakland bar at sixteen and has written some of the music for his films. He played cowboy Rowdy Yates on television's *Rawhide* from 1959 to 1966, along the way appearing in the Sergio Leone "spaghetti Westerns" that made him a film star. When he and director Don Siegel were later looking for possible locations for *Dirty Harry,* Eastwood recalls, he took the director around to various places he knew as a "Bay Area guy." A major box-office star ever since, he has earned considerable critical praise as well for directing such films as *Bird,* his 1988 tribute to saxophonist Charlie Parker, and, in 1992, *Unforgiven,* which won four Oscars, including those for best picture and best director. He lives with his family on the Monterey Peninsula, where he recently was part of a consortium that purchased the Pebble Beach golf resort.

⌒

My parents were both born in California, and so was I. It was 1930, and times were bad to say the least. My parents were living in San Francisco then, I believe, and we later moved to Oakland, Sacramento, Redding, even to Spokane and Pacific Palisades before heading back to

Oakland. My parents were young people, trying to get going, and you just had to go where the jobs were then. There was no such thing as picking your place.

We moved all the way to Pacific Palisades in Southern California when I was very young, because it had the only job available. My father worked pumping gas at the Standard gas station at the corner of Pacific Coast Highway and Sunset. The station was still there until a few years ago—when they replaced it with another station—and I used to drive by with a little nostalgia. Nowadays it's hard to think of a person moving all that way to get a job pumping gas, but maybe they would if they thought there was some opportunity there. That's the kind of time it was.

We had a big old sedan, and a sort of old beat-up trailer. They'd hook the trailer onto the car, and that's how we traveled. We didn't own much. All our belongings, whatever there was, went in the trailer. We rented houses in various towns, and as a kid, you'd just get somewhat stable in a neighborhood and you'd move on, but by the same token, you just thought that's the way it was. My sister and I didn't much care for the moving around, but the family was so small, and we were a unit— the four of us and the dog.

In those days there was no other form of entertainment that anybody could afford, so I would go to movies whenever it was possible. You'd go with the family, something they don't do much anymore, and as you got older, you'd hike down to a theater on the weekend and catch a matinee of Randolph Scott or somebody like that in a Western or a detective movie.

I was always curious about music. When I was in junior high, we had an old upright piano. My mother played a little bit, and I just started fooling with it. When I was in the eighth grade, I guess, I wandered into a place with another kid, and watched two guys playing boogie-woogie on the piano. It sounded wild, and they were having a good time with it. So I went home and practiced a little. A while later I was at a party, and I sat down and started playing. All of a sudden these gals started coming over. I went from being a shy guy who wouldn't say two words to getting a lot of questions and answers.

I don't think that was my inspiration, but I went home and started playing with it more. I listened to records and began imitating records that were popular. My mother had Fats Waller records, which I liked. Those were hard to emulate because of the stride aspect, but I could do a little bit of that.

I tried playing the flugelhorn, but I wasn't a disciplined person. I never really sat myself down and practiced two or three hours a day. There was always some sort of distraction. So I became blasé about it.

I'd go downtown with other guys, there'd be a piano, and I'd play. I started going to a club in Oakland, where they hired me to hang out. I'd get tips and a glass of beer or something, even though I was way under-age. In those days nobody cared.

I first started going down to Central Avenue in Los Angeles when I was in high school. We'd come in from Oakland and cover all the joints in Southern California. Then, when I moved down here, we would go over to the nightclub behind the Ambassador Hotel and listen to musicians, or to Central Avenue. Central Avenue was just a sprawling neighborhood like many of them were. There were a lot of nightclubs, and I went to all of them. It was a hot spot for black musicians, certainly, and some white ones too. My son Kyle got to play with Buddy Collette when I was the recipient of the AFI Life Achievement Award.

I think I first visited Carmel with my parents. We used to go to Half Moon Bay, Stinson Beach, and places like that to swim, even though the water was cold as hell. We were kids, and we'd go jumping in, puddling around in the ocean.

But I didn't really go and spend any time in Carmel until 1951, after I was drafted. I remember you really started appreciating things when you were in the service because everything's taken away from you. You're stuck in the ultimate conformity of being in a military situation.

You'd go down to Carmel and get a breath of fresh air and think, Wow, this is great. I always thought I'd like to come back some day, if I could figure out a way to make a living.

In those days Carmel had a lot of second homes and people who were retired, but there was a nice little community there. I liked it a lot, and even after I moved to Los Angeles and got into a television series, I always kept drifting back. I made Carmel my home and was residing there on a part-time basis as far back as the early sixties. Later on I kind of moved there. I was working all over the world, different places, so I felt I might as well live there.

I lived in Pebble Beach awhile, then I moved kind of permanently to Carmel. I was there quite a few years, owned the Hog's Breath restaurant, and bought another building next door. I went before the city council with my plans, [got turned down], started checking on it, and finally had to bring a lawsuit against them. I decided the place wasn't user-friendly at all. I went to a political meeting where I talked about it, and someone said, Clint, why don't you run for mayor?

So I ran for mayor, and I learned that other people were thinking exactly what I was thinking about how punitive everything was. The opposition tried to paint me as probusiness, which I wasn't. I was proresidence. After all, it was more to my benefit being a motion picture actor, since I'd moved there ostensibly for peace and quiet and to not be in a populated razzmatazz place.

Anyway, I won the election by a healthy margin. I expected maybe the press would do something like "this movie actor is running for office in Carmel," and that would be the end of it. I was trying to keep it on a real grassroots level, but the press wanted to cover everything. The night we won, there were trucks with satellite dishes all over the place. Even today, people come in from Turkey, Italy, France, or wherever and ask if I'm still mayor, even though that was 1986. And I only did two years. Halfway through the second year, I started asking around for somebody else to run in my place.

Pebble Beach is also a wonderful place, and over the years, the Pebble Beach golf course had lots of different owners. Some of them took good care of it, and some of them didn't. When they started talking about selling it again, I thought I could bring something to it. I'd also be working with and partnered with people I know, and I thought it would be nice to have it back in American hands.

The problem with being a second-generation Californian is you're not objective about California itself. I think a lot of people come here for the comfort of it, or to reinvent themselves, and maybe creative people are natural searchers, searching for someplace to be. The lifestyle becomes very appealing. And now that California is so big, you're sort of at the beginning; an awful lot of trends seem to emanate from here. But as I say, if you're born here, it's hard to pinpoint it.

I've always been accused of having a California accent, but I've never known what a California accent is. I do think there's a California mentality, though, which is definitely more laid-back than an Eastern mentality. It's hard to talk about California without falling into the clichés, which are things from the fifties and sixties—Sandra Dee, the Beach Boys—that became synonymous with beach living and beach recreation.

The California I grew up with was very different. I think about it, and I have great nostalgia for it. That California was no freeways. It was two-lane roads and much more rural.

I remember working at a gas station, I think it was Signal Oil, next to General Service Studios, and there was an unemployment office right across the street. At that time I wasn't an actor. I was going to school. I used to be over there, changing tires and stuff, and look across at the people lining up for the unemployment agency. Then, when I became an actor, all of a sudden I was in line. I never collected any unemployment or any kind of benefits, ever in my life, until I was an actor.

When I was under contract to a studio, and got a check every week, I was comfortable for a while. When I went from there to zero checks, I went out and worked. I didn't mind working. But I never got into the normal things that actors do, becoming a waiter or a bartender where you're in contact with the public. I worked for a place called United Pools for a while digging swimming pools all over the San Fernando Valley—Tarzana, Encino.

I did a lot of different jobs. I was always doing something because I couldn't stand not working. My grandmother raised chickens and worked in accounting. She always worked, and she was very independent. I guess she was part of my work ethic.

Acting is a profession where you've got thousands of people trying to get one job, so it's very very difficult. In most professions, you just go to work. You say, I'll be a soda jerk or I'll dig a ditch or I'll wash cars, and you can do it. But in the acting profession, you have to get out and scramble to get a one-liner. So it's more of a feast or famine thing, and mostly famine, unless you get real lucky.

The other day, a reporter called me about the Pebble Beach golf course purchase and he asked me, "How does it feel to have been a kid who in 1951 sneaked onto the course for the Bing Crosby tournament and listened to Bob Hope crack jokes and Crosby sing and scarfed up free food and now, you're one of the owners?" Well, come to think of it, that is the California experience.

Acknowledgments

I must first thank the artists whose stories are in this book. All of them have many demands on their time, and I very much appreciate their willingness to share their memories and observations with me.

I am also deeply grateful to Stephanie Barron, a distinguished art curator whose sense of possibility was in many ways as crucial to this book as to *Made in California: Art, Image, and Identity, 1900–2000*, the monumental exhibition which she is curating at the Los Angeles County Museum of Art and which this book complements.

This book would not have been possible without her support and encouragement, as well as the extraordinary backup of her assistant, Victoria Clare, who was always available, good-natured, and resourceful. My treasured friends Susan Grode and Angela Rinaldi were extremely giving of their time and expertise, as were the similarly generous Barbara Casey, Bernice Kert, and Lyn Kienholz. All believed in this project from the start and helped me greatly to pursue and complete it.

As my ambitions grew, so did my expenses. The California International Arts Foundation made the impossible possible, overseeing grants from the Broad Art Foundation, the Eli Broad Family Foundation, the Lee and Lawrence J. Ramer Foundation, and the Roth Family Foundation, four philanthropic organizations that reflect the progressive spirit of their founders.

I similarly wish to thank the Getty Research Institute, and particularly Deborah Marrow, Michael Roth, Charles Salas, and JoEllen

Williamson, for bringing the resources of that institution to me for four critical months spent as a Visiting Scholar in 1999 and 2000. I would also like to thank the Getty's Valerie Gross, Harold Williams, Sabine Schlosser, Donna Beckage, Brian Davis, Ayana Haviv, Carla de la Paz, Peter Spragg, and Chris Rea. I am particularly grateful to my Getty research assistant Allison Milionis-Gorrie.

The curatorial staff at the Los Angeles County Museum of Art was helpful with background and contact information, research materials, and useful observations and opinions, while the museum's audiovisual technicians graciously provided equipment and expertise in the recording of many of these interviews. At LACMA, I would particularly like to thank Paul Holdengräber, Howard Fox, Sheri Bernstein, Tom Jacobson, Carol Eliel, Jo Lauria, Aya Yoshida, Robert Sobieszek, and Lynne Zelevansky.

Besides working in libraries at the Getty and LACMA, I also did extensive research and writing at the Beverly Hills Library. I am grateful to that library's courteous and knowledgeable staff as well as for its ample exhibition catalogues, magazines, books, and other materials. I similarly appreciate the help of the Academy of Motion Picture Arts and Sciences's Margaret Herrick Library, the Museum of Television and Radio, and Michael Rosen, executive producer at the Archive of American Television. At UCLA, my thanks go to Dale Treleven and his staff at the Oral History Program, Keri Botello at the Graduate School of Education and Information Studies, and the staff of the University Research Library's Department of Special Collections.

Many other individuals and organizations opened their files and Rolodexes to me as well. For their help in obtaining research material, interview appointments, or other courtesies regarding the many artists in this book, I would like to thank: Karen Ames, Debra Bernard, Rena Bransten, Ronni Chasen, Ben Churchill, Mary Daily, Mary Dean, N. Vyolet Diaz, Phil Esparza, Noriko Fujinami, Cathie Gandel, Jackie Green, Cristofer Gross, Nancy Hereford, Karin Higa, Kevin Higa, Selma

Holo, Joe Hyams, Deborah Kelman, Richard Kornberg, Diane Kounalakis, Craig Krull, Karen Kuhlman, Laurel Lambert, Deanna MacCellan, Jason Martin, Robin Mayper, Phyllis Moberly, George Moore, Tobey Moss, Louisa Munoz, Gary Murphy, Kathy Penner, John Pennington, Kira Perov, Tom Rooker, Jack Ruttberg, Yatrika Shah-Rais, Tony Sherwood, Judi Skalsky, Lori Starr, and Raul Vasquez.

I'd also like to express my appreciation to friends and colleagues Stephen Sansweet, Tressa Miller, Thomas Hines, William Holmes, Jack Shakely, John Walsh, Nancy Berman, Ken Brecher, Jan Burnham, Charles Champlin, Richard Cromelin, Elaine Dutka, Betty Freeman, Doug Freeman, Grace Glueck, Robert Hilburn, Michael Kantor, Eric Lax, Susan Loewenberg, Kristine McKenna, Emily Miller, Susan Miller, Neville Morgan, Lynn O'Leary Archer, Norman Pearlstine, Douglas Ring, Robin Wagner, Gayle Wegman, and Narda Zacchino.

While I did all the interviewing and editing on these interviews, I couldn't have done that without a great deal of help. Victoria Kaplan did an excellent job of transcribing my tapes. Minette Siegel and David Inocencio were very generous in providing me space for interviews at their Multi Image studio in San Francisco. Librarian Aileen Tu was invaluable as my assistant on the visual artists' interviews, tackling and mastering the intricacies of digital recording along with me. My incomparable editorial assistant Judith Ryskiewicz brought a keen sense of organization, intelligence, humor, and spirit to her work.

My agent and friend Susan Ramer has once again been a great source of support, encouragement, and wisdom. I can say the same for Tom Dupree, my smart and talented editor at HarperCollins. He was excited by this project from the first time he read my book proposal, and he never failed to convey that enthusiasm to me. His wonderful assistant, Kelly Notaras, shared that excitement, which is so important to a writer, and like her boss was always there for me. My thanks also to copy editor Susan Llewellyn.

Richard Schickel, my loving partner and mentor, continually took the time away from his own many commitments to discuss an artist, an idea, a word choice, or a worry. Besides his willingness to attend too many movies alone, I appreciate his great passion for this project, his graciousness in sharing its long, complicated evolution, and his continuing affection and support.

Barbara Isenberg is a regular contributor to the *Los Angeles Times* and *Time* magazine, editor of three books on theater, and a former staff reporter for the *Wall Street Journal*. Author of the critically acclaimed *Making It Big: The Diary of a Broadway Musical*, she has received the Distinguished Artist Award from the Los Angeles Music Center and was a Getty Visiting Scholar. She lives in Los Angeles where she is associate director of the Institute for the Humanities at the University of Southern California.